Edited by
Lionel Lumb and Deborah Van Veldhuizen

CTR Inc. Publishing
New Jersey, USA
2008

First published in 2008
CTR Inc. Publishing
PO Box 6345, Monroe Township
New Jersey, USA

Websites:
http://www.blairrw.org/ctr/index.php and http://www.bewfoundation.com

ALL RIGHTS RESERVED 2008. No part of this publication may be reproduced in any form or by any means without the written permission of the authors and CTR Publishing.

Copyright to the individual articles will revert to the respective authors one year after publication.

Main entry under title: **The Way We Are**

Subtitle: An Anglo-Indian Mosaic

Edited by Lionel Lumb and Deborah Van Veldhuizen

ISBN (13 digit) 978-0-9754639-4-9

ISBN (10 digit) 0-9754639-4-2

Library of Congress Control Number: 2008930255

Layout design: Ruth Greer http://www.ijin.ca

Cover Design: Harry MacLure Design Studio http://www.harrymaclure.com

Printed by: Thompson Shore http://www.tshore.com

Other books published by CTR Inc. Publishing

Anglo-Indians: Vanishing Remnants of a Bygone Era, Blair Williams (2002)

Haunting India, Margaret Deefholts (2003)

Voices on the Verandah: An Anthology of Anglo-Indian Prose and Poetry,
Edited by Margaret Deefholts and Sylvia W Staub (2004)

The Way We Were: Anglo-Indian Chronicles.
Edited by Margaret Deefholts and Glenn Deefholts (2006)

Contents

Preface · Blair Williams iv
Editors' Note · Lionel Lumb and Deborah Van Veldhuizen . . . vii

Passages

MOIRA BREEN
Never Give In 2

KATHY CASSITY
Distances 10

MARGARET DEEFHOLTS
A Passage to Canada 19

GLEN DUNCAN
Young Man Behaving Badly 27

CHRIS FRANCIS
Just off the Boat 30

LIONEL LUMB
Denial and Pride 35

JOYCE MITCHELL
Journeying Through Life 43

PAMELA S.C. MOORE
The Year of '72 50

RALPH N. MOORE
Upended Down Under 55

PETER GORDON NAILER
"My India" No More 61

SHIRLEY PRITCHARD
An Anglo-Indian in America 64

DANIEL RIGGLE
A Woman from Ajmer 68

BLAIR WILLIAMS
An Examined Life 75

NOREEN WOOD
The Edge of the Page 80

Identities

GERALDINE CHARLES
Inheriting the Patchwork 87

SUSAN DEEFHOLTS
Inheriting Remembrance 90

MARK FAASSEN
Beyond the Raj. 98

SHELDON FERNANDEZ
Unravelling the Mosaic 105

NANCY LILLY
An Epistolean's Legacy 113

DAVID McMAHON
Identity Cadre. 118

DOROTHY McMENAMIN
Collision of Life and Love 125

RALPH N. MOORE
I Say, Men 132

PETER MOSS
Raking Through the Ashes of That Bonfire of the Vanities . . 134

GERALD PLATEL
A Long Journey in Search of an Identity 139

CHERYL-ANN SHIVAN
The Way We Are at Pondicherry 142

SYLVIA W. STAUB
As the Bough is Bent 148

DEBORAH VAN VELDHUIZEN
Becoming Myself 152

JOHN WALKE
My Irish Grandfather 155

Traditions

QUENTINE ACHARYA
Maxwell Piers 164

ROBYN ANDREWS
A Day at St. Joseph's Hostel, Melbourne 170

PATRICIA BROWN
    February 178
JOY CHASE
    Five Flags 186
ESTHER LYONS
    My Bow Barracks 193
JOYCE MITCHELL
    Ginger Wine 199
LESLEY-ANNE RAYMER
    When Two Worlds Collide 206
MARINA STUBBS
    What's In a Name 211

Reflections

ROBYN ANDREWS
    A Calcutta Christmas 216
LIONEL CAPLAN
    Close Families in Chennai 222
    The Boundaries of Anglo-Indian Culture 230
DOLORES CHEW
    Coming Full Circle 238
ED HALIBURN
    What If? 244
ALAN JOHNSON
    Globalization and Anglo-India 252
SANJAY SIRCAR
    Matters of Language 257

Meet the Authors 267

Glossary of Indian Words and Phrases 275

Preface

THE WAY WE ARE
An Anglo-Indian Mosaic

Edited by Lionel Lumb and Deborah Van Veldhuizen
Published by CTR Inc. Publishing

A Note from the Publisher

So here we are again. *The Way We Are* (*TWWA*) is the fifth[†] in our CTR Books series on the culture and way of life of Anglo-Indians, authored by Anglo-Indians and others. We now follow a well-established process, with our invitation for submissions, kept open for a year, conforming to simple guidelines. (For *TWWA* we asked for up to 3,000 words describing what it means to be an Anglo-Indian in today's world.) These submissions are then required to be sent to a central address (in this case mine), where they are stripped of identity, given a serial number, and sent on to a panel of five judges (more later on *TWWA*'s panel). After an exchange of opinion, the judges select about 40 articles, and only after they have reached consensus do they get to know the identity of the writers. Where the judges recognize an entry—and it could be their own—they recuse themselves.

TWWA's judges selected 43 entries from seven countries: USA—14; Canada—11; Australia—7; UK—6; New Zealand—3; India—1; and Hong Kong—1. Isn't that amazing? And the common element is the Anglo-Indian today.

We are not done yet. Our next book, already announced, is *The Anglo-Indian Woman*, scheduled for publication in 2010—and CTR is good for another two to three books after that. (See our website for details: http://www.blairrw.org/ctr/index.php)

When we started to publish books, our primary motivation was to provide a balanced view of the Anglo-Indian community for posterity. We were concerned that the community had been

---

† Following *Anglo-Indians: Vanishing Remnants of a Bygone Era*; *Haunting India*; *Voices on the Verandah*; and *The Way We Were*

the subject of grossly distorted stereotypes. After five books, this concern has been put to rest. We now have a balanced view of the community, written by Anglo-Indians, Americans, Canadians, Britons, Australians, Indians, New Zealanders, and others. In the process, we have given many the opportunity to describe their lives in India (*Voices on the Verandah* and *The Way We Were*) or their experiences as immigrants in their adopted countries (*TWWA*). We have also developed a worldwide audience that has bought the books and enjoyed them. As Ruskin Bond, our premier Anglo-Indian literary icon, has said, "The community has found its voice, and it is sweet." We believe that *TWWA* takes the literary and anthropological significance of these efforts to new heights.

A word about our judges: They put in large amounts of time, all voluntary, and no praise of mine is adequate. Lionel Lumb, our editor, has a distinguished career in print journalism, TV news and current affairs, and teaching at the university level in Canada; Margaret Deefholts, our writer extraordinaire from Canada, in addition to her own book *Haunting India*, has co-edited *Voices* and *TWWW* and will return, after a rest, to edit *The Anglo-Indian Woman*; David McMahon, author of bestseller *Vegemite Vindaloo*, is an internationally known sportswriter and photographer in Australia; Susan Deefholts is an author, literary critic, and editor in Canada, and, along with Kathy Cassity, who teaches literature at the University of Hawaii, represents one of two young, highly talented Anglo-Indian literary figures. Finally, we have Deborah Van Veldhuizen, co-editor of *TWWA*, another young talent, who teaches Communications to college students in Canada. This, then, is the team responsible for the production of *TWWA*. We are, indeed, indebted to each of them for their ability and dedication.

There is, of course, another primary purpose for publishing our books: it is to help collect funds for our charity, CTR, dedicated to "helping indigent Anglo-Indians in India." This is CTR's 10th anniversary, celebrated in 2008 in Australia, the UK, Canada, and the USA‡. It is fitting that the launching of *TWWA* should coincide with this anniversary.

We love the quote from James Ch. 2, v. 14-16: *Suppose there are brothers or sisters who need clothes and don't have enough to eat. What good is there in you saying to them,* "God bless you! Keep warm

---

‡ Sydney August 23rd Cheryl.Chater@gslpl.com.au; London October 4th k.lobo@btconnect.com; Princeton Oct 18th blairrw@att.net; Perth Oct 25th busbyjenny@hotmail.com; Toronto Nov 8th ypeters51@yahoo.ca

and eat well!" *if you don't give them the necessities of life? So it is with faith: If it is alone and includes no actions, then it is dead.* We started out by providing a small pension to a few seniors in 1998. Today, we provide pensions to more than 300 seniors, spread across several Indian cities. In 1999, CTR also started to provide for the education of young children, and today we are sponsoring more than 180 children across India. We are growing, and our efforts around the world continue to provide more pensions to more seniors and education for more children.

If you enjoy our books, we urge you, our readers, to join us in our efforts to help others. Get involved with our incredible group of volunteers across the globe (not one of whom is compensated, either in cash or kind). We are proud to claim administrative costs of less than one-tenth of 1%, so every donation goes directly to those in need in India.

We can and we are making a difference.

Blair Williams, Publisher
CTR Inc., NJ, USA
June 2008
blairrw@att.net

About the Publisher:

Blair Williams, patron and publisher of CTR Inc. Publishing, is a Chartered Engineer from London who emigrated to the USA from India in 1976. He has spent the last 24 years as an executive in manufacturing companies and is now an Industry Professor at Brooklyn Polytechnic. His technical publication, *Manufacturing for Survival* (Pearson 1997), has been used extensively as a reference and instructional textbook by industries around the world.

On a visit to India in 1998, he was appalled to see the condition of some seniors of his Community, evoking the all-too-distressing realization, "There, but for the grace of God, go I." On his return he set up CTR Inc., a USA 501c(3) not-for-profit charity, expressly to help indigent Anglo-Indians in India. Over the last decade, the charity has been helping more and more less-fortunate seniors and children in India. In 2000, he also began publishing books on Anglo-Indian culture, to preserve the culture and to raise money for the charity. *The Way We Are* is CTR's fifth publication.

Editors' Note

Lionel Lumb and Deborah Van Veldhuizen

The Internet has given Anglo-Indians a virtual verandah on which to chat, share memories, dream about the future, and generally replicate the social life that centred on our real bungalow verandahs back in India. It's also given us an important tool to take charge of our own destiny, to record—as only we can—*the way we were and are*.

As wonderful and fulfilling as the Internet's ability to communicate instantly is, the downside is that so much information gets passed around so swiftly that most is soon forgotten or not properly absorbed. That's where this CTR series steps in, to offer a more permanent, tangible record. There's nothing like a good anthology that you can hold in your hands, while you take your time to savour the multi-layered flavours of rich experiences and interesting lives.

Like its predecessors, *Voices on the Verandah* and *The Way We Were, The Way We Are* is a collection as varied as it is vital, as complex in its detail as it is revealing in its honesty, as creative as it is heart-warming. The very first memoir, *Never Give In*, sets the tone for the way Anglo-Indians spread out around the world after 1947, and faced their challenges with guts and ingenuity.

Put to rest are the distorted portrayals of a shiftless people, drifters dependent on the goodwill of a colonial power and uncertain about their place in the world. Indeed, these pages reveal the world is ours, as we bring the strengths of our multicultural heritage to light the way for the increasingly diverse societies in which we've settled.

As editors of this fifth volume in CTR's canon, we chose to divide the articles into four themes. Inevitably, some pieces blur the lines, but we hope our readers will welcome the principle of a thematic approach.

The first theme, *Passages*, deals with the journeys—both physical and spiritual—that Anglo-Indians made as they left their known and mostly beloved India for the unknown "big out there". In exploring their new worlds, they learned not only how to cope, but also something of themselves. The second, *Identities*, focuses on Anglo-Indian attitudes, then and now, and voyages of discovery into what makes an Anglo-Indian. In *Traditions*, the articles centre on efforts to keep alive the old ways, and take pleasure in the community's longstanding values. The final section, *Reflections*, brings together essays that probe the lives and behaviour of Anglo-Indians—sometimes poignant, sometimes humourous, but always thoughtful or even downright provocative.

As with *TWWW*, we decided not to interrupt the narrative flow with instant explanations of vernacular words or phrases. Instead, we rendered these in italics and provided a glossary at the end. However, we allowed a few exceptions, and provided a translation where the meaning became too murky for reader comfort.

We thank all the authors (you can find out more about them at the end of the book) for their comradely responses to the editing process. And for enriching our lives and knowledge about the world of Anglo-India in the past few months. Our excitement grew as one fine piece after another was added to the treasure chest of *TWWA*. We hope it attracts a lot of treasure-seeking readers.

We also thank Blair Williams for his dedicated commitment to CTR's charitable mission, and to his inspirational and continuing promotion of Anglo-Indian literature. With his help, Anglo-Indians have found their voice: there are many singers now, and the song soars.

Passages

Never Give In

by Moira Breen

It was 1949, two years after Indian Independence, and I was on my way from India to America, travelling on a Dutch freighter to New York City. I was a young Anglo-Indian woman, 25 years old, with a Bachelor of Science degree from Queen Mary's College, Madras (now Chennai), and with five years of experience as a teaching laboratory assistant in two missionary-run colleges: Vellore Christian Medical College and Women's Christian College (WCC), in Madras. I was headed for Vassar College in upstate New York, where I was scheduled to teach freshmen students and also work towards a higher degree. Vassar is an elite college, and the first in America to grant women university degrees. It opened during the American Civil War.

You might well wonder how I—with a single-parent mother and very little money—got such an opportunity. My family had been in India for more than six generations. I am descended from at least five British soldiers, who came from the poorest sections of British society. At first they married Indian women and later Anglo-Indian women, and they made India their home; none ever returned to Britain. I was born in Madras, the daughter of Anglo-Indian parents who had married in 1922. Behind the group photograph of their wedding my mother wrote the words: "A Big Mistake!" My father was a physician in the Indian Medical Department (IMD), which was the subordinate branch of the Indian Medical Service and staffed entirely by Anglo-Indian doctors; the senior branch, the IMS, was for doctors trained in England. He was very unhappy with this two-tier system, and often said he was treated like a hospital orderly. In 1927, after five years of service, my father took a leave of absence to study in England, leaving behind his family—my mother, my brother, and myself. He never returned.

Our mother put us in the care of her parents in St. Thomas Mount (near Madras), while she resumed her university education and teacher's training at Madras University. Four years later, she became a teacher at Doveton-Corrie Girls High School, where she had been a student.

My brother and I were very happy staying with our grandparents, but this golden life was cut short when he was six and I was eight years old. For economic reasons, our mother installed us as boarders in the Lawrence Memorial Royal School in Lovedale, in the Nilgiri Hills—commonly referred to as Lovedale. There we were fed, housed, clothed, and educated for very little money. Lovedale was founded in 1858 for the children of orphaned British soldiers.

The school was very spartan and the discipline harsh. It was cold in the hills, and we had bare floors, no heat, no rugs, no curtains. We swept the floors daily, and polished and oiled the dining room furniture weekly. Every year we were inspected by the head of the Indian Army, Southern Command. Both boys and girls had to parade past him and offer a military salute. We were trained by a British Army sergeant. Needless to say, my brother and I were terribly homesick under this regime, but we eventually adjusted.

I was small and thin, and afflicted with a facial deformity[1]. I could not participate in school sports or engage in school plays. An avid reader, I spent much of my spare time buried in books. At the age of 15, I passed the Senior Cambridge School Leaving Certificate Examination with a top grade, and received the class prize. I was admitted to Queen Mary's College (QMC), Madras. My tuition fees were paid by Lovedale. Four years later, I graduated with a first class BSc degree. After QMC, the other Anglo-Indian girls with me went on to study for their teacher's diploma at Lady Willingdon College. But my mother advised me that my facial deformity precluded me from teaching, and with this traditional route closed to me, I had to use other opportunities that came my way. In retrospect, it seems to me that this is what I have done all my life. There have been setbacks along the way, but also rewards.

The first opportunity—and setback—came because I'd studied Nutrition in my last two years in college. QMC girls were bussed once a week to Women's Christian College (WCC). The WCC professor, an American called Dr. Eleanor Mason, was doing research on the South Indian rice diet. Just before I graduated from QMC, Dr. Mason offered me a research position with her, leading to a Master's Degree in Nutrition. I was elated, but when my name went before the WCC board she was told that the position had to go to an Indian. So I went to work in the Christian Medical College, Vellore, as a lab assistant to Dr. Dorothy Jefferson, Professor of Physiology, at Rs. 60 a month. That was a very low salary for my qualifications—it didn't even cover the cost of my food. Though

I enjoyed working in the lab and Dr. Jefferson taught me a great deal, my position was below the lowest rung of the academic ladder, and there was no future. I was the only Anglo-Indian in the entire student body and faculty. After three years, I left Vellore unwillingly and went to work and study with Dr. Mason at WCC, only because Vellore did not have a Master's degree program.

I was a temporary, substitute teacher for two years at WCC, spending half my time as a lab instructor in physiology, and the rest in nutrition research while working towards my Master's. Again, I was the only Anglo-Indian in the entire student body and faculty. Then came another setback: due to unexpected circumstances, Dr. Mason had to take over as principal and no longer had the time to work with me. Because I had been well trained in physiology by Dr. Jefferson in Vellore, I was able to run the labs entirely by myself, but I had to abandon my nutrition research project. At the end of two years, I had no job and no higher degree.

When Dr. Jefferson heard of my plight, she and Dr. Caroline Holt, another American professor at Vellore, came to my rescue, recommending me for the teaching position at Vassar. My mother paid my travel expenses out of her hard-earned savings. Once I got to America, I was self-supporting—I was paid a salary for teaching, and my tuition was free.

I left Madras on July 14, 1949, for Colombo in Sri Lanka, where I caught the Dutch freighter for New York. Almost six weeks later, on August 23, the boat arrived in New York City. Dr Ruth Conklin, Chairman and Professor of Physiology at Vassar College, was there to meet me. I was very thin, small, weighed just 76 pounds, looked about 18, and didn't fit the stereotype of a professor. The Immigration officer did not believe I was going to join the faculty at Vassar and kept me behind on the ship. Dr. Conklin phoned the office of Vassar's president, and they in turn phoned Immigration in New York, and I was finally allowed to enter America. Dr. Conklin drove me to her home—a three-hour journey from New York—and we arrived there at the end of a very long day. But her house companions had dinner ready and gave me a warm welcome. I was given a lovely room in her house, and I spent the next three years as a guest, paying the minimum.

Vassar College has a beautiful campus, 75 miles north of New York City, on the banks of the Hudson river. At the time, the Physiology Department had three senior professors and three assistants, of which I was one. The physiology course was very popular, and more than 100 students elected to take the freshman course; all six of us on the faculty worked together teaching it. The young students of 17 and 18 years of age were most enthusiastic and spontaneous, and it was a pleasure to teach them.

For my Master of Science degree, I was required to study some of the more advanced physiology courses in the department and, in addition, I had to undertake an individual research project. In my first year at Vassar, I won the biology prize for summer study in the prestigious Marine Biology Laboratory at Woodshole, Massachusetts. Within two years I got my Master's in Physiology from Vassar, and I stayed on for another year, working full-time in the department. My time at Vassar was very happy. The experience and an American degree proved invaluable for the rest of my scientific career in America.

From Vassar, I went to Johns Hopkins Hospital in Baltimore, Maryland, to teach nurses physiology and anatomy in their first six months of training. But they only needed me for six months of the year, and for the second six months I was shelving books in the library. I didn't think this was a good use of my time and resigned shortly after the basic science session ended. While at Johns Hopkins, I studied German in night school, and that proved useful later.

My next job was at Harvard University in Boston, where I worked as a research assistant in the Department of Nutrition. They were in the middle of a combined research project with four other laboratories, collecting data on cholesterol levels in the blood of the American population. This was 1953, and the importance of cholesterol was just being realized. It was my job to do the cholesterol analyses on 30 blood sera a day. This complex and exacting procedure required the use of strong acids, rigid temperature control, and timing. Automation of clinical chemistry procedures had not yet been invented, and so I worked as a human robot. Now when your doctor tells you that your blood cholesterol is too high (or too low), he or she is comparing your level to data obtained by me and the other unknown technicians who preceded me at Harvard.

I liked working at Harvard, but my salary was very low—$200 a month was not enough even to afford an apartment, and I had to live in rented rooms. I made tentative inquiries about working part-time and studying part-time for a PhD, but I was rebuffed. I was now 30 years old and had been doing laboratory work for 10 years. I had to do something to earn more money.

An Indian friend passing through Boston suggested I try Northwestern University Medical School in Chicago, which had a new chairman of Biochemistry who might be willing to take me into the PhD program. With recommendations from Harvard and Vassar, I applied and was accepted. I was also given a fellowship generous enough to pay my living expenses, and I had free tuition. I arrived in Chicago in September, 1954, and had a room on the 17th floor of Abbott Hall, overlooking Lake Michigan. It was a lovely room, and my friends said that I had the best, cheapest room in all of Chicago. I took many courses in the medical school and studied more chemistry in night school. In return for my free tuition, I had to grade medical student examinations in biochemistry and monitor some of their examinations, and occasionally run calcium assays on clinical samples. But on the whole these chores were light. My PhD mentor was a specialist in mineral metabolism; I was expected to do calcium analyses on a few drops of blood obtained by cardiac puncture from a rat, but no method existed and therefore my immediate task was to develop one. Little did I realize how difficult this would be. Scaling down the existing clinical method, from a full test tube of blood to a few drops, did not work. I had to try something completely different. I was partially successful when I used fluorescence agents and dyes, but the methods I developed were not entirely satisfactory. Eventually, after six years, I did enough research work to publish two papers in the leading medical journals and got a PhD in Biochemistry in 1960. I was now 36 years old, and once again I was in the job market looking for a real job. But first I took a break to visit my mother and brother, whom I had not seen for many years, in England.

It was my first visit to England, and I arrived carrying a US passport—there's an interesting story behind that. On entering the USA in 1949, I was given a permanent resident visa and a nice letter advising me that after five years I could apply for US citizenship. At the time, I had a British/Indian passport, which needed to be renewed in 1952 because I was still three years away from being eligible for US citizenship. I applied to the British Consul in New York, only to be turned down because, they said, my father was born in Hyderabad, then a princely state, and he was, therefore, not British. At the time of my father's birth, his father, Michael Breen, was a clerk in the British Residency in Secunderabad. Michael was the son of John Breen of County Clare, Ireland, who had joined the East India Company in 1847, during the Irish potato famine, as a soldier. Ten years later, his regiment fought in the Indian Mutiny, and he was wounded in Lucknow on October 6, 1857. This quaint "logic" of British bureaucrats who deemed my father was not British inspired me to apply for US citizenship on the very first day I was eligible.

In 1960, good academic jobs for women were few and far between. There were lots of jobs for women technicians, but very few were employed at the professional level. I applied to many pharmaceutical houses, only to be told that I was "over-qualified". Universities had lots of post-doctoral jobs, but these were temporary positions with low salaries, because they were supposed to offer further training in another area of research. In practice, the candidate often was bringing skills to the job, rather than the other way around.

I took one of these jobs at the University of Virginia in Charlottesville, founded by Thomas Jefferson, one of the founding fathers of America. Then came more setbacks—research funds ran out, and within a year I was back at the University of Chicago, in another post-doctoral position. In less than two years, that lab also closed.

While I was at the University of Chicago, I was invited to spend some time in a new clinical research lab in Northwestern University which had the latest automated equipment. I found to my delight—and chagrin—that there was now a sensitive, automated method for calcium analysis using fluorescence. Here was a method that I had been looking for and had never found while working for my PhD.

One day I was shown a new chemical that fluoresced with magnesium. I knew immediately that if the method for calcium could be automated using fluorescence, the same could be done for magnesium. Immediately, I started trying to work out the fluorescent automated procedure for magnesium. My years of study, in German, of the chemistry of dyes now paid off—I'll omit the technical details, but let's just say my method worked like a charm. I wrote up the procedure and it was published[2] in 1966.

Shortly after publication, I got requests for reprints from

all over the world, especially from Third World countries and pediatricians. From these requests, I learned that babies in Africa were dying, and no one knew why. The deaths were related to babies fed exclusively with Nestlé baby formula. Someone determined that the symptoms in the babies were the same as those seen in rats on diets deficient in magnesium. Nestlé baby formula—unlike mothers' milk—had no magnesium. Now, with my method, it was possible to analyze a few drops of blood from babies in order to confirm whether they were dying of magnesium deficiency.

Some months after publication, I attended a magnesium conference in New York City, and I heard firsthand from doctors, who had been in Africa, about babies dying of magnesium deficiency after they had been on Nestlé baby formula. The two companies that made the fluorometer and the automated equipment acknowledged my contribution, and asked permission to include my magnesium method in their manuals. This was an example of research being done on my own time, after hours, on borrowed equipment—and with no funding. Much research work never sees the light of day and some benefits may show up years later, but my work on magnesium is an example of research having an immediate impact on society, and for this I am very grateful.

In the meantime, in 1965, I was offered a position as Senior Research Biomedical Scientist with the Federal Government. Specifically, this was in the research service of a large veterans' hospital north of Chicago. I was now 41 years old and had been working and studying in laboratories since the age of 20. This was my first permanent professional job with a respectable salary, and full medical and retirement benefits. The labs were new and well-equipped, and I was assigned research technicians and a choice of research projects, on which I worked independently. I went into other areas of research, and had papers published in top peer-reviewed journals. I worked there for 24 years, until I retired at 65.

After I got my PhD and my job with the Federal Government, my economic position improved considerably. I was able to buy a car and a house in the country: behind my house are open green fields and woods, with deer, skunks, raccoons, opossums, and coyotes. I have lived there for 41 years, enjoying life with my pets: two cats and a dog.

I am now 83 years old and often think that I should have

done better with my life—on the other hand, I could have done a lot worse. I could very easily have become one of the old and impoverished Anglo-Indians left behind in India.

My early years in India and in America (after leaving Vassar), were a struggle. But whatever obstacles I had, there was always someone to help me—my mother, grandparents, teachers, and friends. My education in India gave me the foundation for my work in America. Dr. Ruth Conklin took me, a perfect stranger, into her lovely home and helped to integrate me into American society. My old school in India, Lovedale, gave me the backbone to live up to its motto:

NEVER GIVE IN

DISTANCES

by Kathy Cassity

In 1947 my Anglo-Indian grandfather, a police inspector in Tamil Nadu, died. His body was buried and his descendants scattered at sea, washing ashore on distant coasts. Whenever I view world maps, I push imaginary pins into each location where I have a relative, noticing our family's penchant for islands, peninsulas, cliffs, coastlines—Gibraltar, Vancouver Island, Tasmania, Hawaii, Perth, Sydney, Brazil, the French Riviera. Today most of us live on edges, and far apart.

We're a tapestry of contradictions: cops and con artists, preachers and drug smugglers, teetotalers and alcoholics, teachers and dropouts, engineers and artists, nurses and chronic patients, wanderers and homebodies, atheists and true believers, Anglicans and Catholics, family men and bachelors, rebels and conformers. Sometimes the opposites describe the same person. In us, you can find a little bit of everything.

One thing you'll never find is a picture of all of us, together.

June 1984. Auntie Emily and Uncle Reggie's 25th anniversary celebration in Hampshire, England.

This is the closest I have to a portrait that includes everybody. Even with a cast of 25, most of our family is missing. I'm included for the first time ever, even though I'm already grown. My father immigrated to America in 1958, three years before I was born, and didn't travel overseas again until 1982. At 22, this was my first time, both visiting Europe and meeting the family.

The photo was taken after plentiful wine, several hours into the party with several yet to go. Anglo-Indian celebrations rarely end on the same day they begin—unlike the American parties I'm used to, cut short by guests who must rush to get to Costco before closing time. (A true Anglo-Indian would never abandon a party to shop.) On that visit, I revelled in abundant food—aromatic curries, crunchy biscuits and creamy custards, bottomless cups of milky tea, flowing beer and wine. The air pulsed with the tight harmonies of big bands and the dreamy lyrics of standards. Over the music I heard rhythmic stories, tall tales and hearty laughter, with humour that makes the Monty Python troupe seem like dull schoolboys.

That June 1984 trip was magic, even though they all blamed me for Ronald Reagan while denying they had anything to do with Margaret Thatcher. That week in Hampshire, our conversations stretched into early morning, my uncles re-creating India through story. As they talked I thought of my father, an Anglo-Indian boy in Tamil Nadu with a farfetched dream, to build jet planes in America. Each evening I fell asleep curled into a musty armchair, surrounded by a sea of musical accents like lullabies.

September 2005. It's the second most complete photo, with a cast of 15, mostly different folks. We're gathered in the reception room of the Bear Hotel in Hampshire, dressed in black after saying goodbye to Uncle John, the nexus who kept our far-flung family from disintegrating. Many more of us are missing.

It's no longer the 1950s. International travel is no longer just for the wealthy, nor is phoning long distance. We don't wait a week to open letters, penned on tissue-thin blue aerogrammes that refuse to tear open properly. Today we can beam instant messages from one computer to the next, and we all have them, even those techno-resistant eccentrics who for decades managed to resist all 20th-century trappings—cars, CD players, even telephones. We have the World Wide Web. It should be easier than ever for a family like ours to stay connected. So why are we more distant than ever?

Some chasms no technology can bridge.

I arrived in London a week before Uncle John's funeral and stayed with my thin, dark-haired, bearded, and bespectacled second cousin, William, at his flat in Putney. William left India in 1949 at the age of five, and he still remembers the ship pulling out of Ballard Pier in Bombay. He suggested dinner at the Sree Krishna in Tooting, and at first I resisted, anticipating melancholy. Just about everyone who used to join us here is now gone, including Uncle John, who originally found this rare shrine to South Indian cuisine. "But they've renovated the whole interior," said William, "so it might not be as nostalgic as you fear." We walked arm-in-arm from William's flat to the bus stop, neither of us sure who was propping up the other—William guiding his jet-lagged American cousin, or me assisting William, whose right knee doesn't bend. That night he used a walking stick, saying, "It helps with the fatigue."

"You look a bit like Lytton Strachey," I said.

"I assure you, the resemblance stops at the physical."

When the bus dropped us on Tooting High Street, I hardly recognized the Sree Krishna. It had always been dark and brooding, with plush velvet curtains draping the windows and Taj Mahal-like domes gracing the walls. Now the signs were neon, proclaiming "Best South Indian food in London!" Bright marble tiles covered the floors. The cozy hideaway I remember had vanished. "Gone posh," William snorted. My relatives always pronounce that word disdainfully.

We ordered lagers and shared a *masala dosa*. I craved the lentil pancake and the spicy potatoes, the fire that makes my eyes water and nose run. "Best thing in the world for jet lag," Dad said, when I ate my first *dosa* here in 1988. Uncle John had "collected" us at Heathrow after a nine-hour flight and driven us in his rundown Opal—a "banger," he called it—straight to Tooting, without even stopping to drop off our luggage.

When the waiter brought our lagers, I took a healthy swig and relaxed just enough to pose a question I knew William hoped I'd forget to ask. "Did I hear right that Ryan isn't coming to the funeral?"

"Mmmm."

"But that's rather strange. France isn't so far."

"Ah. Yes. Well." William cleared his throat and perused the menu, even though we'd already ordered.

"My God, you sound just like Uncle John. That's what he always used to say when he didn't want to discuss something further. 'Ah. Yes. Well.'"

"You're terribly astute for an American."

"For an American," I sniped, mimicking. "'You're rather astute, for an American. You're rather liberal, for an American. That's rather environmentally minded of you, for an American. I rather like you, for an American.' Must I first and foremost be a nationality?"

"At this point," said William, "you're sounding rather British."

"You are avoiding my question."

"Am I?" William studied the menu. "What question was that, then? Have you ever tried the *idli*?"

"*Idli*, schmidli, you know what question. Why is Ryan avoiding the funeral?"

He cleared his throat. "*Bhindi*—that must be a new item."

"I mean, it's very odd, don't you think," I said, "that one would actually be at the deathbed yet not attend the funeral, even though he lives closer than most of us?"

"A bit odd, perhaps," said William offhandedly. "Now *korma*—isn't that a bit northern for a place such as this."

"William!" I yanked the menu from his long, skinny fingers. "Is it me that he's avoiding?"

"Fancy another drink?"

"You damn British!"

"Ah, but we're not British. In fact, our relationship to the British is a source of much complication."

"The hell you're not," I said, "because your dialogue with me is a model of indirection, classically British."

"Is it? Well, I suppose one could view it as such."

"William," I said, "I want you to do the unthinkable: *Pretend you are an American.*" William winced like a wounded puppy.

"That's right, you are a materialistic, greedy, American capitalist pig who goes to the Baptist church every Sunday and wants to mandate prayer in the public schools. You drive an SUV, you support the war in Iraq, you voted for George Bush and, by golly, you always say exactly what's on your mind—no beatin' around the bush for you, not like them Euro-peeins with their fancy-schmancy talk and phony accents. You, William Smith, are a real live 'Mercan! And not just any 'Mercan—you're the real kind, a genuine from-Texas 'Mercan!" William winced again.

"Now, William from Texas, I want you to tell it like it is." I switched accents: "Tell me then, old chap: Did our cousin Ryan happen to mention that his avoidance of Uncle John's funeral might have something to do with my presence?"

"Howdy," drawled William, "I'm afraid that's raht."

"What did he say?"

"You realize I was simply trying to avoid hurting your feelings."

"Hurt will last about five minutes, then I'll have a few days of pissed-off, then I will go on and live my life. Hurt feelings and momentary pissed-offed-ness, you can recover from. Broken trust, you cannot."

"For an American, you're starting to make rather a modicum of sense."

"Am I, rather?"

"Quite, quite. Now that you mention it," says William, "he did say that your presence would make things awkward."

"What's he talking about?" I can't imagine awkward. Ryan and I were once close friends.

"Because of things that happened in the past," said William. "I'm quoting now. That's all he would say."

"What things?"

"You'll have to ask him."

"He won't talk to me."

"Well, then it seems you have a problem," said William.

"Indeed," I sniped.

"Quite."

"Bloody nuisance, this family." I shook my head.

A few days later, I had my answer—or one as close as I'm likely to have.

I travelled to Hampshire, where my Uncle Robert, the last of our three bachelor uncles—the one Granny used to call "the terror of the lot"—booked me a room at The Bear. On Sunday afternoon he drove me to Uncle John's flat, leaving me alone to rifle through the heaps of used books and photographs, setting aside anything I might want. Among the piles I found an envelope addressed to our late Uncle Staunton, with a return address: the King County Superior Court, Seattle. Uncle Staunton, who had dropped dead in the Havant library on a January morning 10 years earlier, had never visited Seattle. What business would he have with the King County Superior Court?

Dear Mr. B.: We have no record on file of your brother's will. Here in Washington State, there are usually no court records for uncontested wills for small estates, which are processed without probate. Most likely that was the case with your brother. We wish you the best in your endeavours. Sincerely, Clerk of the King County Superior Court.

How odd. I then flashed upon a vague memory from 12 years earlier, a conversation in Pizza Hut on Putney High Street with

Uncle John. Dad had died six months earlier. Uncle John asked, "Have you seen your father's will?"

"Yeah," I said. "It's just the typical will leaving what there is to the kids, and there isn't much. Dad was such a spendthrift."

"No small fortune, then?"

"Are you kidding?" Uncle John had chuckled, and I'd assumed he was joking. Everyone knew that spending ran in my father's blood.

Perhaps Uncle John hadn't been joking.

That night, Uncle Robert and I sat at one of his locals, the Robin Hood Pub. "Perhaps a little rough for a woman," said Uncle Robert, "but they know me here, so you'll be all right. They'll probably ask me later who the bird was. Around here, everyone minds everybody else's business."

I waited until he was on his third drink before asking, "Uncle Robert, do you know if anyone thinks my dad died with a small fortune?"

An ex-hippie who twice hitchhiked overland to India and back, not much can surprise this uncle. That night, he nearly choked on his beer. "What's all this, then?"

"Do you know," I asked, "why Uncle Staunton would write to the King County Superior Court about Dad's will?"

"Fancy another Strongbow?"

How many drinks have my relatives consumed in an effort to deflect questions?

"No, just tell me what's going on."

"Well, your dad said it, didn't he," said Uncle Robert. "He told Ma, 'I have socked away a small fortune here in America, and I've changed my will to leave everything to you lot. If I beat this illness, I'm coming home and renouncing my US citizenship. I've got millions socked away, and someday it will all be yours.'"

"And he said this—when?"

"That fall before he died."

"When he had the brain tumor." I shook my head. "And everyone believed him? Hasn't anyone heard of organically induced psychosis over here?"

"Well, when the will didn't pan out," said Uncle Robert, "the story became that your mother changed it on his deathbed, you see, and kept the millions for herself."

"Surely nobody believed that."

Uncle Robert's silence, and his eyes, told me otherwise.

"Is that why certain relatives are staying away from the funeral next week?" I know my family hates point-blank, but I'm an American.

"Surely you want another Strongbow?"

"Okay, you changed my mind," I said, "but make it a half." Sometimes, there's nothing left to do but order another drink.

No wonder I hadn't gotten many expressions of sympathy when my mother died. And no wonder certain relatives had either avoided me, or acted...well, strange, whenever I visited. No wonder my grandmother's reaction when my mother died, two years later, was: "God struck her down."

A few days later we gathered for Uncle John's funeral. Not everyone was there. Everyone never is.

The procession departed from Uncle John's flat. As we rode by, older men tipped their hats; younger folks paid no attention. Perhaps courtesy is going the same way as the Anglo-Indians.

In a classic Church of England ceremony, we sang "Abide with Me" and "The Day Thou Gavest, Lord, Is Ended", because Uncle John said the lyrics always reminded him of us: *The sun that bids us rest is waking our brethren 'neath the western sky.* At the crematorium, a tape played his favourite jazz. Even though the food at the Bear Hotel reception was all English, it was an Anglo-Indian party to the end, stretching for hours, with endless jokes and stories and, even though we were at a funeral, laughter. When we returned to Uncle John's flat, each of us took a few books, yet the piles didn't seem to diminish. "But then removing books from John's flat," said Uncle Robert, "is a bit like trying to remove sand from the beach, isn't it?"

In some ways all seemed as it had always been, only smaller. There's death, there's emigration, but there's more. Our own crazy beliefs, sometimes, stopping us from gathering together at the times we need it most. I missed Ryan.

One of William's brothers drove us back to Putney. Back at his flat, William and I ordered *samosas* and *biryani* from a takeaway, nibbling wordlessly while old standards on vinyl blared from the stereo. I stayed awake as long as my heavy eyelids would allow, immersing myself in music and food, breathing in the aroma of curry, trying to summon lost spirits. It seems we've lost so many of the ones who remembered, and I'm now afraid of forgetting. I'm afraid of becoming like everyone, even though as a child, I feared not being like anyone.

The next day I found myself on a 747, heading for San Francisco and then on to my home in Hawaii. The audio system was programmed with the Ella Fitzgerald songbooks, and every two hours I caught my breath when she sang "Every time we say goodbye."

Until now, I'd never realized what an unforgivable breach my father had committed. As the eldest son, Dad had taken the helm after my grandfather died. He'd gone to England first and worked for seven years while attending engineering college, to bring his mother and seven siblings to England. He was destined to be the patriarch. Yet he had his own dream, a different one—to build jet planes in America. When he got his chance he took it, leaving the brood twice fatherless. Or so they saw it, anyway. Dad married a Yank and stayed in America, going 20 years without even a visit. How do they square the memory of the boy they remember in India with the man who deserted them?

Perhaps it's easier to believe that my father intended to live out the immigrant's fairytale. Go to America, make a fortune; come home with conspicuous wealth. Perhaps it was harder to accept that he'd really left for good.

And sometimes it's difficult to grasp the degree to which contradictions can dwell within a single soul. It's simpler to have heroes and villains. No one in the family wanted my father to be less than a hero. My mother must become the villain, leaving me the heiress, not of millions, but of divided loyalties.

But then I should be used to that: I'm an Anglo-Indian.

My father lived his vision, even designed the navigation system for the 747 that I'm flying on now. Thanks to dreamers like Dad, our world is now smaller, or so I'm told. We're globally connected, with geography no longer an excuse for separation. This should be the perfect historical moment for an Anglo-Indian family, with technology spanning every distance. Finally, we can be reunited.

If only it weren't for that other breach—the one separating our stubborn, wounded hearts.

A Passage to Canada

by Margaret Deefholts

Old photograph albums—well over 50 of them—are stacked side by side in bookshelves lining the walls of our family room. A couple which belonged to my parents date back more than 80 years, and although some of the photographs have yellowed with age, the images are still remarkably clear. The albums are precious: they are a legacy of my family's lives, and the years that shaped them—the places they lived in, schools they attended, and the friends they knew. Sepia mementos of vanished days.

My parents, my aunts and uncles, and their circle of friends are all now long gone. Yet these images still have the power to evoke that long-ago world of Anglo-India: for instance, a tin-and-bottle badminton tournament—the men in whites, the women in cotton blouses and pleated skirts, playing on the court of some up-country railway institute or club. Memory fills in the gaps, and I see the onlookers sitting on rattan chairs, drinking chilled *nimbu pani* and nibbling on slices of sponge cake, cheese straw twists, and dainty egg sandwiches served by turbaned bearers. Page by page the years unfurl: an ayah holding a chubby baby; men in khaki uniforms wearing solar topees; a locomotive steaming into a station; a young couple hugging each other with exaggerated fervour at a picnic while the rest of the group pose strait-laced for the camera.

The albums are stacked in chronological order. The older ones are turning fragile, the tissue paper between the pages starting to crumble. In the album which once belonged to my father, there's a shot of a bonneted old lady wearing a Victorian crinoline skirt and holding a baby in her arms, while a younger woman also in a long dress with a laced-up bodice stands next to her. Holding themselves stiffly and unsmilingly, they are my great-grandmother, my grandmother, and my father, as a six-month-old infant, the photograph taken in the small *mofussil* town in Uttar Pradesh (UP) where my Dad was born. Dad's album also has several landscape shots of Naini Tal and his alma mater, Philander Smith College. There are pictures of his friends larking around in the snow, and of him, violin on his lap, in the school orchestra. A few pages later, garbed in his university cap and gown, he holds the scroll of his Master's degree certificate with seeming casualness, in his right hand.

My mother's girlhood photograph album displays occasions spent with family and friends—picnics, fancy-dress balls, and one taken in her late teens with her favourite dog, Laddie, in Chunar, also in UP. Chunar seemed idyllic in those days. It was here that she and my father first met, and it was the start of a romance that was to endure for the rest of their lives. Her subsequent albums, each with photographs lovingly sorted and labelled, record the early years of their marriage, my arrival, and later the appearance of my sister, Phyllis. There are pictures of our sprawling bungalows in railway colonies when Dad was a junior railway officer—Dinapur, Jamalpur, Allahabad, and Asansol, and the years following in Calcutta, Nagpur, Madras, Gauhati, and Bombay.

My first photo album was a gift from my parents on my 12th birthday. It has a brown Rexene-like cover, and the photographs are held in place at the corners by triangular stickers. The school friends I once knew still beam at me from between the album's covers, although they themselves have vanished, engulfed by time and distance.

Our bookshelf of old albums includes my wedding album and a couple more consisting of family shots and pictures of our kids, who were born in Bombay.

And that's all for the way we were in India.

A new shelf. A different style of albums. A shift of perspective. India has slid into memory. Canada is now front and centre.

It is 1977 and our first Canadian Christmas. We are dazzled by the shopping malls arrayed in festive splendour. The kids, seven-year-old Glenn and four-year-old Susan, are caught in the lens of my Instamatic camera as they sit, shy and awkward, on Santa's lap.

Over the ensuing years, our photograph albums continue to pile up on the shelves: my parents' arrival in Canada, school and university graduations, family weddings, parties, and celebrations with friends. Those were the days before digital cameras, and a further set of albums bulge with photographs of our holidays in Australia, Britain, Europe, and the US. My travels back to India over the last 20 years occupy an entire shelf of photographs, videotapes, and diary notes.

But the way we are today isn't defined by what's between the covers of an album or recorded on a videotape. No camera, no matter how sensitive, captures the quiet times of the heart's experience. The exhilaration of our children's accomplishments, the warmth of our family circle, the kindness of friends—but also the sadness of final farewells to loved ones—all of which have contributed to our days in this land of our adoption, Canada.

When we first arrived, we took nothing for granted. Captivated by this country's natural beauty, we played tourists in our own backyard, exploring Vancouver and the Lower Mainland, spending weekends on Vancouver Island, and in the Okanagan and the Cariboo—and during one summer vacation driving awestruck through the splendour of the Rockies. It was a delight to watch town parades, enjoy free art exhibitions, join in ethnic festivals, and listen to free summer concerts in the city parks. Canada Day celebrations were especially important and, heads held high, we sang "O Canada" with great gusto.

We haunted our local library, unable to believe our good fortune in being able to borrow books on every subject imaginable—from fiction and non-fiction best sellers to classic literature and more. All of it free! Likewise, we were amazed by the entertainment choices available to us on cable TV. In India during the late '70s, the only English program consisted of flickering re-runs of "I Love Lucy".

My sister Phyllis still remembers the first time she and I went into a neighbourhood department store, Woodwards (sadly now no longer in existence), when I'd stood flabbergasted at the displays in their food and grocery section. Enjoying my dazed expression, she urged, "Go for it! Get whatever you want...I'm picking up the tab!" But it was all too overwhelming. How could I choose among 50 varieties of cheese when the only one I'd ever known in India was Amul. The shelves groaned under a myriad variety of brand-name chocolates I'd only ever read about—After Eight mints, Toblerone bars, boxes of Black Magic. The refrigerated meat counters, with their neatly sealed packages (no mutton shanks, dripping blood, surrounded by blue bottle flies and suspended on iron hooks from the ceiling), and the fruit and vegetable displays all so clean and orderly. Words had completely failed me by the time we got to the bakery, and my sister, chuckling happily, treated us to our first Black Forest dessert.

Sometimes we'd take a picnic lunch to our neighbourhood park, where Leon and I would people-watch, while the kids played on the swings or seesaws. Our Surrey neighbourhood in British Columbia is diverse, and the parks played host to a range of people who, like us, were immigrants from all over the world: India (mainly Sikhs), Bangladesh, the Far East, Europe, the United Arab Emirates, South America, Britain, and Australia.

It was all so very different from our lives in India.

As time went on, we settled into an everyday routine of commuting to work on weekdays and catching up with household chores on weekends. We spent our evenings cheering for the Canucks on Hockey Night in Canada, or watching a movie or favourite serial on PBS. The kids attended music lessons, swimming classes, and learned to play tennis; they went on ski trips and weekend camping excursions with school friends. It was all part of our assimilation process.

Three years after our arrival, we recited our citizenship oaths before a judge and became full-fledged Canadians. A photograph of the four of us standing next to a Royal Canadian Mounted Police officer, resplendent in his full dress uniform, records the momentous occasion.

Changing citizenship is straightforward. Changing inner horizons is not. Although we'd gained much by coming to Canada, there were things we'd forfeited, too. Gone, for example, was the spontaneous social life we'd known in India. There were no servants here to polish, clean, run errands. In Bombay back in the '70s, we'd thought nothing of urging friends who'd dropped in on spec for a drink and a chat, to join us for a "pot luck" meal. Our cook, with admirable aplomb, would merely add a few more potatoes and carrots to an Irish stew, or stretch a mince filling to stuff a few more pan-rolls or potato chops. Or, if we were short of food, we'd send our house peon to pick up kebabs and rotis from a neighbouring *kati-kebab* shop. And after it was all over, we'd head for bed, leaving it to the servants to look after all the washing up.

Not so here in Canada. Social invitations, often weeks in advance, were carefully noted on our kitchen calendar; so, too, were the occasions when we entertained friends at our home.

I began to miss India. I wanted to feel the grit under my fingernails, to breathe the dust and stink of the city streets, and be part of its surging, crowded sidewalks. In our long, dark, and miserably cold and wet winter days, I longed for the hard, metallic sunlight of the tropics.

Discontent is easy to feed on, and at the time Canada seemed to me like a beautifully wrapped gift covered in pretty tinted cellophane and decorated with a huge ribbon, but when you opened it, the contents were bland, unexciting: houses arrayed along tidy suburban streets, supermarkets and shops all in a row, traffic that ran obediently along demarcated lanes, and people who lived their lives behind windows with vertical blinds. I yearned for India's chaos, its colour, and its unpredictability.

Going back after 10 years was a thrill—one that I shared with Glenn and Susan, who were fascinated by the experience even though they were young teenagers at the time.

Did it cure me of my fever? Nothing quite so slick a resolution as that. India was still a part of me (and will always be), but I understood then that she and I had come to a parting of the ways: we would no longer dwell in the same house, but visiting her would always be a joy and a privilege. After which, I would return contentedly home—to Canada.

And so it has been for the last 30 years.

But what of my Anglo-Indian ties?

When I lived in India, particularly in Bombay with its sophisticated and diverse mixture of Westernized Indians, I was seldom conscious of my identity as an Anglo-Indian. My office colleagues and friends were from a cross-section of backgrounds: Goans, Parsis, Punjabis, or Gujaratis, and most of them had been to Anglo-Indian private schools either as day-scholars or boarders. We night-clubbed, went to movies, partied at one another's homes, listened to the Beatles or Ravi Shankar, raved about the same movie stars (whether from Hollywood or Bollywood), and exchanged magazines and novels. We were equally comfortable wearing *saris*, *kurtas*, skirts, dresses, or jeans, depending on the occasion.

As a measure of our attitudes in Bombay back in the '60s, it raised no eyebrows when my sister married Shahnavaz "Myke" Merchant, who came from a Muslim background. My husband Leon was an Anglo-Indian, but that was coincidental—he could just as well have been Punjabi, or Sikh, or Bengali. The only thing that counted was a commonality of values, shared interests, a sense of humour, and a tolerant outlook on life.

Within a few months of our arrival in Canada, Glenn and Susan shed their Anglo-Indian accents; not so Leon and I, who made no effort to sound Canadian. It is the one characteristic that sets us apart from native-born citizens and, even today, I am amused when people stop me with the comment, "You have an interesting accent; where are you from originally?" When I ask them to guess, the response is usually "South Africa" or "Wales" or "The West Indies". Very seldom does anyone come up with "India".

The game gets better when I tell them I have "an Anglo-Indian accent". Furrowed brow, and a quizzical, "Oh? And what does *that* mean?" When I explain the term, they are intrigued. "But your name sounds Dutch or German," they say. "Was your *mother* Indian?" Rather than going into a long explanation, the easiest comparison is to liken us to the Canadian Métis, an endogamous people of mixed French and Indian First Nations descent. "Ah-ha!" They nod in comprehension and add, "Many generations in India, eh? What a fascinating background!"

The friends we made during those first few years were mainly Canadian, and I was both surprised and thrilled to hear a distinctively Anglo-Indian accent on the phone while making a business call from my desk in downtown Vancouver. It turned out that Leonie was from Calcutta, and we excitedly agreed to meet for lunch the following day.

As is often the case, within the first five or 10 minutes of our meeting, there was a flurry of questions. "So…whereabouts did you live in India?" and, "Which school did you go to?" Followed closely by, "Oh, then you probably knew…" Sure enough, we discovered a couple of mutual acquaintances whom we'd known many years ago in Calcutta.

This Anglo-Indian characteristic has never failed to mystify my brother-in-law, Derek Beavan. Born in London's East End, he spent his childhood and teen years in a Brixton neighbourhood, attending the same school from kindergarten to high school. As he says: "If I met someone from my street in Brixton today, the chances of them knowing my parents or any of the kids I was in school with would be next to impossible! Yet out of 300,000 or more Anglo-Indians spread across a vast country like India, you all manage, in no time flat, to find someone in common that you knew back then!"

Hard to explain to someone who wasn't part of Anglo-India at the time, that this was scarcely astonishing: we lived in the same localities in Delhi, Calcutta, Bombay, or Madras, attended the same privately run Anglo-Indian schools in the plains, or up in the hills, spent our childhood in small upcountry railway colonies, and worked as secretaries or managers in old, established companies such as Shaw Wallace, Gladstone Lyall, Imperial Tobacco, and Mackinnon Mackenzie. The network was (and still is) a small, tight one.

Through Leonie, we met several other Anglo-Indian families in and around Vancouver, and shortly afterwards a group of volunteers decided to form an Anglo-Indian Recreational Club, the idea being to organize social get-togethers on a regular basis, and publish a quarterly newsletter.

The club has hosted a lively series of events over the years, all of which have attracted a diverse crowd, including Calcutta Chinese immigrants, and people of Portuguese descent from Macao, in addition to Anglo-Indians and Goans. The New Year's Eve ball has always been a gala affair with everyone in evening attire, a lavish Western-style buffet, and the dance floor thronged at midnight as the crowd links arms to sing Auld Lang Syne in typical Anglo-Indian style.

Anglo-Indian Day on August 2nd has been traditionally celebrated by a picnic on the weekend closest to that date. The "oldsters" play bocce, or sit around my carrom board, trying to recapture their youthful skill by whacking at the striker and getting their "men" into the pockets. The younger generation, having exhausted themselves on a baseball pitch, or at kicking a soccer ball around, crowd in for a look and take their turn. Picnics are also an excuse (as if we need one!) to flaunt favourite nibbles like coriander chutney sandwiches, *kebabs*, home-made *pakoras*, and even *puttu*-rice *dol-dol* sweets.

Pulling back the lens to look at the wider picture, fortunately the sun hasn't yet begun to rim the horizon on the world of Anglo-India. We are now a truly global community that transcends physical boundaries thanks to the Internet and e-mail. Old friends have found one another after decades and now link hands in cyberspace. New Web sites continue to spiral off Google search engines, spinning at us from Australia, Britain, India, Canada, the USA, and Europe. Some like www.Pepperwater.com have burst like Divali crackers across our monitor screens, grabbing the attention of the younger generation. Others, such as the classic Anglo-

Indian Portal at http://www.maltap.com/anglo/index.php, are the touchstone of all that is quintessentially Anglo-Indian in terms of articles, profiles, news stories, and opinion pieces. My own nostalgia site at www.margaretdeefholts.com still draws readers who stroll its corridors into the past.

It isn't only the Internet that has changed our perceptions in recent years. East-West fusions in music, film, theatre, and even food, are popular trends today, and those with blended racial backgrounds are likewise regarded with admiring interest and curiosity. What a difference from our apprehensions of being labelled as "half-castes" in colonial India!

We have other reasons to be optimistic as we look ahead. Books by gifted Anglo-Indian authors continue to hit print. BBC radio and Australian broadcasting stations have run recent documentaries capturing our unique culture, while newspapers and magazines have been eager to feature our history and way of life in India and abroad. Can a newly minted TV documentary on our global community of Anglo-Indians be far behind?

It's an exciting time to be the way we are.

Young Man Behaving Badly

The profligate 20-something and the trip to India that turned out not to be a lie

by Glen Duncan

The winter of 1991 found me stunned and shivering in the aftermath of an imploded love affair. Being 26, I flung myself actorishly on London and, without any intimations of my own ludicrousness, spent two years showing God what I thought of him by letting myself go. I drank and took drugs sufficient to give me bleeding gums and a Parkinsonian head wobble, conditions that compromised but did not prevent my other main hobby—having sex as often as possible. A lot of girls didn't mind. A lot of them had troubles of their own. It was a cheering surprise, the sort of dismal shape you could be in and still get into some maenadic self-harmer's pants. Granted, these encounters never developed—no morning-after breakfast or fun in the shower—but, encased as I was in the armour of nihilism, I wouldn't have stuck around for any of that rubbish anyway.

For the minimum-wager with Caligulan needs, the glory days are soon over. In two brief years of beyond-means living, I went from being more or less viably broke to being tremblingly, authentically in debt. Also, I filled in the alcoholic's questionnaire and discovered that apparently I was one.

I wrote to my father and asked him for a loan. This doesn't sound so bad. But only a month earlier he had sent me a gift of £500, part of the yield of one of the ancient insurance policies he was in the habit of disbursing among his children.

After an ominous pause, the old man wrote back: yes, he'd give me the money, but he wanted to see me. I was being formally summoned to the parental seat (a one-bedroom, retirement flat in Bolton) because manifestly Something Was Seriously Wrong.

My family is Anglo-Indian and, of the four children, I'm the only one who wasn't born in India. Thus the mythic shadow under which I grew up was a narrative of flight and exile, the Indian glory of Those Days (moonlit dances, bootleg liquor, elephants, tigers, steam trains, and servants) set against the English dreariness of

These Days (miserable weather, poverty, lousy fresh fruit, and consistent hostility from the natives). A fertile story, yes—but theirs. I, made in England, felt excluded, miffed, resistant to the idea of even visiting India, a position of increasing absurdity as, one by one, backpacking friends returned from the place with the standard anecdotal combo of nirvanic epiphany and toilet horror.

In Bolton my father and I drank whisky while he gave me the what-in-God's-name-are-you-doing-with-your-life? dressing down I'd expected. It generated a peculiar psychic response. On the one hand: Wow, this is my dad talking. Better shape up. On the other: Who do you think you are—my dad? My mother got the curry and rice ready in the kitchen. What are your plans, for God's sake? the old man demanded. What is it you want to do?

To this day, I'm not sure why I answered that I was planning a trip to India. I certainly hadn't been planning a trip to India, or anywhere else. My dad was initially incredulous—India? You haven't got any money—but within seconds he segued with protean ease into wild-eyed enthusiasm, got out maps, started drawing up itineraries, calling the roll of friends we'd visit. It had become "we"; he would accompany me. It was while I was still reeling from the shock of his self-invitation that he 'fessed up to losing his eyesight. He wanted to show me the old country while he still could.

In India, I watched him among friends he hadn't seen for 35 years. A glamour of England he didn't know he'd acquired made many of them tentative and subdued. He ran his hands over stone walls, doorways, gravestones. The small changes pierced him; in the face of the big ones he lost his bearings. He took my arm to cross the roads. We had frank conversations on the chilly night trains, became people to each other, aside from father and son.

At the end of it all, the two of us stood at the National Express bus stop at Heathrow waiting for his ride back to Bolton. It was cold, windy, raining. We were both suffering from the need to say something in keeping with the scale of what we'd been through. Quite a problem, considering his default of emotional understatement and mine of lapsing into a crying jag at the first sign of human warmth. Standing there, with his collar up and his left eye watering, he looked older than I'd ever seen him look. The bus arrived. We embraced, still reaching for something to say. In the end he just said, "Thanks for looking after me."

I think that was the first time I realized the balance of strength between us had shifted. What had started as me asking him for help ended with him thanking me for helping him. I was a young man, and he was old. It was my world now, not his. I resolved to get my life in order, quit being a waster, do something with my time instead of (or at least as well as) boozing and fornicating it away.

First published in the *New York Times* Magazine, November 2007

Just off the Boat

by Chris Francis

I found myself in seat No. 36B of the Air India flight from Hyderabad to New York on a hot, sunny March morning, staring out of the window, sweating (the aircraft's air conditioning was not working) and wondering—what the heck was I doing on this plane. Had I done the right thing? This was ridiculous! And no, I enjoyed flying. If you left me on an aircraft, I would opt to live on it. Then what was the reason for my panic?

It all started with the decision taken a year earlier to move to the USA with my wife, Anne. She had left a month earlier and, being the resourceful person that she is, finished with all the formalities for settling down and starting anew.

We were both young, successful Anglo-Indians that belonged to close-knit, large families, and this decision to move abroad was welcomed by both families. Being Anglo-Indian meant that we were going to live among people who more or less shared our lifestyle. The future looked bright, with US dollar salaries, infrastructure to die for (good roads and clean surroundings), cars, and fine homes. Oh, and it even snowed in winter…a fascinating event for us, who thought a cold day in winter was 70° F.

And, yes, day shifts…it had to be the prospect of day shifts and good pay that must have done it for me. It was also a chance for Anne's dream to come true, and a couple of mine as well.

Back in India, we were both employed as managers in multinationals that had outsourced their jobs to the "happening city of Hyderabad"—next only to Bangalore in fame for its software and business outsourcing opportunities.

Both of us earned six-figure (rupee) salaries. We had just built a decent-sized home, with a garden and garage, and had a fully furnished apartment in the middle of the city. We loved to participate in any event organized by the local Anglo-Indian community, including the mandatory dances at Christmas and New Year's, and the AGM and other meetings that the local association conducted.

No kids, but a high income and time to spend—we spent most of it travelling and, apart from contributing our bit as loyal kids to our parents, enjoyed a very comfortable life. We had travelled abroad almost every year in the four years we'd been married. To the local Anglo-Indian community, then, we were deemed successful, and perhaps some even envied our lifestyle.

So when Anne got an offer to move to Princeton, New Jersey, for a permanent transfer, we were not exactly enthusiastic about it, and only looked at it as an opportunity to live in another country and experience it at firsthand. Check out the grass on the other side—if it was greener, OK, otherwise forget it.

A far cry from the '50 and '60s, which saw hordes of Anglo-Indians jump into ships and planes to move to the land that many regarded as the only way out of the uncertainty that faced them—England. And then came Australia, Canada, the USA, and New Zealand. We used to hear stories of how a railway town would lose half its Anglo-Indian families in an exodus to these countries, leaving the remainder only with memories to share about the good times the community once enjoyed. For example, if anyone fell ill, the whole colony would turn up to visit them in hospital.

I felt there was more than a touch of irony in the fact that we were able to choose whether we wanted to leave India for a new life, rather than go just because it was the only choice. India had changed a lot from what it was in those early decades after Independence. We had cell phones and services comparable with the best in the world. The economy was booming, and I had personally witnessed a remarkable amount of wealth creation—a turnaround of entire cities.

The city I was leaving, Hyderabad, was the largest in India after the four metros of Mumbai, New Delhi, Kolkata, and Chennai. Bangalore became the latest addition to the list of metros, but Hyderabad was spread out over a larger area. The Anglo-Indian community traced its roots back many generations—a small but close-knit community, with a sizeable number concentrated in "Little England", or Lallagudda, and a smaller neighbour in Mettugudda. These two localities were in Hyderabad's twin city of Secunderabad. Hyderabad itself had a community based mainly in Nampally and Gunfoundry, but also scattered elsewhere in the city. The Andhra Pradesh capital was also famous for its hotels and theatres, and from the '50s to the '80s these were known to have a sizeable number of Anglo-Indian patrons. Of course, there were the usual dances, and Christmas and New Year's saw a lot of excitement, with many venues playing host to Anglo-Indian crowds.

The '90s saw many Anglo-Indians graduating from university and finding jobs with good private companies; at the onset of the new millennium, when the multinationals moved in, well-educated, English-speaking Anglo-Indians were sought after. These jobs boosted the average family household income, and brought a level of prosperity never before experienced by the community.

So times had changed, indeed, by the time Anne and I decided that we would give it a go, and head for the USA. Things moved so smoothly once we had agreed that I actually found myself digging in my heels at the pace of it. Once the visas came through I found myself debating whether we were doing the right thing. After all, we were comfortably off, right? Friends thought we were stupid, gave us 43 (or was it 44?) reasons why working in India was now a fantastic experience, and how many great jobs were available with the best of companies. Former colleagues baulked at the idea and thought I was foolish even to contemplate it.

Days and weeks passed, and then it was time to sell the furniture. Easier said than done: it was tough to find buyers who did not want to rip you off if they sensed any urgency in closing the deal. I was thankful to the few who did end up buying our well-maintained furniture for a reasonable price.

The pain did not stop with the giving up of physical possessions. It was emotional, too. And I now fervently believe that anyone who thinks that moving to another country is a wonderful experience is either lying or is still asleep dreaming about it.

It was bad enough in the early days telling our families about our decision, but then actually leaving them was really hard. We had been away from home in the past, but always returned to our extended family. And coming from India, a country where family is...well, FAMILY. Period. We would get a call from our folks if we missed a single weekend with them. My father-in-law, Lennie Barton, would call me on my cell phone if I was running an hour late for our Saturday evening ritual, familiar to many Anglo-Indians—a couple of pegs of Old Monk rum with Coke, and some *phallies*, followed by some lovely chops and pepperwater with rice. I tried to get him onto some more expensive rum and whisky, but we somehow wiggled our way back to Old Monk. (My biggest regret since I came to the USA is missing this ritual.) Food was another BIG reason why I wanted to stay.

We had to remind ourselves constantly of a vision that we were doing it to improve our lifestyle, learn something new, and to avoid being told when we got older, "You should have gone to America when you had the chance!"

It was a new feeling, a blend of joy and pain—I don't know how else to define it. Joy, because we both loved to travel and visit new places. Pain, because we loved our families and did not want to move far from them. I could not separate the two feelings and was torn by the battle between them to gain dominance over my perceptions.

Looking back now, the clincher had to be the night shifts. While the money was good, both of us worked nights. Not exactly a fun thing to do. Day jobs were available but didn't pay nearly as well as the outsourced jobs we both had, taking advantage of the time difference with America. We had spent around five years working this schedule, and so when Anne received the offer to work in America as soon as we landed (my job would take a little longer), it was inviting to say the least.

I was suddenly jolted by an air pocket and the announcement that we were to land at Newark Airport, New Jersey. The airport looked familiar—it was, after all, the airport I'd landed at the very first time I'd travelled outside India. I rubbed my eyes to rid them of the last remnants of a disturbed sleep and braced myself for a long adventure ahead. Sleek, fast cars zoomed by on the highway parallel to the runway and seemed to compete with the jumbo jet as she gently touched down on the tarmac.

My mind went back to the scene when I said farewell to my family—so teary and emotional. After being blessed by everyone over the age of 40, I finally made it to the waiting taxi. Of course, 15 family members and friends followed. Not bad—had I left from Guntakal (a south Indian Anglo-Indian Railway colony), I would have had at least 150 of the community seeing me off, and there would have been scenes of sadness to rival the passing away of some celebrity. But even in modern-day Hyderabad, this was a decent-sized Anglo send-off. I just loved it.

The aircraft finally came to a halt. This was America. The land of the free. And soon, I came to know, the land of the very independent person. A million possibilities lay ahead, but the only thing on my mind was the fact that my dearest partner and wife, Anne, eagerly awaited my arrival and had arranged for a limousine to pick me up. Talk about a bragging opportunity to mail back home.

After collecting my bags and passing through Immigration, I walked out to the spot that I was told the limo would pick me up. The driver was a burly Punjabi from North India, who grinned at me and said, *"Namaste,* sir." Oh heck, welcome back to India? I laughed loudly and entered the limo. I already felt at home.

Talk about opportunities—it so happened that about a couple of months later, Anne sent an e-mail asking for details of local Anglo-Indians in New Jersey; it turned out that a prominent Anglo-Indian couple, Blair and Ellen Williams, and their son, Julian, happened to live not far from our home in central New Jersey. I had read about, and was inspired by, the tremendous work Blair was doing to help indigent Anglo-Indians in India, through his charity CTR (set up to help Anglo-Indian seniors and students). He not only invited me to join the board but also helped me realize a pragmatic method of practising charity.

So at the time of writing, it is 18 months since we arrived in the USA, and in that period Anne was promoted, I started my own consultancy, and we are now proud parents of our first baby girl, Cathryn; and, yes, we discovered three Indian stores that sold every item needed to make our favourite curries and chops, bought a car, and obtained a good lease on an apartment.

I still have mixed feelings of joy and pain...but much of the pain seems to have subsided, replaced with joy.

Denial And Pride

by Lionel Lumb

The world is going where Anglo-Indians have led the way. The prejudices of the colonial past—when people of mixed-race were shunned as "neither fish nor fowl", condemned as inferior half-castes, and scathingly described as "eight *annas* in the rupee[3]" or far worse—are fading fast. For example, in Canada, a country that openly celebrates its vibrant multicultural complexity, a poll released in August 2007 found that more than 90 per cent of Canadians approve of inter-marriage between people from different groups. That support climbs to 99 per cent among those under 35.

Canada is the most multicultural nation in the world, and Anglo-Indians blend with ease into the Canadian mosaic. After all, we can realistically claim to be the first multicultural community in the world—for us, the "Anglo" includes ancestors from Portugal, France, the Netherlands, Belgium and Denmark, not just those from England, Scotland, Wales and Ireland. Even the "Indian" embraces ancestors from the large variety of ethnic groups which spice the *masala* mix of India.

But we didn't always have it easy in the days of the British Raj. We served the Empire better than it served us, especially at the end, and we suffered slurs and attitudes designed to make us under-perform.

Even those of us blessed with memories of a gilded childhood, of comfortable homes with servants, long summer holidays in cool hill stations, and games of badminton, dances and *gymkhanas* at the club, can also recall the darker side of rejection, cruel words, and condescending or downright snobbish attitudes at work or social gatherings.

When we migrated to our new countries we found not too much had changed, not at first. Not surprisingly, there are many in the community who find it easy to deny their Anglo-Indian roots—if they can get away with it. Many others take pride in their heritage, even if their journey through life has its dark and bright patches, its moments of denial and pride. I have experienced both.

It was a friend in Toronto who first made me think about the difference between the 11 years of my childhood in Lahore, where I was born, and the 14 years I spent in Calcutta (now Kolkata), where I finished my education and started a career as a journalist.

She said: "You always speak so lovingly of your childhood in Lahore but you rarely talk about Calcutta. Were you happy there?"

As I told her at the time, the answer is yes, very much so. I'd been educated at a great school—St. Xavier's—where the mainly Belgian Jesuit teachers imparted an education as good as the best in Europe or North America; I'd worked for the Calcutta *Statesman*, which prepared me for Fleet Street and, later, BBC Television News; met the woman I would marry and love to this day; our first child was born in Calcutta; and as a teenager and young adult I'd packed in enough fun and good times for two people.

But my Toronto friend was right: no matter how many fond memories I have of Calcutta, they will never match the idyllic richness of the way I remember Lahore. It's taken me decades to work out why: in Lahore, I was just a happy kid cosseted by a loving family, relatives, and friends; but somehow—when we crossed the relatively new border from Pakistan to India, and embarked on the long and dusty train journey from Amritsar to Calcutta—I lost my innocence and entered the complex world of an Anglo-Indian.

In Lahore I never knew I was an Anglo-Indian. Nor that my father and his mother, an Anglo-Indian born in Madras, were in any way different from my English grandfather born in Lancashire. The same held true for my mother's side of the family. We were just folks, a large and happy family with many aunts and uncles, and lots of friends from school, church, and club who were also just like us. Our lives were gracious and moved at a tranquil pace.

In Calcutta everything speeded up. Some of the gentility vanished, along with the personal space that was lost in exchanging a large house and garden for a much smaller flat. My father, who somehow managed his billiard table business in ways that never intruded on our lives in Lahore, now showed signs of stress and struggle. Even in school it was possible to sense a competitive edge missing in Lahore.

Class and colour became factors for the first time. Obviously richer boys at school, sons of very wealthy Indian businessmen, were not like the rest of us. Not to say they were snobbish or haughty—many became good friends—but there was no hiding the difference. I became conscious of my meagre wardrobe, handed-down shoes, the fact I walked to school instead of riding in a car with a chauffeur, and could never spend money at the tuck shop with nonchalance.

In the way of Anglo-Indian families, four of my father's siblings were fair-skinned. He was one of three born darker, as was I. A fair uncle in Calcutta had married a woman of Irish descent. She would take her sons, my cousins, to the Calcutta Swimming Club while I was always left behind, to swelter and sulk in the draining humidity before the monsoon. It took several resent-filled months before the family mustered the courage to tell me why: the CSC's "colour *chowkidhars*" would turn me away because of its Europeans-only policy.

It was not our family's only example of the colour wedge that could divide Anglo-Indian families. An aunt had broken my grandmother's heart. She would only go out in the company of my English grandfather because she didn't want her European friends to know her mother was "a woman of the country". The aunt left for England as soon as she could and shunned our family for the rest of her life.

In another example, my mother's sister and her British soldier husband emigrated from India to Australia shortly after the war, well before that country ended its whites-only immigration policy. We never even thought about emigrating to Australia—we would not have got past that country's colour bar[4].

Jolts like these were good preparation for the realities of the world beyond the genteel lustre of Lahore. They toughened me in ways I could not appreciate at the time but for which I was later thankful. So when the novel and the movie *Bhowani Junction*—with its theme of a desperate people caught between two worlds—hit many Anglo-Indians like a blow to the gut[5], I was able to shrug. Before John Masters came along, I'd read Orwell's *Burmese Days*, which churned my stomach with its comments on Eurasians: "yellow-bellies"; "awfully degenerate types...thin and weedy and cringing...I've heard that half-castes always inherit what's worst in both races". Orwell, born in India, did not share that opinion but his characters were voicing the damning prejudice of the era.

I vowed I would never become like his Mr. Francis and Mr. Samuel, pretending to be European because their "drop of white blood is the sole asset they've got". I vowed never to deny my Anglo-Indian roots, and to insist on being judged as an individual, on my own merits. But it took much longer than I expected to achieve a measure of pride in those roots.

A colleague at *The Statesman*, Reginald Maher, set me on the path to a proper appreciation of Anglo-Indians' unique culture and many achievements. That got me reading more about our community and helped develop a scholarly interest in racism in all its evil forms, not only in India but also in Africa, Europe, and North America. Dr. King and the freedom marchers helped me to dream, too.

By the time we immigrated to Britain in 1963, I'd developed a thick skin and an inner toughness. I could ignore the snide and the subtle, and responded to the openly racist with healthy contempt. Like women in the pre-1970s man's world, I worked twice as hard to earn respect and compliments. But both came, especially at the BBC.

One reward was being chosen in 1971 as the producer to head the BBC's coverage of the looming India-Pakistan war in then East Pakistan. Colleagues on the trip were reporter John Humphrys (later news anchor of the main BBC TV news and a terrier of a radio interviewer), cinematographer Keith Skinner, and audio technician Tom Stoddart. Already in Dacca (now Dhaka) was a famed radio correspondent, Ronnie Robson.

We were in Dacca barely a few days when the many foreign journalists were confined to the Intercontinental Hotel, under the so-called protection of the Red Cross—the Red Cross pulled out as soon as the war began, when Pakistan Air Force planes bombed Indian airfields on December 3. Many expatriates—diplomats, their wives and children, business people, teachers, aid workers, and tea planters—also crowded into the hotel.

One night in the lounge I chatted with an English tea planter from the Sylhet district of East Pakistan. He asked my background, I told him, and we were reminiscing about Calcutta when John Humphrys, working on his script for a news item, came by to clarify some details. We sorted out the problem and John went back to his room. I turned back to the planter and found him looking at me with curiosity and surprise.

"You just told John Humphrys what to do," he said.

"Sure," I responded. "It's my job."

"But you're…," he paused, almost blushed. "I mean…," and he went silent again.

The penny dropped. "You mean because I'm an Anglo-Indian and John's English?" I couldn't help laughing. John and I had worked together for several years and our mutual respect for each other's talents couldn't be higher, or our working relationship more comfortable. That night I went to bed thinking that planter still lived in the old world, and this Anglo-Indian was clearly in the new one.

The war ended on December 16. Keith Skinner and Tom Stoddart had shot amazing news film of the liberation of Dacca and the end of the war, John rushed together a compelling script/voiceover, and I befriended a colonel of the invading Indian paratroop regiment. He commandeered a Jeep and transported me with the BBC's film bag—and that of other networks, including ITV, CBC, CBS, ABC and NBC—to the airport for a flight out to India and eventually London.

John and the others returned to London a week or so later, and all of us were fêted for a job well done. But all too soon the old world intruded. Enoch Powell[6] kept raising his racist head and, despite the best efforts to condemn him on the part of media giants like David Frost, caught the imagination of those who favoured his vitriolic anti-immigrant views. We decided to leave Britain and immigrated to Canada in 1973. It remains the best major decision of our lives.

One of my paternal grandmother's cautionary sayings was that "pride ever runneth before a fall". It's ironic that Bangladesh, a source of Anglo-Indian pride for me in 1971, became in 1975 the site of a fall from grace. I was lured out of journalism at Global Television News in Canada by a contract with the United Nations that would send me for several months to India, Pakistan, Afghanistan, and Bangladesh. The assignment was to supervise the making of documentaries for the UN's Habitat summit, scheduled for Vancouver in 1976. The temptation to re-visit the subcontinent, especially Lahore and Calcutta, and tour Afghanistan for the first time, was too strong to resist. I jumped.

Just before I headed for New Delhi I had a long conversation with a friend at Global called Don North. Don had spent some early adult, and probably hippie, years of his life living in Delhi. He'd never forgotten those times, and he badly wanted to go instead of me—he even asked if I'd step aside and let him take the assignment.

"Why would I want to do that?" I asked.

"Because you're an Anglo," he said, looking me straight in the eye as he used the mildly pejorative nickname for our community.

I'd been away from India for so many years, and hadn't thought about the old prejudices for so long, that I didn't get it right off. "What do you mean?"

"They're expecting a Canadian," he said. "When they find out you're an Anglo they'll have no respect for you. You know, Indians despise you A-Is. They may not tell you but they do."

I protested that I'd worked with Indians at *The Statesman* and never encountered that kind of attitude, and I told Don to get lost. Not so easy to lose was the impact of his words. What if he was right? The thought kept me awake in weak moments on restless nights as I prepared for departure.

The plane from Toronto touched down in Delhi on August 15, 1975, India's independence day. That I knew. What I didn't know was that at some time while it was in the air, Sheikh Mujibur Rahman—the charismatic President and architect of Bangladesh—was assassinated in Dacca. All flights in and out of the country were cancelled. When they were resumed a few days later I took the first available plane to Dacca but an airport official, leery of my passport which listed my profession as "journalist", deported me to Bangkok.

Returning to Delhi, I obtained a new passport and a new visa and eventually made it into Bangladesh, where I was assigned to play a more hands-on role in the production of their documentary than the UN coordinator job I was given in the other countries. Because of my earlier flight and deportation, and the long hours spent obtaining a new visa, I entered the country somewhat dispirited.

The Bengali producer with whom I was to work, also called Mujibur Rahman but no relation of the slain leader, welcomed me warmly enough but threw me slightly when he said: "We were expecting someone else. Your Canadian director, Mr. Jim Carney, told me he was sending a Canadian specialist on India and Bangladesh. But it was a different name."

I explained I, too, was something of a specialist because I covered the war in 1971 for the BBC. Rahman nodded amiably but added: "This producer was spoken of as most suitable—this

Canadian."

I didn't know quite how to take this. Was he questioning my qualifications as a producer or my Canadianness? Then I recalled Don North's harsh comments about Anglo-Indians. Was I too dark, too Anglo-Indian, to fit the Bengali's image of a Canadian? Confused and embarrassed, in a moment of weakness, I shrugged and went on to discuss our shooting schedule, never revealing I was born in Lahore, spent many years in Calcutta, and even understood a little Bengali. My caution seemed to be vindicated moments later when Rahman made a disparaging comment in Bengali to his cinematographer about my cheap calculator on the hotel desk. He was clearly a man who made quick value judgments. I kept the conversation in the safe arena of professional matters.

It was late that night, alone again after dinner, I realized that I had denied my origins. My grandmother must have turned over in her grave in pain. I should have corrected the deception the next day but we were instantly busy on a tight schedule and I let it slide.

In the weeks that followed Rahman and Mohbin, the cinematographer, and I became good friends. But still I never mentioned my 14 years in Calcutta—the city of the great poet and Nobel Prize winner, Rabindranath Tagore, and the spiritual home of all Bengalis, even of those now in Bangladesh.

One day I joined them to find Rahman reading a UN newsletter that included some paragraphs on my career and background. Rahman shook his head in disappointment at me. "You never told me about your time in Calcutta. Why did you hide that from me?"

Mohbin said: "I guessed it all along." He had seen my flicker of recognition when Rahman used the Bengali word *falthu* to describe my cheap calculator.

They were not angry but sad. I was both sad and angry. In betraying myself, I also betrayed them. They deserved better and I should have known better.

Of course, I was able to make it up to them over my remaining weeks in Bangladesh. And when Rahman came to Canada early in 1976 to edit the film at the National Film Board in Montreal, my wife Shirley and I spoiled him, had him over to our Toronto home for weekends, and even helped him through some tough times in New York when he was afraid to return to Bangladesh because of yet another coup there.

The memory of my denial rankled for a long time. Years of professional growth working with superb colleagues in Britain and Canada should have given me the strength to toss Don North's taunt in the garbage bin it deserved.

But there was an upside. I developed from an Anglo-Indian with a modest interest in his heritage to one who really cared. My earlier curiosity about the community's origins and history became a deep-rooted research interest, and I began to write about Anglo-Indian mores and issues, attending and/or taking part in three world reunions: Toronto in 1992, Melbourne in 2004, and Toronto again in 2007. I also help the founder of the Anglo-Indian Home Page, Dr. Adrian Gilbert, by co-editing the online *International Journal of Anglo-Indian Studies* and the *Anglo-Indian Wallah*: http://home.alphalink.com.au/~agilbert/indexold.html

Goodbye denial, forever welcome pride in the community. We outlasted the British, we out-manoeuvred the prejudice, and increasingly we take pride in our unique history and culture. In recent years, riding the great freedom wave of the Web, we have made outstanding progress in ensuring that **we** —Anglo-Indians as opposed to others—set the record straight on the way **we were and are.** Our literary efforts to tell our history as only we can, as only we who lived it can know, assuredly help us to leave future generations a solid bedrock of knowledge and pride.

Journeying Through Life

by Joyce Mitchell

Journeys can be exciting, adventurous, joyous, dramatic. Or they can be frightening, tortuous, tedious, unsettling. The journeys I have taken have created the fabric of my life. I still feel elated whenever I am about to fling myself into another adventure, as I cannot wait to experience whatever it is around the corner.

Each winter I leave my comfortable home near Seattle, Washington, to join my sister in a relic of a colonial bungalow in Ratlam, Madhya Pradesh, in the heart of India. As I board the plane, I take a mental shower and step out of my American skin to assume my Indian skin—the only way I can make this enormous transition between two entirely different worlds. I leave in mid-January, when Seattle is dull, wet, and dreary, although I feel a warm glow of affection for the city I am leaving, where I have enjoyed 28 years of good living, and where my life has been almost magical. I have lived here longer than in any other country, including India, whence I took my first leap into the world when I was just 19 years old.

I have plenty of time to prepare for the changes I will encounter on the 20-hour flight to Mumbai (Bombay). When I leave, I usually dress in comfortable jeans, a loose sweater, and walking shoes. In Amsterdam, where I have a three-hour layover before I get the connecting flight to India, I change into a cotton *salwar-kameez-dupatta*, shed the shoes and socks, and don my Teva sandals in preparation for the heat of Mumbai, where we land at the bewitching hour of midnight.

But somehow, dressed as I am and even though I speak Hindustani, the first question the porter/taxi driver asks is, "Where are you coming from, Aunty—America?" Is it because I walk quickly instead of strolling? Or because I use the *dupatta* like a stole instead of draping it gracefully over the breast as it is designed to be worn? (For me, the *dupatta* is a crippling addition to an otherwise comfortable dress: it is always slipping off my shoulder and getting caught in the wheels of an auto-rickshaw, in doorways or railings.) And then there are the Teva sandals—always a symbol of someone who disregards fashion for comfort.

The question of age is the first major challenge in India. In America, the accent is on keeping fit, staying slim, and being active—through aerobics, swimming, walking, or dieting. After all this time, I am still jolted when a two-year-old addresses me as Joyce. I have learned to accept the casual approach from salespersons, waiters, even doctors and lawyers. It seems we must remain young and vigorous and shroud our actual age in secrecy. In India, you don't have a choice. People look at you and place you in the age group that has been designated over the centuries: student, householder, retiree, renunciation (handing over control).

Until a few years ago, I was still addressed as Aunty, Aunty-*ji*, and sometimes Sister. Now I have graduated to *Mata-ji* or Mummy-*ji*. I was not at all prepared when I became *Mata-ji*. I was waiting in a long queue to buy a train ticket in Dehra Dun. The computers were down because the electricity had been shut off. It was midday, hot, and stuffy. We stood patiently and waited. After an hour, the clerks ambled back to their booths and everyone began to surge forward in anticipation—normally there would have been one line for women and another for men, but this protocol was completely ignored when the booths opened for business. A young man ahead of me addressed the queue, "Make way for *Mata-ji*. Have you no respect for the elderly? Make way, make way." I looked over my shoulder to spot this elderly person. Suddenly, I realized he was referring to me. Immediately I took advantage of my good fortune and moved forward to the front of the line and gave the young man my blessing. Children always address me as Grandma, *Nani*, *Dadi-ji*, and recently little Moyna gave me the grand title of *Burri-Dadi*, Mother of my Grandmother. With this comes the added bonus of being bestowed the gift of wisdom by the younger generation. Often you are asked your opinion and generally they will listen deferentially, even if you are talking utter rubbish.

Another amusing experience happened when I was 60 and travelling on the Frontier Mail from Mumbai to Ratlam. I allowed my friend's cook to use whatever methods he wanted to employ to get me my ticket. I felt guilty, as I would never dream of bribing or breaking the law in America. When the train pulled into the platform I checked the reservation chart and could not locate my name. I approached the conductor and demanded to know why. He looked at his list. I said, "Here is the reservation slip, the berth number is 55."

He shook his head and said, "No, Madam, that is not your berth number, it is your age. That means you are not a temptress."

"Temptress?" I asked, incredulously.

He replied, "Yes, ladies over 50 are placed in general compartments since they are not in danger of being harassed." I didn't know whether to laugh or cry. I was pleased the cook thought I was 55, and relieved that I had a berth on the train.

Attitude is also viewed very differently. In America, I find it's better to be assertive rather than passive. I do not hesitate to "stand up for my rights" when I find I am being taken advantage of or ignored. I assume my English schoolmarm accent and get immediate attention. When we first came to live in Bellevue (across Lake Washington from Seattle) there was only a handful of Asian immigrants. I rather enjoyed being considered "exotic". But one day at the dry-cleaners, and before I could say anything, the salesgirl looked up and said, "Do you speak English?"

Quick as a whip, I replied, "I do. Do you?"

She looked at me, dumbfounded. "Of course I do. It is my language."

"And what makes you think it isn't mine?" No answer.

In India, women are expected to speak softly and deferentially, to bow to authority (usually male). They know "their place". In America, I like the straightforward, no-nonsense approach, but this is considered "being too forward" in India, and often meets resistance. My brother always cautions me, "Keep quiet. Don't speak. I will do the talking as you will only get their backs up and they will refuse your request."

When I first commenced my annual winter visits to India in the early 1990s, I was rudely reminded of "my place". One night my sister, Daphne, and I were threatened at gunpoint at the front door, by three thieves shrouded in blankets. Fortunately, they were not professional dacoits and were as scared as I was. I screamed and leapt backwards (a miraculous feat for a non-athletic person like me) and ran back into the house. Daphne, who had no idea what had happened, stood up from her wheelchair and started screaming as well. Our night-watch *ayah*, sleeping on the verandah at the back of the house, heard us and ran and locked the door, screaming even louder. The thieves vanished into the gloom.

We had no telephone, so once we had the servants roused, and Uncle Bertie from next door awakened, we asked our neighbour,

Mr. Khan, to help us call the police. They came an hour later and approached Mr. Khan, who was waiting with us in the garden. Mr. Khan began to tell the story to the police.

"Three low-life bandits came to the door and attacked my respected sisters, these two helpless old women, holding a double-barrelled gun into their chests..." (Here he pranced around, enacting the whole scene as he imagined it.)

"Mr. Khan," I interrupted, "it was a pistol, not a double-barreled gun, and..."

"Stop interrupting," said the chief policeman, "let Mr. Khan tell the story." I was full of indignation at being dismissed and relegated into silence by these men.

To make matters worse, Uncle Bertie asked me, "Did you unlock the door when they knocked?"

"Yes, I did," I replied. "They said they had a telegram, and I thought it might be from America."

"You unlocked the door?" Uncle Bertie exclaimed disgustedly. Then, to the assembled crowd of servants and police, he intoned, shaking his head, "She unlocked the door. She started the chain of events. If she had not unlocked the door, nothing would have happened."

"You unlocked the door?" repeated the policeman.

"You unlocked the door?" wailed the servants, like a Greek chorus.

Sadly, I realized I was not the victim any more, I was the foolish woman who had unlocked the door. I consoled myself by staying up all night and writing a newsletter to dear friends in America to whom I could turn for sympathy and understanding.

I have learned many valuable ways to confront life in America through my experiences in India. One of them is to be prepared to change plans at the last minute and not be critical of other people for not keeping an appointment or a promise. My friend Deben, with whom I shared many philosophical discussions in Paris, explained why we who live abroad tend to be more mellow and able to adapt to circumstances. "In Kolkata (Calcutta), when my friend promises to meet me tomorrow morning at 9 o'clock sharp, I want to believe him but know that some unavoidable event might make him late, or he might not come at all. When he leaves, I call another friend and make a tentative arrangement, saying I might drop in to see him tomorrow. He looks at his calendar, knows he has another engagement, but half promises he will be able to squeeze in a visit. He knows I am not making a serious commitment. I also approach my wife and suggest that I might join her on her shopping expedition tomorrow morning. She has already made arrangements with the servant to accompany her, and has overheard my conversations, but she agrees good-humouredly. When the first friend shows up, I am so relieved, I want to throw my arms around him. I excuse myself and call the second friend to cancel my visit, apologize to my wife, and all is well with the world."

I find myself employing the same strategy in America. I always have an alternative plan: I carry a book or my diary to write in, just in case I have to wait for an appointment; I pull weeds, call a friend, or throw in a wash while I am waiting for someone to arrive.

Among the most precious gifts America has given me are my "wings". I can drive and have my own car. When I got my licence, I was 50. At long last I was truly independent, and I could go anywhere, anytime. When we first arrived to live in Bellevue, I could not drive—in all the cities we had lived, my husband Joe did the driving, and we could afford only one car. Besides, there was excellent public transportation, and it was not important. But getting around in Bellevue/Seattle was a chore: buses ran only once an hour and there were no shelters to protect us from the rain. I took the basic training with the Defensive Driving School and then spent months getting as much practice as I could, driving in parking lots and quiet streets with a friend who helped me screw up enough courage to appear for my driving test (I helped pay for the new roof on her house). Nothing could stop me once I got my licence.

In India, I don't drive. I learned how to drive in America on the right-hand side of the road, with automatic transmission. In India, traffic runs on the left, and most cars are stick shift. I am terrified of crossing a road in Mumbai or Delhi, leave alone confront the chaos that exists in traffic. In Ratlam, there are few cars, and I have an arrangement with young Jude, who owns an auto-rickshaw. He calls at my house every morning after he drops off the schoolchildren. He is available for three hours to take me to the bank, the bazaar, the cyber cafe, or the post office. It is a hot, dusty ride, but Jude is an excellent chauffeur/guide/companion, and it works very well. Sometimes, when we are delayed, we pick up the schoolchildren and take them home.

I use my cell phone sparingly in America and am more comfortable using my landline. In India, everyone has a mobile—even those who look like they can't afford one—and they use it constantly. Chipu, my supervisor[7] (who cannot speak or read English), has taught me how to send text messages, and my generous friend, Homai, has a spare mobile which she presents to her visitors to use while in Mumbai. They know how to select ring tones, ranging from popular film songs to nursery rhymes and tinkling bells, and these are turned on full blast. People talk very loudly on their phones in order to be heard above all the other sounds which are part of life in India.

My life in America is always busy: my sons, my friends, seniors' classes through Bellevue Community College, theatre, ballet, opera, visits to other states and to Canada, volunteer work, garden, church, dinner, and tea parties. You name it, I am involved. I am also operating under a lot of stress as I always take on much more than I can handle.

My life in Ratlam is physically demanding, and I learn the value of patience and how to endure. Each day offers a challenge, since there are constant power cuts and water shortages. Every chore takes a lot of time and energy, but I can afford household help and 24-hour care for Daphne, who is crippled with rheumatoid arthritis. I know I am loved by my vast family and the friends I have known all my life. Each setback makes me stronger and better able to face the next crisis. I have three hours of complete peace, between lunch and teatime, when I can read, write, nap, or have a bucket bath. I have early nights and regular, all-organic, mostly vegetarian meals prepared by the cook.

I am constantly involved in fixing and repairing the old house, our ancestral home. My family on both sides, the Goodes and Ferreiras, were connected with the old BB & CI Railway, now the Western Railway, for the past 100 years. Ratlam is halfway between Mumbai and Delhi, about 400 miles from each. Serving both broad and metre gauge trains, it became an important junction because steam engines were changed and serviced at the large railway workshops there. When my grandfather and father retired, they built large bungalows across from the railway colony. At one time, nine of the bungalows in the Retired Colony, as it was known, belonged to members of our family.

The garden, too, gets my attention, though maintaining it is difficult because of the meagre water supply—we use dish water and bath water for the plants, and they thrive.

And then, almost too quickly, it is time to leave India and return to my other home. One time I was very annoyed when the jeweller I had visited every week changed towards me as soon as I told him I was leaving. He had always treated me to a cup of tea, offered me a chair to sit on, and let me wear my sandals inside the shop. Now, he turned his attention to another customer and offered her all the perks I had become accustomed to. I was dismissed, banished.

When I returned to the house, I heard Uncle Bertie whispering to Daphne (his "whispers" resonated throughout the house), "Don't worry, we will call the Chitles for tea as soon as she leaves. She doesn't like them, and we haven't seen them in three months."

I was furious, and confronted him. "I'm not dead yet. I feel you can't wait for me to leave, to get rid of me."

He answered: "But I am only preparing Daphne for the sadness of your departure. You will get on that train, and you will be planning your week in Mumbai with all the relatives and friends, and then you will fly off to Seattle. I know you have a lovely home there, and I have met your wonderful friends. You have a lot to look forward to. We have to fill the void of your departure with plans as we will miss you. It is hard to get the servants to lock up your wing of the house and feel the emptiness. So we defend ourselves by making plans, so you will not have to worry about us."

What wise words. Now Uncle Bertie has gone to the "Guava Gardens", as our cousin Pat describes the Hereafter, and we are left with a void we cannot fill, no matter how many plans we make or how many memories we share.

The Year of Seventy-Two

by Pamela S.C. Moore

I awake at six o'clock. The cloudless sky in the Western Australian Goldfields is faintly light, and I can hear men's voices in the vicinity of Monty's Cafe round the corner, which is open 24 hours a day. Maybe, I think, they are early morning revellers after an Australia Day party, except it sounds like a New Zealand Maori *Haka*[8]. Unlikely Australia Day revellers, come to think of it.

I begin to focus on a small parcel standing on the bedside table. It's wrapped in silver paper, with rainbow stars. It's my birthday present from my husband, who is still asleep beside me. I decide to wait before I open the packet, but to judge from the shape, it is a bottle of scent.

In the kitchen the two cats crouch, expecting food. The grey cat, 16 years old, with her swollen stomach and tufted, matted fur, makes her usual wail of appeal, in case I don't get the message. She should have been euthanized months ago, but I haven't had the heart to push the issue; I grieve for the life the poor thing leads these days. Fresh mutton from the fridge is cut into minute chunks to help her old teeth. The young one, Cookie, disdains the meat and holds out for biscuits. They eat greedily. Two satisfied cats mean that I can make the morning tea.

"Seventy-two today," the chant comes from the bathroom; my husband is awake.

A dry-lipped kiss is exchanged, and I open my present. It's *Gloria Vanderbilt eau de toilette*. I like it. A very attractive bottle is placed on my dressing table next to the bottles of *4711* cologne, *Cerruti 1881*, and *Je Reviens*, which marked my three previous anniversaries.

After cleaning out the cat litter tray (my daily chore after the old cat became incontinent and unable to venture into the garden), we have breakfast.

"How does it feel to be 72?" asks my husband, he being all of 82 and knowing what it feels like.

"The same as I felt when I was 71."

"The same as I felt when I was 21," I continued. "Nothing changes on the inside in spite of the ravages on the outside."

We eat our cereal and ponder this wisdom, and he assembles

the array of medicines prescribed for him for Saturdays. "These are the only markers for my week," he says ruefully. "My Saturday fix," he adds, as he swallows dutifully.

The manager of the local branch of the State museum calls by to deliver a weekly TV program supplement. It's his kind favour to us because we don't buy newspapers and have no way of deciding what we don't want to watch. He booms out news about the latest activities at the museum and, in a roundabout way, says he could give me a job as Education Officer. They are having the usual problem. Start a career at 72? Not likely.

"I was intending asking you for breakfast this weekend, but didn't get round to it, as usual," I said

"That's all right. I'll come tomorrow."

"English or Indian?"

"I eat anything," he says with a grin, "I went to boarding school. What's the Indian?"

"*Idlis* and *sambhar.*"

He elects to have *idlis* and *sambhar*, still not knowing what they are. Just before he leaves in his well-used Land Rover, he shows us the provisions he keeps in the door compartment. Sunscreen, insect repellent, a polymer for sealing radiators and other breakages, a torch, various tools, an air gauge, air freshener in case Ben, the dog, breaks wind, and rubber gloves; he has anticipated every eventuality. We say we are impressed, and then he's off.

A little later I receive a phone call from my husband's eldest daughter, who's just returned from Goa. She asks what we've planned for today. "Nothing," is my dull reply. "I can't remember when I last did anything special for my birthday, and besides they come round so quickly these days."

His second daughter and her husband, living in Mumbai, telephone to wish me and give us the news that an old friend has died in Calcutta. She was a Parsi, and we wonder what the funeral process is these days. The Parsi Tower of Silence has been overtaken by Calcutta's urban sprawl. It stands among dwellings and is distasteful to its Hindu neighbours.

We try to phone her husband in Calcutta but, as usual, can't get through.

As may be expected, my thoughts go back to the last time we saw our friends. We went to Darjeeling and Sikkim with them in 1998. The drive was hair-raising, on mountain roads damaged by recent landslides. Our late friend, sitting in the "Alice Villa" dining room in Darjeeling, talking normally about things in general, suddenly said: "When are we going to Darjeeling?" We became acutely aware of her dementia.

My birthday lunch is leftover *moussaka*. Perversely, I decided to cook Greek to celebrate Australia Day yesterday.

I am due to teach bridge at two o'clock, so I pack my bag with practice bridge hands, in case beginners come. In the event, there are just eight regulars, so I stay to settle them down and leave to shop for the Indian breakfast tomorrow. I look for a fruit juice other than pineapple, which we have, because Terry has a theory that pineapple juice loosens the gums since it cannot break down protein. He may be right, so I buy guava instead.

When I return home in the late afternoon, my husband is busy in the kitchen preparing a chicken curry. He's still there as I type this, and I can hear the old grey cat mewing at him (like a dripping tap, she doesn't stop) because she loves raw chicken. She's dying and so gets away with murder.

I've had a total of three birthday cards this year, and all from people who haven't sent me any before. If it weren't for them, I'd have no cards at all. One from my cousin in England, one from my goddaughter, and one from an Anglo-Burman woman I was friendly with a couple of years ago. She and her husband played bridge, but he died last year, and I suspect that she is lonely. They moved to a town on the coast, which is 12 hours' drive away, so we're not likely to meet again. Still, it's nice to get a card for my birthday, and I can't think how she knew the date. My two offspring, living in England, may telephone later, but I won't hold my breath. Their cards will turn up in a week's time when they realize they've missed the day.

It's evening. I've had a few jobs to do. One is writing a letter of appointment for an administrator for the family centre where we play bridge, as I'm the president of the managing committee this year. I've checked the employment agreement to make sure we're complying with minimum standards of employment. All's fine.

A call comes from my husband's son-in-law in Perth.

"Happy birthday, Pam." Then, "What are you guys planning to do this evening?"

"Nothing, Chris, we've stopped celebrating just about everything."

"I thought you'd have a few friends over for a drink."

"We've nearly run out of friends, Chris."

Our long-standing Aussie friend (of 15 years), almost our surrogate daughter, has just moved back home to Perth. Over the years, she took us on a roller coaster ride of marriage, baby, divorce, family disputes, and now she's gone. How to fill the void? It's our pattern of life in this remote outback town. We have friends all over Australia, but few left here.

I'm on my third glass of red wine. They say it's good to have two glasses of red a day, but what the hell—today's my birthday. Cookie, the young cat, is prowling around the computer, knocking the lamps flying. She gets restless at this time and wants attention. The lamps topple sideways, and I catch them before they hit the deck, but typing is impossible. I take another swig of red and go to watch the news. Serena Williams has won the Australian Women's Open. Now that's important!

The chicken curry is delicious. It's suitable fare for a birthday girl. Then, to my shame, ungrateful for his kindness, I remark: "By the way, I was in the chemist's today getting your prescription, and saw the perfumes were on special."

He's hurt that I should mention it. "The girl said that if I went to one of the other chemists it would cost me over $90."

What a cow I am! Now why did I do that?

We retire after watching a movie, *Cinderella Man*. It's a good movie and puts our perceived hardships into perspective.

When we are in bed, my husband starts to giggle. I feel the mattress heaving with his uncontrolled mirth.

"What's up?"

"Nothing, it's just that I can't believe you went looking for that perfume."

"I didn't," I protest. Now I'm hurt.

"I couldn't miss the big display in the window. Anyway, it's the thought that counts," I say, as we peck our goodnights.

Our house lights are out. The cats have settled for the night, the young one curled in a ball in the crook of my knees. In the distance, Monty's Café is coming to life, and the Two-Up School in the Friendly Society Hall behind our house is beginning to get into full swing. Its clientele is composed of miners, pensioners, and Asian girls from the Hay Street brothels. Listening to their roars of disappointment and shrieks of delight filling the warm night air, I wonder what the city fathers would have made of this irregular use of their worthy Society Hall.

And then I realize that this is what we both love. Life is all around us. It's a sort of celebration every day living here.

Who needs birthdays?

Upended Down Under

by Ralph N. Moore

India is a great country in which to be born and raised, as I was, but for the insidious seepage into the psyche of most people—regardless of background—of superstitious beliefs, strictures of caste, and ethnic and religious divides that affect personal forms of address, dress codes, and one's choice of trade or profession. I was glad of the chance to leave it all behind when I migrated to Australia in 1979, to the inland gold mining town of Kalgoorlie (population: approximately 25,000), located in Western Australia, about 400 miles due east of the coastal city of Perth.

The informality I experienced there was in stark contrast to everything I'd encountered in India. Religion, for one, is not a trump card. People are unimpressed by ostentation and get by on a first name basis. They judge others by their capabilities rather than their antecedents. I met a man in his forties, previously a bank manager, operating the local launderette out of choice. Later, I discovered that another acquaintance left his job as principal of a primary school because he preferred to weed gardens and mow lawns for a living. The job you do, as I soon learnt, is your business.

While in India, I worked for an American company at their jute mill down river from Calcutta, where I was a supervisor, along with others from Britain, Ireland, and the United States. During that time, I was sent by the company to the USA and, 29 years later, when I resigned to emigrate, I was a mill manager. But that was in the past. I soon found that my mill experience was of no value in Australia.

"Jute, what's that?" people asked, mystified. Well past my prime, with no qualifications and with an accent that Peter Sellers would envy, I had to adjust rapidly to changed circumstances.

There were high-paying jobs available if I was prepared to work in the bush, driving ore trucks or working in other mining-related jobs further afield. But it meant living rough in single men's quarters, and being one of the boys. It was a way of life I had experienced in my youth, working in Canada for an oil exploration drilling outfit in the far north of Alberta, and it had lost its appeal. Besides, I had my wife to consider: she was not prepared to live on her own in a strange town in a country to which she hadn't had time to adjust.

As a result, with a work ethic that rejected accepting the dole, I took whatever unskilled jobs I could find in Kalgoorlie. Some were downright physical. However, there were compensations to keep me sane. For instance, I attended evening classes for five years at the local college, to fulfil a life-long ambition to learn to paint. In the process, I met some great people. It was an exciting new experience to be in a class of about 18 to 20 like-minded people, most of whom were young working women anxious to acquire a hobby, and to meet other bespattered acolytes from the pottery and print-making classes during the coffee break. At times, besides painting vases of sunflowers, I struggled to commit to canvas, with trembling hands, the nude form of a model (a female of course, stupid). Sometimes I'd "go out bush" with the class on a Sunday, laden with brushes and paints, to observe all the vivid colours in the rocks and desert flora, and try to do justice to the amazing landscape.

In addition, besides a leisurely laidback lifestyle, Kalgoorlie's citizens are also sports conscious, with most participating in at least one of nearly every sporting activity imaginable, both indoor and outdoor. There is a covered, Olympic-sized, heated swimming pool, plus squash, badminton, and basketball courts, and fields for hockey, rugby, and Australian rules football. We have go-carts, a gun club, and land yachting on a nearby large salt lake. If you want to twist an ankle or pull a hamstring, this is the ideal country.

Apart from regular jobs, there are many opportunities for part-time employment to augment one's regular income. Once, I thought I'd try to cut wild flowers (which, in spring, grow for miles) to supply exporters in Perth. I obtained the necessary licence, but the logistics were insurmountable, and it didn't work out. Neither did the taxi driver's licence that I carried for a few years. The more I learned about the trials and tribulations of driving a cab the more disenchanted I became.

A few harried, hectic months after arriving in the country, to earn some extra *paisa*, I innocently accepted an after-hours job as a census taker. That turned out to be not only tedious, but the money didn't match the effort involved. But I did find that knocking on doors and handing out numerous forms was a good way to gain insights into the mores and humour of people whom one would not otherwise meet. It was also an introduction into some surprising new forms of living. There were egocentric men strutting around in sparsely furnished houses that lacked any creature comforts, yet they had high-priced, late-model cars parked outside. There were young, single, unmarried mothers, models of rectitude. There were bewildered, aged widows and retired, single men aching with loneliness, shuffling around in poorly lit homes. There were drunks, illiterates, and yobs, and dogs that came in all shapes and sizes, some damn big, snarling monsters. Buddha could have served his apprenticeship as a census taker to attain enlightenment.

During the state and federal elections, I worked at the polling booths. Starting out as a dogsbody, helping to point confused voters in the right direction to place their compulsory vote, I eventually ascended the totem pole to be in charge of a polling station. I was surprised how many people complained about the inconvenience attached to a five-minute ride in their cars from their homes to mark a ballot—which they'd receive on arrival without any undue delay: I remembered the many times I spent in the hot and humid conditions of India, standing in a mile-long queue waiting to vote.

I became friends with the Returning Officer of the Australian Electoral Commission for the Division of Kalgoorlie (which happens to be geographically the largest electorate in the world—trivia for the next quiz contest).When I retired at 65, he employed me as casual help for the federal elections, held every three years. I worked in the office, packing an unbelievably vast amount of voting paraphernalia to be sent out by courier to distant towns, some hundreds of miles away. Towns with quaint names like Useless Loop, One Arm Point, Grass Patch, and Marble Bar, to name but a few.

A few days prior to an election, with a pleasant female assistant in tow, we visited the nursing homes for the aged as well as the local prison, to get the inmates to cast their ballots. It was a bizarre experience trying to get drooling, comatose nonagenarians to mark a ballot. Or, for that matter, muscular, tattooed convicts with glazed eyes and a two-word, "da, da" vocabulary. For me the fun began in earnest after the election, when the ballots were returned from the outlying towns. For two weeks, I supervised 14 high-spirited young women, employed to scrutinize the ballots.

Each morning, without fail, the girls arrived at the eleventh hour, diving out of cars and taxis. It was quite a sight to watch their mad, frenzied charge into the building: cigarette packets, keys, apples, and tissues spilling out of their shoulder bags, wind-blown hair flying, batik skirts flapping, and beaded necklaces jangling as, giggling and cursing, they tripped and stumbled on the stairs leading to the upstairs room where we were ensconced, to painstakingly pore over the ballots. Sometimes a burst of laughter followed as someone read out aloud the occasional hilarious comment, usually abusive and misspelled, that a vexed voter had written to express disapproval of the voting system and politicians.

I did three such elections, with a different group each time. By the end of two weeks, we were firm friends. On the last day, I'd invite them, with the three permanent office staff, to a buffet lunch at my house, across the road from the electoral office, and we'd relive the highlights. Gradually, over the years, computers have taken over. Some girls have moved on. Others I see while out shopping, and we stop to exchange the latest news.

Another interesting part-time pursuit I enjoyed every Saturday was when I worked from March to September for 15 years, no less, at the race-track, as Clerk of Scales. It entailed weighing the jockeys for each race (but not, as I was once asked by a kindly old dear, the horses). Some of the Runyonesque characters I came in contact with, most of whom spoke an incomprehensible form of English, were truly exceptional. These days our paths only cross in the street or supermarket, and I'm still recognized with a smile and a friendly, "Hi Ralphie, how ya goin'?"

Many people, when I made it known that I was from India, frequently surprised me by stating that they had either been there or acquired a taste for the food. Others, harking back to a bygone era, claimed a distant relative who had served there in the army, or worked as a missionary. The wizened female descendant of one of these recited the familiar lullaby in a quavering voice, "*Makhan, roti, chini,*" she'd learnt as a child. It was through such casual meetings that I became friends with a tall, laconic, Australian who had backpacked through the Indian subcontinent. He was managing an isolated petrol station and roadhouse at Caiguna, on the highway that runs east to west across the vast desert known as the Nullabor. I went out there over a few weekends by Greyhound coach, to visit him and his crew of about eight zany staff—average age about 24.

To break the monotony, every so often my friend declared a fancy-dress day when the staff outfitted themselves from a large Aladdin box stuffed full of costumes and accessories (the envy of any theatrical company). I was there once when the roadhouse was awash with costumed characters. There was a barefooted, hip-swinging, veiled harem beauty complete with ankle bells; a leering sheikh; a shy, freckle-faced Swiss maid; a big game hunter in safari suit and solar topee; and assorted clowns. The best-dressed reveller was a well-endowed waitress wearing a low-cut frilly blouse and a World War II German army helmet, from beneath which two thick, flaxen plaits descended. And to complete the ensemble she wore a Hitler-type moustache. Unsuspecting coach passengers trooping wearily into the dining room couldn't believe their eyes.

In the end, my friend found the strain of running the roadhouse too much and is now living with his young family much closer to civilization, and I no longer have the joy of looking forward to those wacky visits. Nor do I have the fun these days of following a four-piece band of expatriate musicians I came to know during the '80s. I'd accompany them when they played for dances and weddings at the town hall and clubs, and at small, outlying mining towns overflowing with rumbustious vitality. And later, too, when they had a regular booking at one of the pubs from Friday to Sunday. They played music from the '60s, mostly a mixture of country and western with the songs of Roy Orbison— a favourite of the jean-clad, leather-jacketed patrons, both men and women, because Kalgoorlie is unashamedly a cowboy town.

The pub would be abuzz with bearded geologists, miners, drillers—some of whom were Maoris flexing their biceps—truckies, and of course their partners. They knew the words to every song, and would stay after dinner to relax and enjoy themselves, drinking beer as fast as they could be served by "skimpy" barmaids—sleek, sinuous young women, wearing tight, shrunken shorts and flimsy see-through tops (after municipal do-gooders outlawed their wearing g-strings and going topless). The barmaids, steely eyed but with great smiles, would admonish pie-eyed customers: "Look—but don't touch."

So these are the experiences that have moulded me in Australia. I make frequent journeys back to India to visit family, but I'm happy here, with no feeling of alienation and, despite the changes and adjustments, there is the compensation of a hassle-free, leisurely pace. With my wife and two cats to keep me company, and painting and writing to keep me occupied, I appreciate the clear blue skies and warm dry weather, as well as the readily available spices, pickles, tropical fruits, and vegetables. I have both a curry leaf and a drumstick tree growing in the backyard, along with flamboyant bougainvillea and jasmine adorning the wall. In the surrounding trees, I can hear the persuasive call of doves that were, like me, also introduced from India, and I'm glad for the way we are.

"My India" No More

by Peter Nailer

The last bars of *Jana Gana Mana* drifted across the Rajpath in New Delhi. It was a cold, crisp, clear January morning: January 26, 2006, to be precise. At one end, emerging from the morning mist and smog was the outline of the rose-coloured domes of the Secretariat Buildings flanking the Rashtrapati Bhavan, home of the President of India. At the other, glinting with a golden hue in the morning light, was the majestic India Gate.

It was Republic Day in Delhi and there was I, Anglo-Indian by birth, wearing a Tee shirt emblazoned with the Australian flag, sitting with my Australian-born wife and tens of thousands of Indians waiting for the Republic Day Parade to begin.

It was ironic that this very same day was also Australia Day. If we had been at home in Perth, Western Australia, we would be making our way to the banks of the broad Swan River with our blankets and picnic baskets. There we would join with family, friends, and more than 300,000 other people to watch the "Skyworks", a spectacular display of fireworks set to music that would mark "our" national day. There would be no parade of marching troops, elephants, tanks, and missiles, but celebration in the typical laid-back "Aussie way", with impromptu cricket and football matches, filled with lighthearted banter, in and amongst the picnicking groups.

I couldn't help but think that we Anglo-Indians had come a long way since our ancestors' first liaisons with this incredible India. Here was I in Delhi, one half of me filled with pride at the spectacle of modern India, "my India", that passed in front of me; the other half filled with the pride I felt for Australia, "my Australia", on her national day.

I guess this is the way we are, we Anglo-Indians; but for how long will this divided love last? Will our children and grandchildren have the same passion for India, or will the term "Anglo-Indian" die with our generation? Will our generation be absorbed into our adopted countries?

Although born in India, I left at an early age. I had been back to India once before, 33 years earlier, but at the time I hadn't become interested in genealogy and didn't really appreciate my roots, or question why there was a part of my heart that held this love for India, a land I knew only vaguely.

But there I was, back again, possibly for the last time. Only the week before, with tears in my eyes, I had run my fingers along the deeply carved letters that spelt out my surname on the impressive tomb in Madras that housed not only the remains of the first of my English ancestors to arrive in India, but also those of his Indian wife and two of their Anglo-Indian children.

I was in India this time as part of a self-indulgent pilgrimage to the land of my birth. I needed to satisfy the longing within and to share "my India" with my wife, and also to celebrate my 60th birthday in the town of my birth.

The first weeks had been an emotional journey for me through south India, visiting the many churches, cemeteries, and tombs of long-forgotten ancestors. There I revelled in the sights and the sounds, and greedily indulged in the tastes of India, "my India".

Our Australian-born son joined us in Calcutta, and together we savoured the charms of "The City of Joy". Everywhere there were the visible remnants of the impressive British past mingled with the modern present, and crammed into it all was India, as it always was and possibly as it will always be.

On the train to my hometown of Kharagpur in West Bengal, I was bursting with anticipation and emotion. I had this feeling that there were people I knew—or had heard about—riding along with me on the train (not ghosts, just their presence). Not even the ubiquitous cries of *"Chai, chai"*, "Nescafe", and *"Garam* omelette" of the train vendors could distract me and blot out this feeling.

Kharagpur station saw me in tears yet again (silly, emotional, old fool) as we were met by people I knew only through e-mails. They greeted us with flowers and smiling faces. I was home! This was my hometown; this was "my India".

However, time changes everything, and this was no longer the small Anglo-Indian railway colony it had been: this was Indian India. This became clear when we stopped at the spot where my grandparents' bungalow had once stood on the outskirts of the railway colony. Where once there existed a street lined with graceful bungalows set in large gardens, there was now a typically crowded, narrow Indian street lined with shops and stalls. A large, ugly, yellow building housing the municipality offices had replaced the bungalow and its lovely rose gardens. All that was left was the outline of bricks from the foundation sticking out of the red clay compound. Anglo-Indian India had been almost completely absorbed by modern India.

On the last day, a visit to the cemetery to place flowers on the grave of my grandfather and others made me realize what I really was now: neither Indian nor Anglo-Indian, but Australian.

The cemetery was small and overgrown, and we spent a long time walking up and down the rows of graves, reading the many familiar names, but with no success. That strange presence was still with me and, in desperation, I whispered, "Big Dad, lead me to your grave."

Just as I uttered those words, three Indian Air Force jets in formation screamed overhead.

A voice inside me said, "Why are you looking for the dead in the land of the living?" With that the presence disappeared, and with it all the emotion that had burdened me for weeks drained out of me.

Was it my grandfather, known as Big Dad? Was it my imagination? I don't know. I like to think that it was my grandfather, a wise sage who had long ago told his family, "One day you will either have to put on a *dhoti* or a *sari*, and be absorbed into this country, or you will have to leave India forever."

We Anglo-Indians are a strange amalgam of a race, an anomaly with a comparatively short history, who were caught up in that strange but wonderful love affair England had with India. Not willing to be absorbed into the land of our birth, we have spread into many lands. There we, like our ancestors, have intermarried with the locals—only this time we have willingly allowed ourselves to be absorbed into our adopted countries.

Maybe for a little longer there will still be a generation that will remember the "India days". But to our children and grandchildren, Anglo-Indians will become almost a rumour, a rather quaint story in a book, something other than an ancestor.

An Anglo-Indian in America

by Shirley Pritchard

For Anglo-Indians, our family's trek was not uncommon: from an India that was no longer British to the so-called "Motherland", even though India was our land of birth and most of us had never set foot in England. Others chose Canada and Australia, countries still under the umbrella of the Commonwealth, and a few left for British colonies in Africa, clinging to what was left of a colonial lifestyle.

My father and mother, Walter and Lilian, opted for England. Canada was farther away and colder; Australia, with its "whites-only" policy, was difficult to enter without a British passport; and Africa was an unknown quantity with no connections...so damp and chilly England it was.

Eventually, I married an Englishman, and we decided to immigrate to the USA. California shone clean and bright in the sun, and what a golden state it was in the '60s! Los Angeles, where we chose to locate, had a surfeit of apartments for rent with enticing incentives, such as the first month free, including utilities. Gasoline (petrol) was 28 cents a gallon, and that included having your windscreen cleaned, tires and oil checked, and S&H Green Stamps—which, once you had collected the required number, could be traded in for useful items.

We drove down the famous Pacific Coast Highway, watching the surfers in the sparkling blue Pacific, and gave rides to hitchhikers without a thought of danger. It was the time of the Peace and Love Generation.

Connections to India were tenuous as compared to England, with its abundance of Indian restaurants and *jhat bhais*. There were only two or three Indian restaurants in L.A. in those days and very few Indian grocery stores. Even now, we have only one Indian grocery store in our immediate area—we also had a restaurant but that burned down a few months ago. However, in greater Los Angeles the Indian footprint is much larger—in fact, the town of Cerritos in Orange County is like a Little India, with shops selling colourful *saris, salwar-kameez*, and beautiful jewellery, and with the ineffable spicy scents of a bazaar.

My husband, Brian, found employment with Trans World Airlines, and it really was trans-world in those days. TWA was very generous with passes, not only for us but also for Brian's parents, who visited from England at least twice a year, especially after our children, Tina and Mark, were born. We took advantage of the free flights and travelled all over the globe with the children.

We bought a house in Westlake Village, a planned community situated halfway between Los Angeles and Santa Barbara, and about a 20-minute drive through the canyons of the picturesque Santa Monica Mountains to the beach at Malibu. We have the best of both worlds: access to the exciting venues in big-city Los Angeles, the quieter beaches north to San Francisco, about a 10-hour drive on Pacific Coast Highway, and snow in the winter, two hours' drive east to the Sierra Nevada. When people ask us, "How do you like living in America?" we always say, "Well, let us qualify that. First of all, we live in California; secondly, we live in Southern California; and, thirdly, we live in Westlake Village. Yes, we love it!"

Before I relate a couple of amusing incidents, let me explain for those who might not know, "mango fool" is a delicious drink made from *kutcha* (raw) mangoes, boiled in milk with sugar, and served ice cold. The drink takes me back immediately to balmy nights in India, sitting on *morahs* under the stars after coming back from the Railway Institute, and being served this delicious and refreshing drink by our beloved *ayah*.

In the early '80s, we were at an Indian restaurant in California with my sister, Moyra, and her husband, Brian O'Loughlin. He was of Irish descent but had become somewhat familiar with Anglo-Indian cuisine and culture through his association with our family and friends.

Moyra asked the waitress, "May I have some mango fool?" whereupon Brian, who was very witty, said, "That was pretty rude. How would you like it if she replied, 'I don't have any, stupid!'"

Well, we all cracked up at this witticism and were still giggling when the waitress returned and Brian said, "I'd like some *kulfi*," which she misheard as "coffee". She enquired, "Do you want black or white?" Brian's face was a picture as he turned to Moyra and asked, "There's black *kulfi*?" Well, that took us right over the edge.

Our local Indian store in Thousand Oaks is *Apna Spiceland*, where we get our Indian "fix". Our family has long considered Bolst's Pickles as the "Cadillac" of Indian pickles but, over the years, they have been more and more difficult to obtain. I had a "private reserve" of Bolst's at *Apna's* but, once that ran out, they were unable to restock. In desperation, I wrote directly to the company in Madras, obtaining their address off the last precious bottle's label.

I eventually got a reply, via regular mail, on a tiny sheet of letter paper, typed on an ancient typewriter with uneven keys, providing me with the name and address of their representative in Essex, England. Undaunted, I contacted them and they provided the name of a representative in Carson, California. Ah, now we were getting somewhere.

We e-mailed this contact, who informed us that it was very difficult to get Bolst's Pickles these days, suggested we switch to Patak's brand, and that we should go to our closest source...yes, you've guessed it, *Apna Spiceland*. So we had come full circle to no avail. What a pickle!

One day I was looking for a local art teacher and found a wonderful artist, Carol Heyer, who has a studio in her home where she gives classes. When Carol found out, in the course of conversation, that I had been born in India, she exclaimed, "Well, I must introduce you to my mother and aunt because they, too, are from India."

So, after the class was over, we went into the living room and I was introduced to the two ladies. They asked me what my mother's maiden name was, and when I said, "Lilian Dorsey," they burst into tears, hugging me, exclaiming, "Shirley, we knew you when you were a baby!"

What were the odds of my picking that particular art teacher? The connection with my mother was re-established, much to everyone's delight, and they all met again when my parents came to California for a visit. No friendships as sweet as those crafted in far-off days on the subcontinent.

I think the connections will, however, slowly end, partly because of the inevitable and relentless passage of time, but also because subsequent generations of Anglo-Indian children, born in countries far from their parents' land of birth, have little or no connection with India. Our children, I am sad to say, have never been to India—we were too nervous to take them when they were children and, now that they are grown, although they love to eat Indian *khana* and are interested in our stories, they have no real desire to visit present-day India.

As of this writing, Brian is semi-retired, keeping himself happily occupied race-directing. He was elected Chairman of the Long Distance Running Committee for Southern California for many years, ran the London Marathon and a few others, and also helped inaugurate the Siberian Marathon, held annually in Omsk, so it was an easy transition from his avocation to his present occupation.

I work a few minutes from home at beautiful Sherwood Country Club. In my spare time, I paint, write, go to the movies, garden and take our beloved dog, Charlie, a German Shepherd/Chow mix whom we rescued from the pound, for daily walks.

We also own a condo overlooking the Pacific in Baja, Mexico, about 40 miles south of the border, and go down there occasionally. It takes approximately four hours—depending, of course, on the notorious Los Angeles freeway traffic.

On a recent trip there with Moyra and a school friend, Dot (née Jones) Juarez, I remarked: "You know, when we were *chota batchas* in Ajmer, if somebody had told us that, umpteen years later, we would be living in America and driving down to Mexico together, we would never have believed it."

So, here we are, connected by the wondrous Internet to friends and family all over a world that has shrunk into a global village. We had a marvellous time at the 7th World Anglo-Indian Reunion in Toronto in 2007, meeting old friends and making new ones from that most special time in our lives—a small but important chapter in the history of the British Empire and her most prized possession: India, the Jewel in the Crown.

A Woman from Ajmer

by Daniel Riggle

Would anyone want to hear perceptions of Anglo-Indians from an Anglo-American? I think that's a valid question. Maybe reading this will suggest whether or not I have anything to add to such a discussion. I have learned most of what I know about Anglo-Indian people and traditions through a woman named Janice, who came to the USA from Ajmer, went back to India briefly to marry her teenage sweetheart, and then returned with him to America (for which I and many others are now forever grateful). To me, Janice stands for the strengths of the Anglo-Indian community and its traditions, just as she epitomizes what has made America great as a nation through the many fine people who have immigrated here from many countries.

I'd like to believe that some of my ancestors also represent such good people, coming here from various European countries over the last couple of centuries (my nearly 80-year old mom is researching the genealogy of our family, something in which, I'm ashamed to admit, I had not shown too much interest before meeting Janice).

Janice came to this country in 1974, to be with her sisters and father. Through her, I would later learn not only more about her family and traditions, but also how to appreciate my own in ways I never had before. I learned that her father, Patrick D'Sena, a carpenter who worked for the Indian Railways (as did so many Anglo-Indians), was the father of 10 children, that his wife died a month after the birth of their last child, that he remained faithful to her memory, loved his children more than anything in his life, enjoyed a good joke, a good party in his younger days, a strong mug of tea with toast, and in his latter years built a strong affection for his adopted country, the USA—as did his children who came here.

In Janice and her surviving sisters, all of whom I would meet, I witnessed a similar devotion to family, as well as a love of both India and America. In truth, their love of the USA still strikes me most poignantly, since this affection appears stronger in them than it does in many Americans whom I've known or with whom I've grown up. Janice's sisters here include Norma, Annette, Pat (aka 'Iyne), and Juanita (aka Nita). Among family, Janice is also known as Janu, though her father called her Pidgy. Another sister named Judith (Midgy), unfortunately, died at 14 of a heart condition, more than 40 years ago.

Here was another of the early lessons I learned about Anglo-Indians: that familial affection sometimes appears in the form of creative nicknaming. At times, I'd find difficulty in following conversations, often charged with humour and punctuated by crescendos of laughter, in which appeared characters with names like Sunnu, Bunnu, Buddie, Tootsie, Shugie, Coo-Coo, and Bobbin. Some stories were filled with great local colour, depicting family and neighbourhood scenes, or parties and dances that might become a bit too raucous, often with a beautiful girl or woman caught up in the whirlwind of men battling for her attention; the story would reach its *denouement* at a dance, in which tempers flared (usually harmlessly enough), and life returned to a more normal (sometimes a chaotic normal) state once the melodrama ebbed. Then it would be back to the dance floor or food, to commence the festivities all over again.

Here, too, were areas in which I'd grown to appreciate aspects of Anglo-Indian tradition that I'd never experienced to such a degree before I met Janice: these cultural features were food and social gatherings at which music and dance *must* be present. I actually enjoy the former as much as Anglo-Indians (my mother is half-Italian) but admit that the latter, in my blue collar, Midwestern upbringing, is a bit less practised. Still, it was initially through stories of these social gatherings, and later through attendance at several, that I was allowed to meet Janice's wonderful sisters. At this point I should add another observed Anglo-Indian trait— at least if Janice and her sisters' physical beauty reflects that of other Anglo-Indian women—and perhaps this trait would explain why those male passions got stirred up in parties and dancehalls in India (and in the USA, I might add). Janice and her sisters, I couldn't help noticing, are all striking. But to avoid stirring up any misunderstanding reactions among anyone who might read my comments, I should turn to what I grew to love as much as any Anglo-Indian, through meeting Janice and some of her family and friends: that is, Indian food cooked in ways I'd never tasted before.

There were curries, of course—chicken, ball (*kofta*), and egg—

the famous (or some might say infamous for how it affects some digestive tracts) *dāl*, plus rice, potato cutlets, *chappattis*, mince, pepperwater, and a specialty of Janice's, which I call "spicy tuna" sandwiches. Even traditionally "American" or other ethnic dishes, such as spaghetti and meat sauce (my favorite before meeting Janice, as you might imagine), took on a decidedly Indian quality, with the addition of a touch of cilantro and a diced-up chilli or two. I love Janice's version as much as my own and my mother's—but don't tell Mom I said so.

Truly, though, what struck me the most in getting to know Janice, who by the time we met found herself deciding to end her marriage, was her devotion to her immediate family, something she'd learned from her community. When this devotion was tested, it emerged more strongly than ever, through a spiritual faith I'd also never encountered before, and a work ethic almost unimaginable in retrospect.

Perhaps I should mention here that Janice might be misperceived as unimposing, since she is barely five feet tall, and her closeness to her roots and community challenged any notion of terminating a marriage. The future she faced as a single mother appeared fierce, and the reaction among her loved ones and closest friends would test her often in the coming months and years. She would inherit tens of thousands of dollars in debt, and a house near foreclosure, one that she had attained and could only keep at great cost. She also faced the raising of two teenaged children, with little hope of much assistance from their father (at least for some time), and even the care of five large dogs. A decision to step into this apparent maelstrom, in a sense defying the same family and religious principles on which she was raised, meant she would simultaneously espouse and remain bound by those traditions. Her action entailed a number of consequences, expected and unexpected. In the end, I'm glad to report, her reliance on principle and her belief in God did lead to outcomes to which most would attest—her family and community *had* taught her well in the ways of doing what was right in the eyes of God. How could someone such as I, still struggling with agnosticism, not gravitate towards bearing witness to these events?

I found her oddly not embittered towards marriage as a whole, and not vindictive in any way towards her soon-to-be-ex-husband. Instead of wringing child support and alimony out of him, she "set him free", in a manner of speaking, to find a cure for whatever ailed him while they were together. For their privacy's sake, I'll leave those things unsaid. There are many people here and in other countries who would just as soon see an "ex" slow-roasted over an open pit than let him go to his own devices (and to God's), while quietly taking on themselves whatever wreckage remained of the past, and also lovingly raising the children.

That same God knew, if no one else did, what obstacles Janice faced other than debt: she experienced much second-guessing and criticism from family and closest friends, ridicule from others who proved less-than-friends, gossip, ostracism, and offers of mediation from those who thought she could and should be brought around (even intimidation and threats from the worst of those whom she'd once felt were close). And where she could find less judgmental voices, she found help and guidance, but even those bits of advice sometimes conflicted with her instincts and past experiences. Again and again, she would turn to God. Isn't it fitting that her own Anglo-Indian community and traditions had reared her to hold faith in God? Perhaps her actions should have made sense. Yet, a major challenge for Janice was in how her belief in family and God appeared to conflict, at first, with those around her, those from whom she'd learned those ideals. In watching this transforming experience for her, I, in a sense, became transformed myself, and was drawn closer to my family back in Chicago, and to God.

As her friend since the first days in which she assumed the responsibilities of a family and household, I watched as what was conflict, in most cases, became resolved, mostly because Janice was resolute. More than anything, she saw her actions as a means of keeping her family together, a notion unclear to those who lacked awareness of how difficult she considered life prior to her divorce. (How difficult this life had been for her might be suggested when one considers what she faced once she stepped out on her own.) It was a choice that she told me she'd come to over the course of years and hundreds of experiences that told her there could be no other way. Can anyone really appreciate the dire nature of such a choice: to be thousands of miles from your birthplace, with the father upon whom you once leaned so heavily gone since just before your marriage (a marriage that same father had warned you against), and your community, a link to your past and identity, feeling itself threatened by the decision you believe that you must make? The inner, emotional struggle was as great as the financial one. During an especially difficult stretch early on, even her precious children, Trevor and Heather, were being urged to rebel against her. I'd never seen anyone pushed further into a corner.

Still, it was hard for me to understand this level of devotion to family and community. As I mentioned, even coming from a family that had lived many generations in the USA, I'd lost much of what could be called a heritage (save my obsession for pasta and tomato-based sauce). I'm not sure even now I appreciate the depth of loss Janice felt when she initially stepped outside her community. But she did, and what did it take for her to succeed, to show herself and all of us that her choices were right and, indeed, God-inspired? More work, and tears, and a struggle to maintain her renowned good humor, which, I've learned, is also an Anglo-Indian tradition (as much as it is, in many ways, an American tradition), to laugh in the face of adversity, and to make do with less when more is not an option.

So she hunkered down (as a running joke we had referred to "hunkering down, like Winston Churchill in his bunker", during World War II). Soon enough, her children came around to trust and support what Janice hoped to accomplish: to keep the house, get out of debt, and get them into a place where their own dreams could come true, in the adopted country she'd grown to love. But as I said, this meant struggle.

Every weekend for eight years, Janice travelled back and forth across the 14th Street Bridge, linking Washington, DC, where we both have day jobs, to Arlington, Virginia, where she'd work Friday and Saturday nights. She missed or took off fewer than 10 of those weekends. Her second job was at an assisted living facility for the elderly, called Goodwin House, where she ran the front desk. I drove her across that bridge for seven of those years. She almost never complained, except when she was so tired that even *she* didn't think she could continue, but she kept going so that she could manage the household, provide for her children (and the dogs), and pay off those old debts. That first year of the eight she worked the second job, I didn't have a car, so she had to take a combination of buses and Metro trains, travelling two extra hours each way, losing precious sleep time, sometimes missing connections at the Pentagon, sometimes running up the last hill to Goodwin House. And still, at Goodwin House and at her full-time job, she managed to earn the love and respect of dozens of co-workers and those elderly folks whom she served on weekends (some of whom were less-than-lovable at times).

That second year, I bought a truck, as much so that we could ride together as to ease what was becoming an almost unbearable commute for her. This gave her two or three hours of sleep. All this time, her priority remained Trevor and Heather, providing for them as best she could, and from this devotion she never wavered. Not only did she keep the house stocked with food, she cooked regularly (to our delight), even digging into her pocketbook for spending money when the kids needed it for a night out, graduation fees, proms, birthdays—you name it. In the end, which is why I now know she prayed so much to do what was right, it was always about her children, her family, what would be best for them, and in the end, the results are what I believe proved her right.

When Trevor announced he wanted to be a police officer more than anything, at first she baulked. He was her baby boy, her only son. Then, when she was convinced that this was what he wanted above all else, she stood behind him, riding along with him to take physicals, written tests, psychological evaluations, a college course with the police academy, and eventually completion of the course. He is now a police officer in the town in which they live and in which he grew up; in his first year, he was decorated for valour for apprehending a criminal. He has already bought his own house, and is rightfully her pride and joy.

For Heather, Janice paid for semesters at community college, modelling classes (Heather is as beautiful as her mother), even a trip to Ireland, so that growing up in a single-parent home wouldn't mean growing up deprived of what a two-parent home might have provided. After learning of Heather's desire to become an accountant, she again overcame her own initial misgivings (she'd always wanted Heather to be "my doctor", like any good parent of such a brilliant child), and she came to fully support her daughter's goals and plans. Eventually, through Janice's help, Heather got a full-time position in an accounting office at a non-profit in Washington, DC, which is also paying for Heather's college courses in accounting. Once again, it appeared, following God's will and her true belief in her family, the results were best for Janice and her family.

Perhaps ironically, by letting her ex-husband find his own way to a resolution of his inner struggles, which he appeared to project onto the relationship, he was led to find help for his demons. In fact, he is quite successful and has played an expanding role in his children's lives as his success has increased. Moreover, his children are more proud of and connected to him than they'd been for significant periods during the years they lived together. Finally, Janice's extended family, her truest "Anglo-Indian community", which was once a primary source of her strength and identity, has been restored to her in ways that no one might have foreseen. From most accounts I've heard, friends and family now see someone stronger than they'd imagined her to be—though many thought her quite strong before.

It provides great joy to see the sisters together; to hear that laughter, heads thrown back without care; to smell the curries cooking; to watch them drinking tea, dipping a biscuit or two; to hear them remembering, bringing back their father, or their three living brothers—Colin, Eugene, and Norman—who are still in India, their deceased brother Dan, their mother, and Midgy. The community in which she was raised, which gave her values of family and spirituality, has returned to her, and now understands her devotion to those values in doing what she needed to do.

In a big way, witnessing this reunion is what has taught me most from the experience of watching what Janice went through. I, too, was brought closer to my own family, a brother in Virginia with his wife and two kids, and my parents and other brothers and sisters in Chicago. Indeed, she encouraged me in this pursuit of family ties. Through her example, I could see that struggle need not break the bond of brother and sister and parent, and that even when a consensual relationship ends, even if we are not always understood or treated fairly when we decide to change our lives, truth does seem to emerge after all. Right decisions emerge as right decisions in the end, through results that all can see: children finding their paths in life, accepting back a parent once thought lost; a woman holding onto her home and her children, holding on to herself and her God, being led and leading others in steps guided by faith, facing darkness, and stepping out into the light.

An Examined Life

by Blair Williams

"The unexamined life is not worth living"
– Plato (The trial of Socrates, 400 BC)

Do we ever belong? I have never felt that I belonged to anything, at anytime, or anywhere. Even now as a senior, and more comfortable with who and where I am than ever before, I still wonder if my feelings of spatial and emotional unease are natural, experienced by most, or if this is a legacy of my mixed ethnicity. (I felt much better when I recently read an extract of *Man Is Not Alone*, in which Rabbi Herschel stresses the need for "constructive discontent".)

Anyway, at some point over the last decade, it became less important for me to belong and more important to make a difference. This change in paradigm helped to steady my restlessness.

Perhaps a little background is in order. I grew up an Anglo-Indian in India, separated from most other communities partly because our culture was exclusive, and partly because my family was living in the Andamans—an isolated group of islands in the Bay of Bengal—where there were very few companions, either Anglo-Indian or Indian. It was only in my boarding school, Montfort, that I met boys my own age, and they were mostly Anglo-Indian. Being underage for my class and completing high school via the Senior Cambridge examination, as it was called, at the early age of 15, I grew up lonely, awkward, and somewhat isolated. My parents' financial struggles had a major effect on me, leading me, for a large part of my life, to define success as the acquisition of wealth. Study in an Anglo-Indian college helped establish a little of my identity, but here again I was underage and very immature, which did not help me to associate easily with my colleagues. By the time I left, however, I was somewhat more secure and comfortable with myself.

After college, I joined the Indian Railway Service of Mechanical Engineers (IRSME) as an Officer's Apprentice, and was plunged into an environment of boys from every community other than Anglo-Indian—and into a culture that was totally foreign to me in terms of language, food, and way of living. This made me tentative and unsure of the prestige my status provided. I lived in privileged circumstances, like a *sahib*, a term which, in colonial India, meant a male of some social or official status—in other words, a gentleman. Having servants at my beck and call—which, in turn, meant never having to cook a meal, wash a plate, or even polish my shoes—did little or nothing to alter that awkwardness and insecurity.

This state of being out of tune with my own cultural environment persisted for the next dozen or so years, during my association with the Indian Railways. Towards the end of our time in India, I was posted to Calcutta, a big city, and there my wife and I associated with many Anglo-Indians, with whom we felt comfortable, both socially and culturally. Since I continued to link success with wealth, when an opportunity presented itself to emigrate to the USA, I readily accepted it. Here was my chance to achieve my life's goal of financial independence.

Immigration meant having to adapt yet again, in my early thirties, to a totally different culture in an alien setting. The environment in the USA was obvious—huge energy and seemingly limitless opportunity, with constant striving for more. It rewarded initiative and effort. (As I was to discover, it was the closest approach to a meritocracy anywhere in the world.) Naturally endowed with energy and drive, I thrived and advanced in this climate. By design, we associated mainly with native-born Americans, and this accelerated our understanding of the country. Nonetheless, it took about five years before we were fairly settled, and we were often lonely. The Anglo-Indian culture, which espoused a quasi-Western lifestyle—in dress (our women wore dresses); in food (we ate beef); in drink (we loved our Scotch-and-soda); and in entertainment (we enjoyed ballroom dancing and jiving)—helped us assimilate easily into the mainstream. Despite friendly advice, we did not change our accents and continued to speak (as we do even today) like educated Indians. Having English as our first language helped tremendously. I joked that my ability to speak and write it, which had been my greatest strength in India, was my greatest strength in the USA, too.

We found the culture generally more subtle, explicitly kind, but without emotional backing—most Americans never quite mean what they say! This is not a criticism, merely the way

American culture is, stemming from an effort not to be candid if it is likely to hurt a person's feelings. The culture was also Darwinian, and "natural selection" seemed to operate continuously and without compunction. This could be brutal, and coming from an environment where responsibility was so diffused that no one was ever held responsible, this harsh reality was quickly understood.

It helped that I found rewarding employment and enjoyed material prosperity early and fairly easily. Despite being laid off a couple of times, I was able to bounce back and continued to flourish. I earned well, saved, and invested in some of the numerous financial instruments so easily available to the common man. (Investing was new to me and had to be learned.) We travelled extensively and enjoyed the good life that the USA makes possible. I used to tell people that, after 30 years, I had become a *sahib* in America! We made many friends but never felt that we had really merged into the mainstream of society, never felt fully comfortable—just too many basic differences in culture, values, and backgrounds. This assessment may be subjective and personally biased. On discussing my assimilation with an American friend, he said, "You are as much American as any American I know. I see you as totally integrated."

And so we come to today, in the first decade of the 21st century. I have realized that success is not financial abundance but freedom of choice—to be able to live your life as you want to—anyhow and anywhere. Success brings a variety of options. Some degree of financial success is necessary, but one must define *enough*, and once that has been done, *more* has minimal impact on the process of fulfilment. I retired at the age of 60 and was offered a job as a university professor. I felt I had died and gone to heaven. Teaching at the university level was a relief from the pressures of the business world, and I enjoyed the interaction with bright young minds. I am still at the university, teaching part-time.

About this time, on a trip to India, I discovered a whole community of destitute Anglo-Indians, some very old and some very young, who had no resources and depended on help from wherever they could get it. There is a concept in Hinduism known as *dharma*. Translated loosely, it means one's calling, or what one has been born to do. Hinduism defiled this concept by creating a caste system and using it to suppress and exploit its people. In its pristine version, it is a wonderfully refreshing concept, as it demands that we ask the question, "What is the purpose of my life? Am I fulfilling it?" On seeing these indigent Anglo-Indians in Calcutta in 1998, I was immediately struck by the thought that this was my *dharma*, to create a means of relieving some of the human suffering and degradation I had witnessed in the community of which I was a part.

I also realized that, but for good fortune and a favourable roll of the dice, I could have been one of them, and they could have been me. It was a traumatic moment, a huge shift in my paradigm of life. I was confident I could provide substantial and sustained help, not only for the seniors and children of Calcutta, but also for impoverished Anglo-Indian elderly and children all over India.

I returned to the USA and spent a year setting up a 'Not for Profit' organization with official approval from the US Revenue Service (IRS), to "help indigent Anglo-Indians in India." In the USA, the tax laws encourage charity by allowing tax-deductible donations to registered organizations. We called the charity Calcutta Tiljallah Relief, the reasoning being that Calcutta was internationally known and would attract more patrons—the "City of Joy" was the subject of both a best-selling novel and a movie based on it. Tiljallah is the name of a slum where a large number of poor Anglo-Indian seniors live in abject poverty, in sub-human conditions. In retrospect, the name was a mistake, as many thought that the charity was associated exclusively with Calcutta when, in fact, it was applicable to the whole of India. (The charity is now referred to as CTR.)

Starting with a group of like-minded Anglo-Indians in Canada, CTR established additional centres in Melbourne, Sydney, Perth, and the UK, each run by a coordinator. Money is raised in all these centres and sent to projects in India, with hardly any administrative fees withheld (less than 1%) because volunteers do all the work. CTR supports two types of projects: it provides monthly pensions to seniors and sponsors the education of children in Calcutta, Madras, Bangalore, Hyderabad, and Delhi. In 2007, CTR covered more than 300 senior pensioners and more than 200 children.

Establishing, spreading, and sustaining CTR has proved challenging but very rewarding. Particularly gratifying is the work of CTR's group of volunteers, who spend considerable personal time organizing fundraisers and maintaining their groups of supporters. Each of the coordinators has, in turn, developed a team that helps run the fundraisers. Surprisingly, we have had no turnover among the coordinators: every one of them who came in at the start is still involved. We have also had no scandal or any hint of impropriety at any time, in spite of the occasional and regretfully inevitable rumour and innuendo.

One has to marvel at how a community with a reputation for being hedonistic and self-centered has, in fact, found a cause, and how so many volunteers have dedicated themselves to it. More support is still needed, and maybe part of the community is embarrassed to recognize this development, because it is guilty of not supporting the effort.

The great 20th century psychologist and thinker, Erik Erikson, postulated that most persons leading fulfilled lives reach the point where their greatest satisfaction in life is giving. The same thinking can be applied to a community. History will record that the Anglo-Indian community abroad, in some small way, has made the transition from success to significance. This is part of the Anglo-Indian Diaspora, and it is part of the way we are.

At the beginning of this article, I mused about belonging. My conclusion is that neither geographical nor ethnological belonging matters. It does not matter where you come from or who you are. What matters is what you do. You have to ask what your *dharma* is and then try to fulfill it. I am privileged to witness and participate in the dedication of our numerous volunteers in India and abroad, all working selflessly, in very difficult physical conditions, to make life a little better for their fellow humans. Helping others seems to transcend the need to belong, as it fills a void and fulfils the spirit.

"I am what survives of me." (Erik Erickson)

The Edge of the Page

by Noreen Wood

The undercurrents of change had been flowing swiftly below her for some time now. At first she hadn't noticed, because it was just a gentle nudging at the unconscious level of her mind, and the exciting world around her was grabbing all of her immediate attention. Mary Beth was swept up in the madness of the '80s, when the emphasis was on acquisitions of all kinds—money, status, technology, and the American culture that was just a short distance away from the small Canadian town where she lived. The '90s were consumed by an effort to hold on to all of the acquisitions of the '80s. Buffeted on all sides by people and events that had nothing to do with her roots or culture, it was easy for her to get lost in the hectic pace of life in North America, where everything had to be done yesterday, and the laid-back lifestyle of her youth, where everything could always be done tomorrow, was forever gone.

Mary Beth had no idea how much she had changed. So getting back to her roots was an exacting task she had set for herself, once she realized what a useless thing it would be to gain the whole world only to lose her self in the process. Preserving one's Anglo-Indian heritage after marrying out of the community, and raising a child in another country, would no doubt confuse the issue. Keeping the threads that bound her to her family, and her Anglo-Indian roots, was like keeping the words from falling off the edge of a page that was frayed from age and neglect. She found it so much easier to melt into the culture of the West, where she could be a little bit of this and a little bit of that. She was part and parcel of the Canadian scene, and the familiar question, "Where's the accent from?" became more amusing as the years went by. It was not until the year 2006 when she began to contemplate her own mortality (for no special reason) and the possible demise of her ethnicity—whether it happened by design, neglect, or just plain bad luck—that she forced herself to look back into the past.

The latest issue of the quarterly magazine *Anglos In The Wind* had arrived in the mail and was lying on the kitchen table. Mary Beth's daughter, back home from university, picked up the magazine and flipped through the pages without much interest, until she came to the page with the matrimonial ads. Giggling at the conditions imposed on young men to have clean habits, "sans vices", before applying for the hand in marriage of "A-I girls", she casually turned to Mary Beth and asked, "What does A-I mean, Mom?"

"What?" Mary Beth spun round, shocked by the question. "What does A-I mean?" she repeated. "Not Artificial Intelligence, I am sure."

It took her a few moments to realize that her daughter was serious about the question.

How could 20 years have passed without her ever alluding to her heritage, so that even her daughter did not know her true background? How could she have lost herself in another culture, another world, and another dimension of life so easily?

Mary Beth went back to her journal, filled with colorful pages reflecting her moods and the events of her life unfolding in a new country. The secret book lay in her antique writing-desk drawer, with the bound side facing away from her. This allowed her to see the multi-coloured edge of the pages, the multi-faceted pages of her life.

The flaming orange pages were filled in at the time of her arrival in Canada. So much activity: a new career, another university degree or two, learning to drive a car. Life was good and glowing with excitement.

The pale pink pages recorded the graduation ceremonies of her daughter, her 21st birthday party, and the nights spent talking to her child about that first date, puppy love, and the loss of it.

The blue pages—and there were quite a few—held memories of home, her family, close friends, and all the little nostalgic moments in her life.

But the pages she loved best were those mellow, yellow ones, with excerpts of the letters from her sister Sally Ann, who still lived in India. The frayed and somewhat torn edges of these pages was an indication of how many times she had read them, over and over again. They always made her smile.

February 4, 1989
My dear Mary Beth,

The Gladstone family has finally decided to move to Australia to join their son Danny. While Uncle Johnny seems sad to leave India,

Aunty Katie can't wait to get her things packed to leave this "God-forsaken", town as she puts it. However, she has not forgotten to pack her old blue rubber slippers, the ones often held together by a safety pin, just in case she needs them in Sydney, as those Australian shoes will most certainly hurt her bunions.

Love, Sally Ann

May 21, 1993
My dear Mary Beth,

You will be sad to hear that Uncle Jimmy passed away last week. You remember how he used to hit us on the head with his knuckles when we were kids, each time he caught us stealing his guavas from the tree in his back yard? Holy Mother of God, you should have heard the wailing and lamenting that went on at his funeral! Uncle Jimmy would have loved the send-off that he got, if he had but turned around to watch it before checking in at St. Peter's gate.

Love, Sally Ann

June 19, 1998
My dear Mary Beth,

India's high-tech industry is making waves, and with it comes the hope of much-needed jobs. Our Anglo-Indian children are inspired to do well in school and to further their education in good universities, with the hope of working for these computer companies some day. The other day, at a birthday party in Aunty Dolly's house, there was no talk of the youngsters going to Australia or Canada, like it used to be in the old days. They are now looking to make their mark in India, and I am so hopeful that they will succeed. You should make a trip to India some day soon just to see how well everyone is doing.

Love, Sally Ann

November 16, 1999
My dear Mary Beth,

We are on the verge of the new millennium, and the Anglo-Indian community in India is thriving. It seems that every family you meet now has their own car and home. In fact, Patti and Kenny were just back from visiting his sister in Australia, and they say that we are much better off here. We have the time to drop in and chat and cook pepper-fry and pepper-water whenever we like. Gracie, who had gone to Toronto to see her cousin, said that most of the Anglos that she had met were careful not to cook curry in the winter months as the smell stayed in the house for days. And the horrible Canadian winters that she told us about! Much better that we stay here, where the sun shines brightly and the sky is blue, even though on most days you have to look at it through dust and smog.

Love, Sally Ann

December 28, 2000
My dear Mary Beth,

Both the Barton family and the Campbell family have bought their own homes and have moved away from our street. You should see the call centres that have sprung up! All our Anglo-Indian boys and girls have now got well-paying jobs and are able to build their own homes. In fact, a whole section of the new development has homes owned by Anglo-Indian families. On a Sunday afternoon, you can hear the songs of Jim Reeves, Buddy Holly, Johnny Cash, and other songs we loved, wafting down the street mixed with the aromatic smells of Anglo-Indian food being served on the verandah to anyone within sight. Every Sunday it's a party on that side of town.

Love, Sally Ann

April 2, 2002
My dear Mary Beth,

I love this thing called the Internet. I can't imagine that I can send my letters to you, all the way in Canada, in a matter of seconds. Now fancy that! David is a great son-in-law, and he spends a lot of time showing me how to use e-mail. I wrote a long letter to you last night, but then I forgot to press the send button and foolishly closed the computer. Now I have to write that letter all over again. But I did learn something. Always press the save button and never forget to press the send button.

Love, Sally Ann

October 8, 2004
My dear Mary Beth,

Isn't it wonderful how the Internet has managed to bring the Anglo-Indians together no matter where in the world they live? I hear that a group based in the USA is trying to use it as a tool to collect funds to help less-fortunate members of our community in India. Foreign currency, after conversion to Indian rupees, goes a long way, doesn't it? It is nice to feel connected in such a special way.

Love, Sally Ann

February 15, 2007
My dear Mary Beth,

Thank you for sending me the link to the Web site of the World Anglo-Indian Reunion to be held in Toronto this year. I spent hours going through the list of names to see if I knew anyone. Except for a few, I did not recognize the names. Maybe they left India a long time ago. Maybe their lives are so different, and India is a faraway place in the echo of their minds. Maybe they have melted into the global society of the countries that accepted them, and as a result will be almost unrecognizable to me. But I am sure that where there is an Anglo-Indian gathering there will be fun, good food, and dancing, and the passage of time will no longer matter.

Love, Sally Ann

Some day, Mary Beth thought as she leafed through the yellow pages, some day I will tell my daughter all about my Anglo-Indian heritage. But for now she put the journal back in her desk drawer, locked it, and returned the key to its hiding place.

IDENTITIES

INHERITING THE PATCHWORK

by Geraldine Charles

I am the thread
I am the line
I am the story written through time
I am the song my ancestors sang
I am the new path
I am the line

Some years ago, I read Sheila Allan's autobiography, *Diary of a Girl in Changi*, which dealt with her years as an internee in a Japanese prisoner-of-war camp. In the book, she tells the story of the Changi quilts—the patchworks that were made by the women interned in Changi, on the island of Singapore. Those who contributed a square embroidered their names, and often within the design of their squares were images that acted as hidden messages. The quilts were then presented to hospitals in the military camps, and were a means of communicating details of the women's location and safety to husbands and friends.

Three of these quilts survive, one of which was on display when I visited the Changi museum in 2002. With its hidden messages, I found this quilt a powerful image, and it inspired me to use the metaphor of the patchwork quilt when I talk about Anglo-Indian family history. I explain that, to me, the individual squares that make up a patchwork represent the Anglo-Indian families that survive today, and they are sewn together with a thread woven from shared experiences and a common history.

With a real quilt, if one examines the individual squares, each piece differs in pattern, in material, or in texture. Often the patches are associated with the individual members of a family, and they sometimes have stories attached to them. In terms of the Anglo-Indian patchwork, the differences we see between the squares represent the unique story not only of how each particular family survived disease, war, and discrimination, but would also symbolize the aspirations, successes, and achievements of each generation of that family. As in a real patchwork, sometimes one might spot similarities between patterns: these are the clues that indicate common roots, the family links that existed in earlier times.

For some of us, simply knowing that the patchwork exists is not enough. We not only want to understand how the unifying thread came to be formed, we want to unravel the weave of the individual squares. This would help us to find when the strands of the patterns with similarities diverged from each other, and to follow these individual strands back in time, and perhaps thousands of miles across the ocean.

It is curious that many of the pieces of the Anglo-Indian patchwork, and their individual strands, can be found in two rather unremarkable white, metal cabinets, in the Asia, Pacific & Africa Collections Reading Room of the British Library; and that the key to unlocking the secrets of this Aladdin's cave is contained within a set of indexes held nearby. Captured in the drawers of these cabinets are the records of the life and death of thousands of Anglo-Indians. For some, their time on earth can be measured in a handful of days, whilst others were destined to become the forefathers of today's community. Here they remain, frozen in time, waiting to reach out across the generations and speak to you, their descendants: "We were here, we strove to survive, we gave you life—remember us!"

I still find it incredible that a plastic reel and a length of film can, in seconds, bridge the gap of decades. Fleetingly, through these records, we are able to share in their joy at a baptism or a marriage, and their despair at the loss of a loved one; and, yes, it does give one pause for thought, when reading the burial record of a child, to reflect that if their sibling had also succumbed, one wouldn't be sitting in front of the screen reading that record.

However, though death causes strands of the individual squares to break, it is marriages and births that resulted in the interweaving of new strands, the strands that today form an intricate relationship between many of the Anglo-Indian families from whom we are descended.

Just occasionally, a strand one is following doesn't stretch back across the seas; instead, its origins are rooted in India. Such strands probably reach back into antiquity, to a time before St. Thomas the apostle brought Christianity to the East, before Alexander the Great crossed the Indus, perhaps even as far back as the first settlements in ancient India. These are the loose ends, the strands that can never be followed because no records exist.

What lies beyond will remain tantalizingly out of our reach as nameless shadows, men and women whose way of life we can only guess at, yet whose blood mingles in our veins with that of our European ancestors.

Today, the treasure in those nondescript drawers is being made available worldwide, through databases such as those of the Families in British India Society and the Genealogical Society of Utah. We can also reach out across the oceans electronically, and share with long-lost cousins the stories of what happened to our families after they divided. The fragments of an original broken strand can now be repaired, and family threads that separated decades ago re-woven.

Some patchwork quilts become heirlooms and are passed down the generations. Let us hope that the memories of the Anglo-Indian community will also be cherished, and handed on to our descendants yet unborn.

Inheriting Remembrance

by Susan Deefholts

What does it mean to grow up Anglo-Indian, in Canada? It's a question that demands a complex answer.

We moved to this country when I was three years old. I have a handful of memories—each the size of a Pocket Instamatic photo—of my formative years in India, and a teacup's worth of sensory impressions.

I also have several suitcases of memories that don't belong to me.

Those memories—fragile, crumbling, secondhand—are my legacy. They're all I've got to link me to a world that has now disappeared—the Anglo-India of the early and mid-20th century. Grounded in Anglo-Indian culture, those memories are also unique to the experiences of their original owners.

My grandmother was one of those. The suitcase she left for me is elegant, with a patterned fabric exterior of Victorian-style flowers and curlicues. When I open it, its contents are neatly packed, beautifully pressed and folded. Any rips or tears are mended with tidy stitches.

She was that kind of person.

She used to spend every second weekend with us. On Sunday afternoons, she would make me scrambled eggs exactly the way I liked them—she had the magic touch, because no matter how I've tried to make them like that since, they never turn out quite right.

Everyone else would already have eaten, and so Granny and I would sit, and she would take out a few of her memories so that I could have a peek at them. I cherished those afternoons, for they provided me with a privileged glimpse into a present that is now long gone—a present that I would never have access to otherwise. I also valued them because they hinted at the person my grandmother was, long before she became my grandmother—and in some cases, before she was even my mother's mother. I'd see the girl she used to be, growing up in India.

There were stories of her brothers. Of how Jim used to tease her, but he was really her favourite. Of how Eric was always a little different.

"He followed his own path, once we were grown. No one knows what became of him."

The thought of losing track of a sibling—someone you had grown up with, who was so much a part of your childhood—disturbed me deeply. I was barely out of childhood myself, at the time.

She talked about her first encounters with my grandfather, and how he had been something of a mischief-maker in his youth.

She spoke with a smile on her face, her skin soft and astonishingly young, her irises dark, but rimmed with a border of grey.

Some of the memories she showed me might once have had a darker side—a sadder undertone. But they had been eased by time, the damage mended by perspective and her desire to see the best in people.

And all of them were steeped in—and profoundly shaped by—the Anglo-Indian world that she had inhabited.

She talked of how she used to discuss the day's menu with the cook in the mornings. Then she would see to her correspondence at her desk. In the afternoons, she would call on friends and have tea. Hearing those stories, I thought of the English classics, like *Pride and Prejudice*, and the lifestyles they depicted—except that every now and then, I'd be reminded that this was, most assuredly, not England at all.

"It would get so hot that you'd have to leave the windows and doors open. But then you had to be careful. I remember going into our bedroom at dusk. This was in Chunar[9]—there was no electricity up there in those days. I saw a long, thin object on the bed. I assumed it was one of grandpa's ties, so I reached out to pick it up—only to scream when I touched it." She grinned at me. "It wasn't a tie, it was a snake—a krait—that had slithered inside, to get away from the heat."

Or,

"Our compound in Gauhati[10] was right above the Brahamaputra River, and on sunny afternoons crocodiles would climb out and sun themselves on the stone steps leading to the water."

Or,

"Your mother was off on a trip with her friend. They arrived late at the *dak*-bungalow they had booked into. They were exhausted, so they settled in for the night with minimal fuss. As they were drifting off to sleep, they felt something dropping on the thin sheets they were using as covers. Your mother turned on her flashlight and said, 'Oh, it's just baby scorpions,' then turned it off and went to sleep."

"Baby *scorpions?*" I was horrified.

Granny shrugged. "They don't develop venom until they're older, so there was no danger."

Snakes, scorpions, crocodiles: not quite the usual components of an English comedy of manners.

So this, then, was one of the ways in which I acquired my sense of Anglo-Indian culture: via my grandmother's reminiscences.

My dad showed me a different perspective on the Anglo-Indian world. His father used to work on the Railways, checking and ensuring the integrity of the rail tracks and ballast. During school holidays, Dad and his older brother Colin would go along on these trips. They'd bring their guns.

"We would only ever shoot for the pot. We'd bring home whatever we took down, and the cook would clean it and dress it for dinner the next night."

He never quite said as much, but over the years, I managed to infer the larger story: on one income, with six children to feed—not to mention school tuition, uniforms, and sundries to pay—finances could get tight. His parents used to pare down their expenses, in order to pay for their children's education.

School itself was rather different, too. This was back in the days when it was accepted—and perhaps even expected, as part of a good, disciplined education—that a teacher would cane his students. Then, there were the meals.

"The butter was often rancid, so when the master wasn't looking, we'd put it on our forks and shoot it up at the ceiling to see who could make it stick." Nor was there usually enough food at mealtimes to sustain the appetites of growing boys.

"We'd get our tuck boxes from home, though. We'd each have our group of friends, and when anyone got a tuck box, he'd share it around with the rest of us."

All this presented quite a contrast from my own life at school.

Food was never short and the public school system provided my brother and me with solid educations—and no extra cost for tuition and books.

Of course, there were other things that hadn't changed. Bullying, it would seem, is an inevitable part of childhood—though at least I could escape from it in the evenings, at home. Still, it was my dad who advocated the direct approach—the one that had served him so well at boarding school, when the torment was endless and inescapable. He taught me how to fight—how to throw a punch and how to undermine your opponent.

As a result, the bully who had been tormenting me all year—stealing my bag and throwing it in the ditch, hiding my glasses, snapping my bra strap—had his comeuppance one lunch hour. With the entire class as witness, he was beaten up by a girl. The bullying stopped.

Dad had other, sadder stories as well.

"Aunty Peg was out in the garden—she was just little at the time—when a rabid dog somehow got into the compound. We didn't know. We thought the gate was closed. When it tried to attack her, our dog interceded, and their fight was what drew our attention to what was happening. We shot the other dog. But our dog had to be put down, too. I was the one who called him to me. He sat down and rested his head in my lap as he died."

There was a touch of moisture at the edges of his eyes as he swallowed and grimaced.

"He trusted me."

When he told it, I imagined my dad as he had been, based on the photos I had seen of him at that age. He'd be black-and-white and two-dimensional, and would have a small edging cut out around him, like I'd snipped him from one of the pictures—which is exactly what I had done, in my mind's eye.

I don't remember ever having learned the dog's name, nor his breed, so I imagined that he had probably looked something like Old Yeller, from the movie.

That's what most of my inherited memories look like—odd pastiches of old photographs, film images and fabrication, like those Victorian collages that are strangely flat, and have everything thrown in all at once.

As the years went by, it became more difficult for Dad to remember. It was as if all his memories were stored in crowded, jumbled rooms, and over time, each of the doors got locked. Sometimes he could find the keys, and sometimes he couldn't.

But, more and more frequently as the years went by, the doors remained locked. Often, he'd even forget that he had become forgetful.

After he died, and we went into his apartment to clear things out, it became obvious that at some level, he had known he was losing the ability to open the doors to his memories. To compensate, he kept every piece of paper, every article, every note he had ever written, read, or received. It was as if the apartment itself had become the storehouse of his memories. But there was no system to his collection—no files, no catalogue, no order. And so, over time, those rooms became like his mind: an irretrievable jumble of memories, piled on top of each other, with no way of sorting through them to find the particular one you required.

At that point, he only ever told the same 30 or 40 anecdotes, only ever quoted the same sets of phrases that were most familiar, and only ever asked the same questions, though he rarely remembered the answers I gave.

But then, sometimes, we'd be talking, and Dad would find a key. He'd unlock a door and go into one of his rooms, emerging moments later with some new treasure.

At those times, I felt like I'd been gifted. Once, he told me of an uncle who lived with his family while he was growing up. His uncle had been a young, hearty fellow whose main interest was sports, not studies. He had just begun working when he broke his leg. It never healed quite right, and for the rest of his life, he was unable to walk properly. He couldn't work after that, couldn't support himself. He never married, and so he lived out his days with his brother—my grandfather—watching his brother's family grow, his brother's children become adults and go off to live lives of their own.

I had never heard of this uncle before—and it saddened me to realize that, if not for this lucky chance, I might never have learned of him at all. I brought out the album and asked Dad to show me his uncle's photo, so that I could add him to my mental image of the family.

"That's him, there. Though he was much younger, then. This must have been taken not long before his accident."

That was the only photo we could find of the shadowy uncle who had lived in their house and watched them all grow up. It was as if he, like the life he might have lived, had disappeared after his injury.

Dad also told me about the dances at the Railway Club. It used to take two hours to walk from their home to the club.

"You'd never dress before you went because by the time you arrived, you'd be covered in dust. Instead, we always brought our clothes with us and changed once we got there."

Growing up in a country of frequent rainfall, paved streets, and closed-in cars, the notion of arriving at a dance covered in road dust seemed as foreign to me as baby scorpions dropping from the ceiling.

All these details—the backdrops of railway colonies, alfresco dances, hill stations, and boarding schools—these are my inherited memories, now carefully stored away in rooms of my own. They're faded already, with details missing—and it makes me sad to realize that I may never be able to fill those gaps, except with my own inferences and fabrications.

This, for me, is what it has been to grow up Anglo-Indian. Those stories were what helped me forge my own Anglo-Indian identity—because there were no other sources. When I was growing up, people didn't know what Anglo-Indians were.

I was in the multicultural club at school. In junior high, I went off to multicultural camp with a legion of other kids from all over the district. It was fun—and fascinating—to learn about so many different backgrounds.

On our second afternoon, just after lunch, one of the teachers stood up. "I'm posting sign-up sheets here at the front. If you think you've got an unusual background and feel comfortable talking about it, fill your name in. Tomorrow night, we'll choose a number of you to go up and give a brief presentation about your culture. Then we'll ask questions."

I figured I had something interesting to say—that my background was sufficiently unusual to qualify me for this opportunity. I wrote my name on the sheet. Under "culture" I wrote:

"Anglo-Indian (mixed British and Indian)."

The next day, when I checked to see who had been selected to speak, I was startled to learn that my name wasn't on the list. I asked the teacher about it.

"Oh yes, of course." She smiled kindly. "We already have someone from Britain and someone from India to talk about their cultures. We thought it would make more sense to have a different person from each place who knows about that culture specifically."

She had, of course, jumped to the wrong conclusion. She'd assumed that my background was simply the sum of its British and Indian parts. But it wasn't. Mine was a sub-culture—neither wholly British nor wholly Indian, but something quite different. A unique and inextricable hybrid that was quintessentially multicultural.

Years later, in university, I read *Under the Volcano*. Geoffrey Firmin, the protagonist, was supposed to be Anglo-Indian. But as I read, I realized that this was not my version of Anglo-Indian. Geoffrey Firmin was British and had lived in India. So, too, were the Anglo-Indians of Forster's *A Passage to India*.

These, then, were the Brits who once were *called* Anglo-Indians before that became an official name for people of mixed heritage. There were also others—people who walked on the other side of the two-way street.

Growing up, I had been told with some pride that Merle Oberon and Cliff Richard were Anglo-Indians.

I have to admit it was a number of years before I learned who either of these people were. Still, as a result of hearing their names bandied about, I had a vague impression that these two, at least, had put Anglo-Indians on the map in some way. When I finally learned a little more about them, however, I also discovered that Merle had only ever let it be known that she was from England, and that Cliff's family had moved there from India when he was just a kid. The world saw them as British.

Of course, I know perfectly well that times have changed. Back then, mixed ancestry might have hindered the career of a woman like Merle. I can understand why she instead chose to emphasize a background that would enhance her status.

But for a young girl, trying to construct a sense of where I came from and what my own background was, the fact that Cliff and Merle were Anglo-Indians had become irrelevant. Though they were public figures, they didn't give me a sense of how others perceived the Anglo-Indians, nor of how our sub-culture fit in with the rest of the world, because in their public lives, they were British.

Then again, perhaps this detail was actually key: perhaps the reason it was so difficult to uncover a public profile of the Anglo-Indians, and to figure out how they were regarded elsewhere, was that, historically, many Anglo-Indians had chosen to efface themselves and blend in with the British whenever they could.

Growing up in Canada, I also knew how little effort was required in order to blend in. Aside from my dark hair and my olive skin, my background was no more—and often less—prominent than the backgrounds of the other kids in my class, at least half of whom were also either immigrants or the children of immigrants. But where my native language was English and my cultural paradigm largely European, there were other kids who were starting from scratch, learning English in kindergarten and navigating the complexities of a culture that was completely different from that which they encountered at home.

In fact, it was only through the idioms, the recipes, and the get-togethers, which often as not ended with a sing-along, that I would even glimpse my Anglo-Indian heritage in the course of my everyday life.

And so I often found myself kneeling before those suitcases of memories that weren't mine. It was thanks to those precious, priceless heirlooms, lovingly passed down to me for safekeeping, that I am now able to define myself: as a grandchild, as a daughter, and as an Anglo-Indian.

Beyond the Raj

by Mark Faassen

January 1, 2006, was an interesting night for me. My first time in India, it was also my first exposure to the fabled Anglo-Indian dance, on Indian soil. Though I had been to an Anglo-Indian dance in my native Canada once before, nothing could have prepared me for what I was about to witness.

The car picked us up at around 8 p.m. and took us to a local community hall. People were milling around outside and slowly began to filter in. While not the Taj Mahal, the hall was decorated neatly with an abundance of coloured streamers and banners. At its front end a stage housed a six-piece, all-Anglo-Indian band. Standing guard at the foot of the stage was a charismatic emcee—an elderly gentleman with a voice as smooth as silk, clearly a veteran of these types of events, who presided over the evening's proceedings. One half of the long hall was reserved for large parties—who pre-arranged a table and chairs for their respective group of friends—and long, neat rows of chairs lined the other half of the hall. The crowd soon thickened, and the band began to play.

The music was totally Western; no time was permitted for even a couple of cursory Bollywood or *Bhangra* numbers. There was, however, the noticeable inclusion of hip-hop and reggae—not even played, I might add, at an Anglo-Indian dance in Canada; at least, not at the dance I attended. The dance floor throbbed with the old standards, inviting the older generation with the foxtrot, waltz, and other slower dances. After a little while, however, the mood shifted, and it was apparently time for the jive. The older crowd thinned and, to my surprise, the floor became packed with younger Anglo-Indians and their dance partners. Not only were we about to begin the jive, we were in the midst of a full-fledged "contestants take your mark" competition.

I sat at a table on the edge of the dance floor and watched, almost tickled pink with what I was seeing. I can honestly say that I have never seen such vigorous, serious-minded, and unrelenting dancing in all of my 28 years. These were not casual participants. These young people knew the steps and knew them well. I remember thinking to myself, in this day and age, where on earth do they learn how to jive? Watching them, I broke into a sweat.

After the jive came the fancy dress competition (or costume competition, for those of us who have never heard the term "fancy dress" before), which was then followed by a beauty pageant. Yes, a beauty pageant, complete with a panel of three guest judges. The pretty girls, virtually all in mini-skirts, flashed their best smiles and took turns at wooing spectators with their responses to a skill-testing question. The boys—most wearing shirts and dress pants, with some in suits—sat grinning, happily taking in the scenery.

Glancing around the room, I would say that one-third of the mature women wore *saris*. I enquired and learned that they were indeed all Anglo-Indians. A woman casually explained to me that one change in the community in modern India is that it is considered appropriate and respectable to wear a *sari* on special occasions—and what was more special than breaking in the New Year? What a charming sight it was to see a dance hall full of *saris* dancing the waltz and foxtrot with seasoned flair.

It is important to add at this juncture that this was not a large metropolis with a sizeable pool of Anglo-Indians, such as Bangalore, Kolkata, Chennai, or Delhi. This was small-town South India, where New Year's apparently still brings in a crowd numbering in the hundreds.

I'm not sure what it was exactly that served as the tipping point, but as I sat observing the scene, it struck me that while some things may change, other ways die hard. Sure the hall may be slightly less shiny than in the past, the suits on the men may carry a wrinkle or two more, and a number of women may be dancing in *saris*, yet in spite of all that, I realized firsthand that the tradition continues.

If anyone told me two years earlier that I would be submitting an article for inclusion in an anthology about Anglo-Indians, I wouldn't have believed them. In fact, the conversation would never have taken place because I wouldn't have any Anglo-Indians to talk to. Let me explain. My mom is Anglo-Indian, my dad is Dutch, and I am made in Canada.

The only Anglo-Indians I've known my entire life have been my family, until late 2005. That's when I started working on a documentary film about the community. I travelled to India for the first time and eventually had the chance to speak to Anglo-Indians from India, Australia, the U.K., the Netherlands, Canada, and the United States.

I suppose I have a unique perspective of what we are, because I wasn't around for what we were. I'm part of this Anglo-Indian thing, but also apart enough to be an appreciative observer.

This is the question I pose in my documentary: What does it mean to be Anglo-Indian in today's world? It's been written that the Anglo-Indian community is but a drop of water in the ocean that is India. So where does this leave us in a multicultural, globalized world?

Today Anglo-Indians are scattered around the globe—being everywhere and nowhere, visible and yet invisible simultaneously. The community spans several countries, and Anglo-Indians have shown that they are law-abiding, dependable, and willing to integrate into whichever country they live in. Whereas, in British India, to be Anglo-Indian was a sort of quasi-nationality unto itself, today's Anglo-Indian is a loyal Canadian, Australian, or Indian.

One advantage Anglo-Indians say they have, and I heard this over and over again, is that we can mix and get along with any ethnic group or people. In many ways we're model citizens of a multicultural society. Ironically, this ability to integrate, to understand, and to socialize with others is also a cause of worry to some in the community.

Anglo-Indians integrate so well that many believe the community will assimilate itself out of existence. The Anglo-Indian of today, and particularly the younger generation, is either too Canadian or too Indian to be "real" Anglo-Indians. Is this conclusion based on what Anglo-Indians are actually like today, or is it perhaps in part more emotionally based?

On the one hand, if we compare the younger generation today with the typical Anglo-Indian from Bombay in 1927 then, yes, we don't seem to make much of an Anglo-Indian. Take myself: I don't go to Anglo-Indian dances, I don't play cricket or field hockey, and I don't dress like an Anglo-Indian would from that era. But is this the standard or criteria by which we should measure Anglo-Indianness in 2008?

Everything in life evolves, and identity is no exception. From what I've seen and heard, the children of Anglo-Indians abroad tend to consider themselves Canadians or Australians foremost, rather than Anglo Indian, and understandably so. Most of us were born outside India, grew up with friends of other ethnic groups, and we tend to have limited knowledge of the history of our own community; a topic that for many of our parents was not of foremost importance. However, while my generation is obviously attached to the countries we were born in, I found that lurking beneath the surface lies a more subtle, personal, and complex set of attachments toward our families and background.

How do I know? Every younger person I talked to would always start by saying the same thing: "I don't know anything about Anglo-Indians," and then he or she would go on to talk for three-quarters of an hour about being Anglo-Indian! If they didn't care, then presumably they wouldn't have anything to say.

Some from the parent generation explained to me that their children have no interest in going to community functions like Anglo-Indian dances. On this delicate point, I would suggest that the older generation ought to understand that it needs to offer us something more to gain our interest. Shying away from a dance does not necessarily mean shying away from our heritage. It simply means that we don't want to go to a dance. So while the younger generation may have little formal knowledge about the community, and may not always have equal interest in attending the same social events as their parents, the idea of coming from a mixed-race culture that combines India and the West is relevant to our everyday identities. We may not always put the name "Anglo-Indian" to it *per se*, but we do recognize that we have a unique background of mixed heritage that stemmed from colonial India.

I discovered what some might find an intriguing paradox in India. The biggest thing that struck me when talking to younger people there is that they know they are Anglo-Indians. It sounds obvious enough, but younger Anglo-Indians in India are more aware of their Anglo-Indianness than those in the West. Whereas I may be an Anglo-Indian once removed, they are Anglo-Indian—period. And yet the younger generation in India is also probably the most integrated generation of Anglo-Indians ever when it comes to merging with the Indian mainstream. They can speak their respective regional languages with ease, they have any number of non-Anglo-Indian friends, and they can chitchat about the latest Hindi film star or television programme with ease. Yet these very same individuals can be found, come Christmas and New Year's, on the dance floor at an Anglo-Indian gathering. Rather than being this or that, or one or the other, Anglo-Indians in India today are a good example of how several identities can co-exist effortlessly.

I would like to emphasize that I disagree with characterizations that the community in India is dead or dying. The community may be smaller and humbler than it used to be, and to be sure it faces challenges, particularly with respect to alleviating the condition of the less fortunate of the community; but to say that it is on the verge of extinction is, in my experience, an exaggeration. Instead, I was unexpectedly impressed to see a core segment of the community working hard to keep people connected and re-connected; individuals who are negotiating a space for themselves in modern India yet mindful of maintaining some kind of balance between past, present and future in preserving an Anglo-Indian ethos and outlook. I think it's understandable, perhaps, for some to accept the demise prognosis if they migrated long ago and are unaware of how things have evolved. India has changed a lot since 1947, and especially since the 1990s.

Changes for the better at the national level are paralleled within the Anglo-Indian community. After a number of tough decades readjusting to life in independent India, the community is rebounding. Opportunities are increasing. This is not to suggest that life is a bed of roses for the everyday Anglo-Indian, but amidst the trials lies ample room for optimism. One of the most effective examples to illustrate change is the increased number of Anglo-Indian youth obtaining university and even postgraduate degrees. An important page seems to have been turned with respect to higher education. Access may still pose a problem for some, but desire is unyielding. The only way to prove it is to go and see. Or, if you can allow me some self-promotion, watch my documentary when it comes out.

My impression is that the days of having an Anglo-Indian cultural checklist are over. Once you had to (a) be, (b) speak, (c) dress, and (d) play like one to be a *pukka* Anglo-Indian. The checklist was possible for decades because of the insularity of the community. But as people moved out of India and settled elsewhere, and as people within India moved out of the railway colony or a particular part of town, the community became less inward-looking and more exposed to the outside world. Today we may be more varied than the typical Anglo-Indian probably used to be, but does being different necessarily mean we stop being Anglo-Indians?

Change does not necessarily mean a loss of identity; it's how we respond to change that is more important. Our extent of integration with the societies we live in is not the issue. The issue is how we choose to define ourselves and then take the steps to preserve it. Writer Amotz Asa-El[11] once described the unique condition of the Jewish people as being "geographically diffuse and culturally fluid." Speaking about the migration known as the Jewish Diaspora, he writes: "In the course of that migration, the Jews merged with myriad local cultures but at the same time vigilantly maintained their Jewish identity. Since then, Jews have been found in almost every corner of the earth, bringing with them their heritage, education, and skills, while displaying an ability to adapt and contribute to local cultures..." Jews are an interesting example of how "joining the mainstream" does not necessarily translate into a loss of identity. I also don't think many can accuse individuals of that group of taking the passing down of culture for granted.

Now I'm going to put the older generation on the spot and ask: Are we truly doing everything we can to sustain the Anglo-Indian community internationally?

A lot of positive things have happened in the past five years alone. Anglo-Indians from all over the world have come out of the woodwork, myself included, and are documenting our history, our stories, and, through book publishing, online journals, academic research, charitable organizations, multimedia projects, and magazines, things are vibrant. This is a constructive start, and there is always room to grow.

But if there's one thing that I realized over the course of my travels, it is that together with putting our full breadth of history down on paper, we ought to actively support the community in India. And when I say support I don't necessarily mean financially—it could be morally, symbolically, educationally, professionally, as well as financially.

Any discussion on the lines of, "What is the future of the community?" is inseparable from the 150,000 or so Anglo-Indians who live there as an officially recognized people. They represent the anchor and the homeland of the community, and as long as the community in India is healthy and sustainable, they remain the best prospect for the continuation of Anglo-Indians as a recognized group. If we truly are an international community, it would help to be unified as one.

Where we go from here is naturally open to debate. The future of the community may not be guaranteed, but neither is its alleged extinction. How individual Anglo-Indians choose to respond will make a difference. Some may stray further from the flock, some may return, and others may seek to remain firmly in the fold. If enough people want to preserve something of the Anglo-Indian experience or identity, it will still take some work.

The future may very well be a question of perspective. If we uphold the typical Anglo-Indian lifestyle of yesteryear as the standard for defining Anglo-Indianness today then, yes, it seems likely that the community will fall victim to what some have termed "living in the past"—with extinction not far down the road. In contrast, an emphasis on a specific Anglo-Indian lifestyle may need to be replaced with an emphasis on an Anglo-Indian ethos, or way of thinking, which would continue to distinguish the community, particularly in India, and that could possibly supersede one specific moment in time or geographic location.

Similarly, do we continue to adhere to a legal definition crafted in a different era and in a very different social context, or do we choose to adopt a more pragmatic approach? For instance, should we define an Anglo-Indian as anyone of mixed European and Indian descent, without stipulations? Some of our children and grandchildren no longer qualify as "authentic" Anglo-Indians because of newer cultural combinations of intermarriage. If we would like them to remain in the fold, then along the way we will need to consider whether it is possible to put firm boundaries and markers on an internationally scattered community that is itself already mixed; and, if not, whether we should even spend time trying.

Altogether, the possibilities for re-defining or modernizing the way we think of ourselves are numerous; the only thing that remains to be seen is whether we have the will to do it.

Unravelling the Mosaic: Musings of a Young Anglo-Indian

by Sheldon Fernandez

My paternal grandfather was a proud man. I never made it to the homeland during his lifetime, and I often wonder how our relationship might have changed had I done so. He was the closest of my grandparents because we shared a love of history, and among my most cherished possessions is the family tree he created to commemorate our heritage. He would trace through its branches in loving detail, like an architect describing his masterwork. Gesturing gently with his finger, he would bring me to the tree's root of 1823, when Salvador Fernandez voyaged to India and fathered the family. Although the historical record testified to Salvador's Portuguese descent, granddad explained that the spelling of his last name suggested he was, in fact, of Spanish blood. I asked if that meant we were Spanish or Portuguese so I would know who to cheer for in the FIFA World Cup. "Neither," he replied firmly, "we are Anglo-Indian."

In sifting through the branches of generations past, I think about my grandfather and the ancestors to whom he paid tribute: what would they make of people my age and the extent of our "Anglo-Indianness"? Would they smile at a culture embodied or sigh at a heritage lost? Would our commonalties be embraced or our differences emphasized?

When I put this question to my generation, a vague consensus slowly developed. Yes, being Anglo-Indian was significant and, yes, there were aspects of our heritage we'd pass on to our children. The qualifier, one that might seem laughable to our elders, centred on the topic of values. Our culture is important, we said, because its core values will find expression in subsequent generations. To this end, let us turn to the thorny topic of value differences in our community, because it is here where the future of our heritage lies.

My mom laments that she was born in the wrong time period. There is an inward sadness when she speaks at such times, an inconsolable disappointment at the erosion of morals and the boundaries of our conceit. In true Anglo-Indian humility, she'll insist the problem is not an incompatible present but an incompatible mother, and that if her children are thoughtless and materialistic, it is because of inadequate parenting. Yet behind her words there is a rueful air, a yearning for a quainter and gentler time, uncorrupted by the coldness of modern ways.

For my dad, talk of my generation elicits nothing more than amused resignation. We will never understand, he tells me, because we are enchanted by the falsities of our time. We exclaim that moral values are relative, while forgetting that we are relatively ignorant. We cast aside the insights of old because we have yet to realize that the knowledge of books cannot encompass the wisdom of time. "You are all smug and arrogant," he says, in his smug and arrogant voice. We will never understand.

In the same way, I often wonder if my parents understand. For many of us, growing up was wrought with a strange ambiguity, that of being different, the same, and yet generally not belonging. From earliest memory, the term "Anglo-Indian" itself was more an emblem of historical ancestry than a conscious way of life, a hint of heritage loosely bolstered by parental tales of tradition and hardship, and a childhood experience that had us sitting on the knife's edge of assimilation and exclusion. Assimilation, because of the fluidity with which our parents integrated into the Western world; exclusion, because we were still subjected to pangs of intolerance during our childhoods. To narrate the story of my generation is to describe a tight-rope walk between cultural tradition, adaptation, and alienation.

For example, you were called a Paki to be sure, but sensed that you were different from the even more ridiculed Pakis across the street, with unpronounceable names, circus-like clothes, and malodorous foods. Your mom was equally skilled at cooking lasagna and curry, and while your dad spoke nostalgically of Indian field hockey and cricket, he was also into rock and roll, Western cowboy films, and American baseball. You remember extended family outings to Loblaws and K-Mart, but can likewise recall sporadic trips to the Indian grocer, where a real Indian in funny dress sold your mom fancy spices and vibrantly coloured sweets. If whites thought you brown because of your skin, browns thought you white because of your name, and confused, wide-eyed children of all colours were forever asking, "What are you?" Attempts at explaining your confusing heritage did not demystify your background so much as it confirmed its uniqueness. But it is on the question of values that we really diverge. To the extent that my parents trumpet the traditions and teachings of old, I labour to demonstrate why they are also irrelevant. And so we eye each other from opposite sides of the fence; there is acknowledgement, but not understanding; respect, but not reciprocity. The time is ripe, I believe, for clarification.

People my age are selfish, and we are selfish because we were born into a society that has trained us to be so. We are taught that even the most formidable obstacles can be conquered with sufficient effort and channelled passion. We are told that the world is for the taking if we would only have the courage to grasp it. And we are given a worldview that dares us to dream beyond it, lest we squander the sacrifice our forefathers made in bringing it to us.

These are all praiseworthy principles—the pride and promise of our democratic structures—but take note of their individualistic flavour. Our societal aspirations today are focused on the fulfillment of personal potential: my right to a higher education, his right to equal pay, her right to choose. In the modern mindset, the individual is premium, and we assert this prejudice unapologetically amidst the historical shadows of oppression and intolerance.

It is our modern constitution distilled, this pursuit of opportunity, this quest for equality. Such great promise and innate content, but in the end—to what end? To what do we direct these smug ideals, so anxious in their adolescence, so lonesome in their autonomy?

Ask my generation about our rights and you'll get an earful; enquire about the desired ends and you'll get a telling pause. Is it to a greater good, to a higher cause, or to the liberties themselves? Because this question remains unanswered, our thought process often runs in the negative, and we wallow in the "have-nots" of our privileged lifestyles: the possessions we can't afford, the breaks we don't catch, the soul mate we can't find. We don't purposefully think this way—it would be less exhausting if we didn't—but we can't help it: it's the product of inhabiting a world of boundless opportunity that idealizes earthly accomplishment.

In the context of this cold calculus, the advice of our parents can seem laughably outdated. A single example will suffice. One of my mother's more jarring claims during my childhood was her assertion that "the family that prays together stays together". She would utter this proverb constantly, to compel us to go to church, to recite the rosary as a family, or to reiterate her simple belief in the power of prayer. I would usually humour her sentiments, but on one occasion I went for her jugular with every ounce of elitism I could muster.

It's an uplifting thought, I told her, but poor philosophy; optimistic rhetoric ignorant of the very realities that prompt us to lean on faith. Religious families do fracture, often irrevocably. The poisons of abuse and jealousy are sometimes too venomous for the bonds of belief, and we remember with regret those God-fearing individuals who never taste the fruits of their fidelity: Hutus and Tutsis in Rwanda, peasants in Central America, women in Afghanistan, and ... a certain carpenter crucified at Calvary.

I told Mom she was being hopelessly naïve: faith does not always overcome; it's an antiquated euphemism masquerading as a truism. She didn't argue, whether out of hurt or disgust, I'm not sure.

Or perhaps mothers simply know what their sons do not, as many years later I would see firsthand the world that had given her such values. "I've been thinking of you all morning." she wrote during my travels, "My world in Chittagong is so small, you will wonder how I even got out."

On the plane ride to Bangladesh, I remember being as anxious as I'd ever been, and as we approached our destination of Chittagong my stomach tightened with unexpected anticipation. I had heard about this city endlessly as a child, of tumultuous times and inescapable poverty, and of unpretentious lives modelled in faith and fellowship. My family had left this place years ago in search of the prosperity that now enabled me to return, but lamented that the values of the old world were being eclipsed by the extravagances of the new one. I was a product of their struggle, but had never really understood their sacrifice. In a moment, that would change; I was going to see the world they had left behind.

The aircraft slowly descended, and as my mom's birthplace came into focus, I peered out the window with warm anxiety. After years of storytelling and exhausting travel there, finally, was Chittagong. The heavy sunlight illuminated an unusual mixture of urban concrete and plush vegetation, and the idyllic sea rippled gently aside the metropolitan buzz. My eyes moved from building to building as I tried to connect the urban scenery with parental tales of old. Perhaps that was the street where mom had bargained for purses or where grandfather had laboured unfailingly for the family. The elderly man beside me, a Bengali with whom I had conversed during the trip, smiled and said, "It's a wonderful thing to come back to your roots."

One event from my trip stands out above the rest, and it happened one evening at my Uncle Bunu's after I had taken a nap. As I walked downstairs, I heard the words my parents had taught me many years prior. "Hail Mary, full of grace, the Lord is with thee," they all said in unison. There they were in the living room—my relatives—kneeling, praying, and focused. My two little cousins sat dutifully beside their mother in unwavering respect, and their soulful words gave their meagre surroundings an indescribable integrity because something was profoundly different: their adoration was genuine.

As a lifelong student of religion, I had dissected questions of faith from all angles, but this was the real article, as authentic a spiritual appeal as I'd ever seen. They were really "Hailing Mary", not for her benefit it seemed—but for theirs. And so they continued, praying together, staying together. Mom's sentiments didn't seem so naïve.

The danger with such a powerful encounter is the temptation to reduce it to parable; that of the anxious foreigner who by rediscovering his roots reignites his faith and is moved to "just believe". But that would be a disservice to the complexity of our existence, one that allows faith to find hope but permits tragedy to annihilate it. For every family that finds strength through faith, there is a counterpart that perishes in spite of it, and both constitute equally vivid facts of our reality.

Is there, then, a subtler message that we can garner from our predecessors?

In theological circles, we begin with a simple question: "What would Jesus do?" It is this inquiry, we are told, that should frame the Christian ethic. But in studying the subtleties of the faith, you realize that the hypothetical is misguided and that the real question is more practically rooted. Specifically, how is the person of Jesus relevant to the challenges of today? In the same way, I would submit that the cultural question for my generation is not, "What would our ancestors do?" but rather, "How should what they've done inform our lives?"

As applied to the question of values, the key observation, I believe, is that there is a liveable truth between the moral assuredness of our parents and the swords of cynicism we wield to discredit it. Real maturity recognizes that regrettable counter-examples do not invalidate the circle of wisdom so much as they are a part of it, and that optimism is not a cradle of the weak but a tool of the experienced. Or, as one scholar put it, "That hope has appeared in this universe of ours is itself a ground for hoping that hope is at home in the universe."

If this wisdom is truly timeless, the majority of my generation will find it. We will rediscover it through the memory of example, the trials of parenthood, and the plain pains of time. The rules of right will come full circle: goodwill may not always triumph, but it sometimes does; steadfast prayer does not always hold a family together, but it sometimes can. We will teach our children to respect their elders because one day we, too, will bear the wrinkles of unacknowledged wisdom.

Yet in what ways is this quest for wisdom, or the manner in which it is traversed, distinctively Anglo-Indian? Is there an ethic or value unique to our people? We might speak sincerely of Catholic morals and Christian ideals, but our community is but one of many whose conduct is premised on the principles of faith. We could leverage romantic terms like "character" and "chivalry", but the seeds of tradition are planted by the elders of all cultures. What is it, then? What is the ideal that threads our community together?

In visiting my father's birthplace of Calcutta a year ago, I had the privilege to tour the tomb of Mother Teresa, and engraved in one of the memorial stones was a quote of hers that remains close to my heart. "Do no great things," she said, "only little things, with great love."

It is a saying so outwardly simple and so seemingly wise that I wonder if only so sublime a person as Mother Teresa could meaningfully assert it. We might imagine Jesus himself imparting such wisdom, so elegant and enigmatic is the teaching. Elegant, because the value of humility is self-evident; enigmatic, because both Christ and the Saint of Calcutta achieved greatness in the very way the statement cautions against. Undoubtedly, there is an implied link between love and modesty, and it is on this point that I believe the spirit of our community can be found.

When I examine the lives of my parents and grandparents, aunts and uncles, both blood and honorary, and Anglo-Indians both at home and abroad, I see in them much virtue worthy of emulation: integrity, sincerity, spirituality. But the most reliable commonality, that which makes me most proud to call myself Anglo-Indian, is a trait at once revealing and at first underwhelming: an authentic, unwavering, and everlasting humility.

It's a quality unappreciated in our modern climate precisely because it exists in opposition to those spectacular talents that captivate us, and that this attribute goes unnoticed makes it all the more praiseworthy that some people truly embody it. This, I submit, is the river that runs through our community: a majestic modesty, if such an oxymoron can be used.

I saw this quality in my paternal grandfather: a quiet dignity and understated manner that commanded respect. I sensed it when he pleaded with my parents to be tolerant of my failings, lest they forget that they, too, were immature children once. And I felt it when he tenderly showed me our family tree and retraced the lineage of generations past. He was forever proud, but never boastful; wise so as to be understated, understated so as to be wise.

It was this sense of moderation and integrity that punctuated the lives of my grandparents, and I see it duplicated in my parents and their priorities. The Catholicism communicated to my siblings and I was many-sided: routine, ceremony, and discipline were all elements but, mostly, it was Catholicism by example. To the extent that we routinely went to church on Sunday, my parents embodied the ideals of faith in themselves: mom, through her compassion and quiet strength; dad, through his integrity and raw will of belief. It is their example that prompts me out of bed to church on Sunday and fuels the pangs of guilt when I miss it.

To my parents' generation: my father was right—we will never understand. You have spared us from hardships of real political turmoil, of gross inequalities, and appalling wrongdoings. Words such as "independence", "liberation" and "bigotry" are for most of us but abstract terms—far removed from the deep-seated realities they represent for some of you.

If it is the measure of men to exceed the ambitions of their fathers so their sons may do the same: you succeeded wholeheartedly and have set for us high expectations. But the torch must be passed and the responsibilities extended. The journey is ours, the roads are many, and the anxiety is real.

To my generation: I, too, am right—our parents will never understand.

> Of life at this pace and the prosperity race,
> Of its ethical wrenches and the obscuring of fences,
> Of the whirlwind of change and ideological range,
> Of generational tension and scars we can't mention.

But it is one of the joys of a generation to discover in the conduct of their children the example of their parents. Let it be so with us, so that it may be true for them. May we in time comprehend the power of faith, the promise of goodness, the sacrifices of parenthood, and the splendour of humility.

May we personify our heritage with the pride of our ancestors as we endure the struggle of the challenging present, in hopes of an emphatically different yet prosperous future.

An Epistolean's Legacy

by Nancy Rixon Lilly

My Dearest One,

Imagine yourself snuggled close to me. It could perhaps be thundering outside, as my quiet voice tries hard to muffle the crashes that might frighten you. It could be a cold wintry night, as we sit wrapped in your mother's blanket, which has, until now, been perched invitingly on the sofa just for this occasion. Then again, it could be a Texas summer day, with inactivity and reading being the only welcome respite from the hot, glaring sun outside. Close your eyes for a moment and imagine me with you as I relate the way we are.

The story of me is also the story of my son, your father, and it will continue with the story of you. Our story is filled with warm and loving characters, each bringing a tie that nourishes and strengthens the family tree. This tree was planted in India 150 years ago; despite it being up-rooted and transplanted many times, it remains strong and fruitful, as it begins a new saga in the United States of America. You are the new branch on this tree.

We did not dream of coming to America. Like most Anglo-Indians, we wanted to go "home", except for us it would have been Calcutta or Shillong, my parents' home-towns. Since we could not decide where it would be, we remained for some time on neutral ground in Dhaka, Bangladesh. The impetus to settle elsewhere was spurred by the proverbial foot in the door: as with most family migrations, we followed the one who left before. Imagine our delight, tinged with an equal measure of sadness, as each one of us boarded that Boeing 747 for a new life in a foreign land.

As a child discovering the joys of reading, I would voraciously devour my father's Max Brand cowboy-western paperbacks; now here I was, starting a new life just like the early pioneers of America. I relived their sorrow of leaving family and friends behind as they boldly, but with some unspoken trepidation, traversed west. The trepidation was short-lived as the surge of empowerment was intoxicating. I was excited. Fear was furthest from my mind as I kept my unblinking eyes focused on the spot where I had left the rest of the family; on the ground at the airport's observation deck. As the jet rose ever higher, that changed to a patchwork quilt of variegated greens, changing again before long to an enveloping azure. It was only then that the emptiness in the pit of my stomach spread like the incoming tide, as it washed over me. I wanted to go back! I whimpered mutely, wishing to be safe again on hard-baked earth, and at home with my family. Soon, they would be gathered in the single room that we all shared; the faded, checkered curtains pulled to darken the room, and the ceiling fan whirling at the topmost speed. Dad would be sitting on the director's chair he had made himself, Mum and the others on the bed. They would all be talking as we had so often done, wondering what I was doing, what the flight and America were going to be like. And they would all be missing me. Too late! There was no going back now. I had taken a giant leap into the unknown.

I concluded that there was truth in the saying about safety in numbers. For the first time in my life, I am afraid to be alone in a hotel room. With my parents' warnings playing on an audio loop in my head, I inspect the room, checking every nook and cranny, and especially under the bed. I double-bolt the door and prop a chair under the handle for good measure. Even with these precautions, I am bleary eyed at the airport check-in the next morning, waiting in the queue for the second leg of my inter-continental flight.

Like a baby, one of the first things one learns has to do with one's feet. I had to learn to use an escalator with grace. Images of me being unceremoniously ejected from the escalator for vacillating were enough to master it with a silent mantra of 1-2-3-step. It was nerve-racking, and for a few months I opted to take the stairs. That soon changed as I, too, began to change.

It seemed to take longer to learn the American monetary system. There was never a plausible answer to my question, "Why is the dime (10 cents) smaller than the nickel (5 cents)?" To my relief, at some stage of my metamorphosis, I stopped mentally converting dollars into *takas* and vice versa. When did that happen? I'm unable to recall. But after mastering money, I was able to fly solo into supermarkets and department stores.

The world really opened up for me when I learned how to drive. I enjoyed my freedom to explore the neighbourhood, and finding new routes from point A to B. Although I flunked parallel parking, I was handed my driver's licence and told: "Be careful out there." Driving for me did not have the hype most teenagers accorded it. I found it stressful, and I seemed to be on the defensive from the moment I backed out of the garage to my safe return home. I missed being chauffeured around on a rickshaw or baby-taxi, which allowed me to sit back, day-dream and enjoy the ride. Nonetheless, I took to driving like a duck to waddling, and remember with fondness the firsts: my first drive in the rain, and my first outing on the highway with my son, breathing a sigh of relief on reaching our destination. "We have to go back now, don't we?" he had asked, with a quiver in his voice.

My first drive at night came while we were living in England for a while. I forgot to turn on my lights. No one honked but I finally noticed everyone giving me a wide berth, and I shuddered when the realization finally hit home.

Another hurdle came when I was forced to pump my own gas. For as long as I could, I would drive up to Wayne's Gas Station for a "full-serve". He would pump my gas and check my tires. Approaching Wayne's one morning, with my car dangerously at E for empty, I was floored to see they were closed. I hesitantly made my way over to Exxon, pulled over to the side, and studied others executing a "self-serve". When sufficiently confident about the gas-pumping modus operandi, I sallied forth.

In general, the stress of driving made me a cautious driver. How cautious?

"Ma'am, did you see the speed limit posted on the sign back there?" one of Texas's finest, a law enforcement officer, asked.

Smiling weakly, I replied, "Yes, I did. But I thought I was driving within the limit."

"Well, ahem ... you were driving too slow." he drawled.

Fully expecting to receive my first ticket, I began to sweat. I awoke to find myself in bed. Yes, it had been a very bad dream, and it stemmed from the challenge of maintaining a speed of 20 mph when picking up my son from kindergarten.

Before my son began school, our only contact with the outside world was hanging out in the mall. He called it our second home. After a bout of chagrin at being recognized by a store clerk, I vowed to change my ways. Darkening the doors of the mall was held in check till I decided to seek gainful employment and make it worthwhile.

When we did go shopping, I missed bargaining so much. There

is an art to it, one that my mother executed with such panache. In America, it was a shock to learn that the price printed on the tag was the amount that had to be paid. No quibbling, haranguing, or walking away from the merchandise. Not if you really wanted it. "We accept cash, cheque, or any major credit card, Ma'am." The only stores in Dhaka that I remember giving us *bâki* were the neighbourhood *dukans*; they knew where you lived. Here, one's only chance to impress with those bargaining skills learnt at your mother's side comes at the Saturday garage and yard sales.

Besides locating the bank, post office, and grocery store, one of the first things an immigrant does is look for stores carrying "comfort food". So, it wasn't long before we scoped out and found an Indian grocery store. I then went wild, stocking up bags of rice, *dāl*, and the pantheon of Indian spices; I was keen to cook our kind of curry, quite unlike the heavy, tomato-based ones at our local Indian restaurant. I make a mental note always to remember the green chillies. They made dishes taste so much better. When homesickness washed over me and threatened to pull me under, I whipped up a pork vindaloo, or a snake-gourd curry stuffed with ground beef, and all was right with the world.

Ours was not the kind of family that had servants taking care of our every need. We had a maid who worked for us occasionally, and I use "worked" loosely. She'd show up one day but then disappear for months on end. We were taught to use "elbow grease" and do our household chores, besides learning to cook. Imagine my joy, when I learnt that I wouldn't have to hand-wash towels and sheets, and that these could be thrown with everything else into a washer. The conveniences of American wealth and technology awed me. I learned how to fold fitted sheets by watching strangers at the laundromat handling theirs. After weekends of surreptitious observation, I thankfully spied—and copied—the one who had mastered the art of corner-to-corner folding. I watched and learned.

I was grateful for the opportunity to be a stay-at-home parent for the early years of my son's life. I'd come to America with years of secretarial experience, and when I set out to find work I progressed from a maid service, to a cafeteria employee, to a volunteer secretary of a non-profit organization, to retail sales, and finally to human resources.

Twenty-six years have elapsed since that first inter-continental flight. I have matured, mellowed, and, like fine wine, have peaked. I have a new homeland now. I am glad to be here, and thankful for the opportunities afforded my family. And as each one of us goes through the process of becoming a US citizen, we vow never to forget the past and the way we used to be. Life wasn't easy in the land of our birth, and it is still a struggle sometimes in our adopted land. But we are all settled, with homes of our own and loving families. This, then, was where we were meant to be.

Every so often, I marvel at strangers' quizzical looks and preconceived ideas of who I am. I can now laugh at their repeated, "No...really, what is your name?" Like a forgiving and indulgent parent, I shrug it off, all the while praying, "Lord, give me patience. They don't know me, why should they? Let them think me a Mexican, Filipino, Thai, or whatever. I know and have accepted who I am, and I know who they are. That is all that really matters."

I close with the hope that others will not have to encounter prejudice in their lifetime. To be accepted without a raised eyebrow would be a long-overdue blessing. I can only wish they will know *who they are*. I know I'm proud of the way we are.

All my love, your Nan.

Identity Cadre

by David McMahon

Who we are is defined by our heart and soul. It doesn't depend on our postal code.

At the age of 12, I didn't become a substantially different person when my father retired as traffic manager of the Calcutta Port Commissioners, and we moved from Kidderpore to Behala. I might have had a sudden growth spurt. I might have knocked off a bit of puppy fat. I might have noticed my voice breaking as maturity (or what passes for maturity) kicked in. But it didn't for one moment alter who I was.

Likewise, nothing changed in my psyche when I moved from India to Australia. I was an Anglo-Indian in Calcutta. And I am still an Anglo-Indian here in Melbourne.

Get my drift? I'm still the same person that I've always been. Proud of my family. Proud of my friends. Proud of my ancestors. Proud of my heritage. Proud to call myself Anglo-Indian.

For the first 30 years of my life, I travelled on a blue-and-gold passport that said "Republic of India" on the front. From that point on, I have travelled on a blue-and-gold passport that proclaims "Australia" on its cover. But it hasn't altered who I am.

One of the funniest examples of family-related geography took place when I was 14 years old. There is a substantial age gap between my older siblings and me—Keith, Michael and Brian got a head start of 15, 12, and 10 years, respectively. Because my brothers were in boarding school at Sherwood College, Naini Tal, I only saw them for three months each year. By the time I was six years old, all of them had left the family home: Keith and Brian to join the merchant navy and Michael to become a fighter pilot.

When I was old enough to go to boarding school, I chose to go to St. Joseph's College, Darjeeling—the school famous for its compass orientation, North Point. By then, Keith had spent time in England before moving to Australia. Shortly after I started year 10 at school, Keith returned to India on holiday, travelling on an Australian passport.

As Brian just happened to be in Calcutta at the time, it was decided that he and our mother would travel to Darjeeling with Keith. Since Keith was now a "foreigner", he had to get special permission to visit Darjeeling because of the sensitive political situation in the region. The necessary paperwork was completed without a hitch. Once they arrived in the beautiful Himalayan town, it was decided that they would spend a day or two extra—which meant that Keith had to apply for an extension.

While I was in class one morning, Mum and Brian accompanied Keith to the official who would review his case. They explained they just wanted a couple of extra days because they were spending as much time as possible with me while I was at boarding school. Very efficiently, Keith was given permission and the necessary paperwork was completed.

As Mum, Brian, and Keith rose to leave, the official politely stopped Mum. He wanted to know if he could possibly ask her a "very personal" question. Mum, who was never flummoxed by unexpected roadblocks, told him to go right ahead.

Clearing his throat, the official cut to the chase. "Madam," he said, "how is it you have one Australian son, and the other sons are Indians?"

Which brings me back, rather neatly and conveniently, to my original assertion. Where you live doesn't necessarily define who you are.

Obviously, I had great difficulty accepting this fact of life when I was little. A neighbour's daughter, Radhika Batra, often used to come to our house to play with me, even though she was probably a year or so older. Apparently (so I have been told) if we ever had an argument about who would get to play with a particular toy, and if I stood my ground, Radhika would say, "Okay, then I'm going home."

The lesson must have slowly sunk into my consciousness. One day I was coming off second best in a test of wills. So I stuck out my jaw, put my hands on my hips (such as they were) and announced, "Okay, then I'm going home."

Radhika burst into peals of laughter. "But this *is* your home," she said, trying hard to speak as mirth enveloped her.

I've been told I had a hard time coming to grips with the concept. However, in my defence, I should point out that I was probably only four or five years old at the time.

So where is my home? I lived the first 12 years of my life at 3 Dumayne Avenue, just a stone's throw from the Kidderpore docks. Then we moved to Behala. In between, I spent my adolescence in

Darjeeling. As newlyweds, my wife and I moved to Melbourne. We spent two years in a unit[12] in Box Hill. Then six years in a house in Endeavour Hills. Then we built our dream home, in the same beautiful suburb.

So where *is* my home? This is my home, this graceful abode where my wife and I have raised three children. But I have a special place in my heart for everywhere that I've once called home. In 2003, during a holiday in India, I took my wife and children to see the sprawling, magical home at Dumayne Avenue, where my mother first carried me through the door as a newborn.

It was a very special moment for me, to be able to show my children all the nooks and crannies in that rambling house and the huge garden, so special to my early years. It was truly a great privilege because when you think about it, how many parents get to show their children where they grew up? There could be no greater way to share a sense of place and a consciousness of belonging.

Both those factors are so integral to the Anglo-Indian experience. By extrapolation, they are also crucial to establishing who we are. I am blessed with a sense of place. Likewise, I have no trouble working out where I belong.

Both these trends have been a favourite theme of all the noble chroniclers who have flocked to India in the past six decades to make "The Definitive Anglo-Indian Documentary". They have always tried to induce members of our community to explain, on camera, or into radio microphones, where they really fit into the great scheme of global communities.

Yet there is an outcry every time these documentaries are aired. Allow me to play the devil's advocate here. I am an Anglo-Indian and I am a journalist, so I can see both sides of the argument. If members of the community are happy to speak their minds freely and in a non-controlled environment to a film crew and an interviewer, both parties are acting in the truest spirit of democracy. The interviewer can ask any questions he or she wishes. Similarly, the person being interviewed can answer those questions in any manner they deem appropriate.

Likewise, the person being interviewed can choose not to answer a question. But if you've spoken to a film crew and said something that (a) you might regret, or (b) is likely to cause angst in the wider community, that is not the fault of the interviewer, the camera crew, or the producer. They didn't feed you the quote.

But here's where we run slap-bang into reality. The reality of media is that many hours, many days, many locations, many interviews, and many divergent points of view are presented in the course of filming a documentary. A documentary crew might spend a month traversing the country, accumulating several hundred hours of film or videotape. That "footage" is subsequently edited down to form, say, a half-hour documentary.

This is where the editing version of the Venturi effect takes place, where something of immense volume must face the cull, making way for only the minuscule representation that actually makes it through to the final version. Perhaps as much as 90 per cent of the original footage is left on the cutting-room floor, leaving only what the editing team and the production team must skilfully weave together in a logical sequence.

There is another factor to take into account. If the documentary is to be presented on commercial television, there is a further avenue of restriction. If it is to be presented in a half-hour format, the actual program will run for a total of between 22 and 25 minutes. Why? To make way for the commercial breaks.

Don't like the concept of ad breaks? That's too bad. They make media outlets commercially viable. If those outlets were operating in the red, they wouldn't have the budgets or the funds or the technology or the human resources to send experienced crews out to make documentaries.

There is another salient point to take into consideration. No one is forced to speak to the documentary makers. Their opinions are sought freely. They are not told what to say. They go in front of the camera of their own volition. That's the essence of free speech in every sense of the phrase. If you volunteer to speak to a documentary maker, you can't say later that you were misrepresented. They're your words. They're your opinions.

That's the spontaneity that documentary makers or feature writers want to see. You know why? Because they're not platitudes. Because they're the honest opinions of Joe Public. Because they're different from contrived spin, which as we all know is one step removed from propaganda.

Do people sometimes present a very negative view of Anglo-Indians? Yes, indeed. There is a duty that should apply to every journalist: the overwhelming need to present a balanced point of view on any subject. This, alas, is not always the case.

More than 40 years ago, a British crew spent time in Calcutta, interviewing Anglo-Indians of all ages and from every economic category. There was widespread consternation among the community when one teenager brightly observed that she couldn't wait to go "home". Naturally enough, the interviewer asked where "home" was.

"England," said the teenager, who had been born and bred in India and who had never been closer to touching England than when pointing to the country on a map.

At the same time, the British crew visited the Dalhousie Institute, an Anglo-Indian sporting and social club. They asked permission to film some of the people playing tennis on the three clay courts. Permission was readily given. Unfortunately, one of the men had a gaping hole in his shirt—and it was generously but inadvertently exposed every time he threw the ball up to serve.

Among the horrified onlookers, it was the greatest underarm controversy until Trevor Chappell's last-ball delivery against New Zealand almost caused a diplomatic incident.

In the mid-'80s, I thought I had run slap-bang into a diplomatic incident all of my own. My fiancée and I had just arrived at Gatwick Airport in London, after stepping off a flight from Brussels. Because we were travelling with just hand luggage, we were the first passengers to reach the Immigration counter.

The officer behind the desk did not wave us through. He examined our passports carefully. There were a lot of entry and exit stamps to peruse, because I travelled a lot as a sports journalist, and my fiancée flew several thousands of kilometres every week as a flight attendant. Her passport and mine had concertina-like extra booklets of pages to accommodate all the stamps from the various airports we had visited.

Next, he flipped back to the front page of her passport and mine, poring over the details.

This was not looking too encouraging. But we both had valid British visas and had flown out of London only a week earlier, so there could not possibly be a problem with our documentation. There was a growing line of passengers behind us, becoming increasingly restive.

Eventually he spoke. "Can I ask both of you a personal question?"

I spoke for both of us. "Go ahead." My mind was racing. I could not imagine what could possibly be the problem.

All he wanted to know was how my wife's surname was Welsh and mine was Irish, although we were both travelling on Indian passports. I nearly laughed out loud because the question was so innocuous.

So while the rest of the queue waited for these two youngsters to clear Immigration, we stood there and gave him a potted history of the East India Company, the Raj, and how the Anglo-Indian community came about.

It was also an important lesson for me. Until that point in my life, I simply assumed that everyone in the United Kingdom would know what an Anglo-Indian was. That incident at Gatwick was a great reminder that I should not operate on the basis of assumptions.

A couple of years earlier, I witnessed an interesting example of how even the most logical assumptions could be totally misleading. At that stage, I rode a motorbike and wore one of the first locally manufactured full-face helmets. It was a Studds helmet, produced in Madras. After a couple of years, the sliding visor cracked when someone dropped a cricket bat on it.

The only way to replace it was to take the helmet to Madras and have a new visor fitted by the Studds staff. Because I travelled a great deal, it was not long before I found myself booked on a flight for a two-day trip to Madras. I took an overnight bag with me, and carried the helmet in my hand. A very good friend of mine, the sports journalist Ashok Kamath, met me at Madras airport, and we walked out in deep conversation.

At the exit, someone asked me something in Tamil, a language I do not speak. The man was immediately rebuked by someone standing next to him. As we walked past them, I asked Ashok what had just transpired. He chuckled and gave me a translation.

The first man had asked me if I wanted a cab or an auto-rickshaw. The second man had chided him for his apparent stupidity. "Don't you have eyes? The fellow is carrying a helmet, so he obviously has a motorcycle parked outside."

It was a great eye-opener for me, and during my journalism career in two countries, I have never made assumptions. I edited a national magazine in India and a morning newspaper in Australia, and I have always operated on the basis that proof outweighs assumptions, 24/7.

I ran into another assumption once. I have always worn my Indianness like a badge of pride. Some years ago, when I worked at *The Sunday Age* in Melbourne, I was on vacation when a Queenslander joined the paper. She was introduced to all the members of staff and was told that I would not be back for five weeks as I was visiting family in India. When I returned, her jaw dropped and I couldn't work out why. Weeks later, she confessed that her mental picture of me was a "little fat bloke with a pink turban". We still laugh at the incident, for there was no rancour involved. See what I mean about assumptions!

Much has been made of the weight of expectation on the next generation of Anglo-Indians who are born overseas as a result of widespread migration. All three of my children were born in Melbourne, but have experienced India up close and personal, in the course of many trips back to the country where I was born. My wife and I have not forcefed them a compulsory diet of pride in India, but it's been interesting to see how they, in turn, have developed their own deep sense of affection for the country. By intellectual osmosis, they have absorbed our pride in who we are.

Where to from here for the world's Anglo-Indians? Alas, I am not clairvoyant, but I do believe that the policy of regular reunions around the world has created a crucial rallying point. For a community that has bloodlines from every conceivable nation, there has to be a strong sense of belonging.

Like every other Anglo-Indian, I am a genetic cocktail. Not that it worries me in the least. Last time I looked, even Britain's royal family, the Windsors, had strong Germanic ties.

Collision of Life and Love

by Dorothy McMenamin

The softly crooning voice of Jim Reeves singing in the 1950s, "That's what happens when two worlds collide," will be remembered with nostalgia by many older generation Anglo-Indians. The word "collide" usually conjures up ideas of a crash and damage but, of course, that is not the mood and image Jim Reeves evoked. His songs droned on gently about love and life...timeless themes in any culture. Anglo-Indians came into existence with the collision of life and love between European males and Indian women as early as when the first European males arrived in India in the 17th century. Their Eurasian offspring bloomed on Indian soil amidst the many Indian cultures of the subcontinent, but ensuing generations maintained the language and culture of their paternal ancestors. Buffered and privileged by opportunities later made available via the ruling British Raj, Anglo-Indians formed yet another mixed-race group amongst the teeming multicultural Indian milieu. They followed the usual endogamous marriage practice of Indians, marrying essentially within their own group... then came the withdrawal of the British in 1947.

With the end of the colonial era, Anglo-Indians faced decisions about their identity. Were they born-and-bred natives with their home in India, albeit having followed a Western lifestyle under the paternalistic eye of the British rulers? Or, should they continue to align themselves with the British, in which case it was time to follow in their footsteps and depart for foreign shores. Very few Anglo-Indians owned property in India. Therefore, their roots in Indian soil were shallow, more like pot plants thriving in a tropical climate. Gradually, more and more Anglo-Indians transplanted themselves out of the subcontinent, the forever-loved land of their birth.

The choice was determined by the belief that their children's future was best served out of India. Few of the older generation really wanted to end their carefree lifestyle, where money had not been the price of comfort. Where employment seldom offered large salaries, but instead came with free or subsidized housing, good schools, and local clubs where friends gathered to play tennis, cricket, hockey, cards, Housie, and sing and dance.

Those gloriously sunny mornings, early to work or school, shading from the midday sun, having a *charpoy*-bash during the long, hot afternoons with the bamboo chicks lowered over the verandahs, and then rising for a high tea; then the balmy evenings, the birdsong, and chatter with friends late into the night.

None of these was easy to leave behind, but leave the Anglo-Indians did, in droves, in the decades following the 1950s.

Like most Anglo-Indians, my relatives departed for England and former British colonies such as Australia and Canada. My immediate family went to England, and in the 1970s I emigrated to Australia. Life was a lot easier and warmer Down Under. However, it was still difficult to choose to live far from one's immediate family, even though Anglo-Indians are used to a relatively peripatetic existence and had, early in life, formed the good habits of letter writing (probably begun during their boarding school days). So, I travelled and kept in touch through letters, receiving news of old friends in India, Pakistan, Bangladesh, Canada, the USA, Australia, and, yes, even in New Zealand.

Eventually, I met my husband-to-be, a New Zealander. His ancestry was not really very different to my paternal ancestors—the Irish who had fled their homeland because of the famine due to failure of the potato crops. Whereas my "spud-Irish" ancestors had stopped at India, his went farther, to the bottom of the South Pacific.

When I first came to New Zealand in 1977, my impression was that no Anglo-Indians lived in Christchurch. Family friends had migrated directly to Auckland in 1948 but later moved to the warmer climes of Australia. Many streets in Christchurch, and other cities I later discovered, had familiar colonial names, such as Colombo and Madras Streets, and even the nearby hills were named Cashmere Hills. Some of the early settlers came from India, such as the Craycroft Wilsons, who purchased an estate in the Cashmere Hills, and even built a home for their Indian servants, the now popular Stone Cottage. But there were no fresh curry spices in the shops in Christchurch, not even an Indian restaurant when I arrived. That meant letters from mother came with lots of recipes, and there were many parcels of spices and curry pastes

In the 1980s-1990s New Zealand became an attractive destination for tourists and migrating families, so gradually we began to have lots of Indian and South-East Asian restaurants, together with the necessary spices, since everyone has taken to curry like ducks to water, as in most parts of the world.

In the 1990s, mainly tied to the home with four young children, I began my so-called university hobby and graduated in World Religions and Indian History. Since my youth and schooling in Rawalpindi, I thought I understood much about the Indian subcontinent and its many religions and cultures, but soon realized that I had only scratched the surface of the complexity and diversity of Indian cultures. However, when it came to studying modern Indian history and anthropological accounts of colonial life in India, my hackles rose when I encountered descriptions of the British and their "poor relations", the Anglo-Indians.

Meanwhile, my research interests were growing. For some time, I had been collecting the memoirs of the older generation who had experienced the violence and tribulations associated with the Partition of India and Pakistan in 1947—I suppose growing up in the Punjab with its Partition horrors had left its indelible mark. So, in 1996, I expanded my questionnaire to elicit details about their pre-1947 colonial lifestyles. I wanted to embark on postgraduate research into Anglo-Indian society but was told there were no primary sources available in New Zealand. By recording oral histories of elderly people from colonial India, I was creating primary archival material for posterity, as well as my own sources. Anglo-Indian friends overseas had been my first interviewees, but gradually I began to discover people who had come to New Zealand from India, hardly discernible from ordinary New Zealanders, or Kiwis as we are often called—although being likened to a flightless, nocturnal bird is quite unflattering.

My oral histories recorded the collision of the two worlds of Anglo-Indians and New Zealanders, which appears to have been one of integration. Some individuals initially struggled to adapt and fit in, but the chameleon characteristics of Anglo-Indians meant that was a private struggle, and outwardly they soon appeared to be regular Kiwis. In fact, the Maori and European mixed-race people in New Zealand are a group whose features are not dissimilar in appearance to Anglo-Indians. However, mannerisms and speech are distinctively different and immediately recognizable at closer quarters.

The first person I tracked down from India was a lecturer who I heard reminiscing about his young years in a distant land and the aroma of spices, and learnt that his parents had come to New Zealand soon after Independence. His mother, Christene Evans (1919-2007), had been taken to India at the age of three and loved her childhood and young married life there. She put me in touch with the widow of another lecturer who had served in the Indian Civil Service. Joan Flack (née de Penning, 1915-1999) had grown up in Darjeeling, married an ICS officer, and they immigrated to New Zealand in 1949. Joan was a great raconteur, especially about her family, who had made fascinating contributions to British India. Her Anglo-Indian ancestor had assisted in surveying the subcontinent, known as the triangulation of India, with the famous surveyor, Sir George Everest, after whom the highest mountain peak in the world is named. Another of Joan's relatives established the first patent office in India and registered the first patent: a machine for pulling a *punkah*. However, the machine was a financial failure because the local *punkah wallah* operating the old cloth fan by a string tied to his toe was vastly cheaper.

The extraordinary experience of finding and meeting people to interview from old India revealed, as many people have found, the close ties within the Anglo-Indian community. When Joan Flack learnt my family name was Doyle, she recalled a Terrence Doyle at her teachers' training college in Darjeeling, who turned out to be my father's elder brother, long deceased. She even told me a heart-warming tale about being in his class and reading a book hidden on her lap, when suddenly she felt his hand on her shoulder and heard his voice asking, "Good book?"

"Yes," she replied, continuing to read, and my uncle moved on. However, when she read the engaging novel in the next class, the book was snatched from her lap, never to be seen again.

My next Anglo-Indian was found across a table in a restaurant. A woman I had not met before asked where I was from, and I eyed her back with equal curiosity. Of course, we both turned out to be Anglo-Indians, although she had come to New Zealand in 1951 as a child. It turned out that our fathers had both won medical scholarships and, although my father was a few years' senior, they had trained together at Calcutta Medical College. My father died many years earlier, but my mother had trained as a nurse at the same college. Upon introducing my mum to her dad, Norman Barnett, over half a century later, a world away in New Zealand, my mother asked whom he had given his autograph to during the "ragging" that took place with new medical students and nurses. Apparently, the "autograph" was a sooty imprint of the new recruit's backside! A cheeky exchange between a couple of octogenarians far away from home. A variant of today's carbon imprint perhaps?

With the burgeoning use of the Internet, I was now able to keep abreast of research and worldwide interest in things Anglo-Indians. It was on the web that I got my real breakthrough locating Kiwi Anglo-Indians. I discovered the fifth triennial Anglo-Indian Reunion was to be held in Auckland, New Zealand. I bought my tickets straightaway, and contacted the Anglo-Indian host association, run by the late Gene Leckey. It turned out that the Leckey family had come from my part of the world, their father being a train driver in the Punjab, and Gene's sisters had attended St. Denys's school in Murree, just "up the *khud*" from us in Rawalpindi. I interviewed Gene's elder brothers, never dreaming that, in fact, it was Gene who was to die first and suddenly of a brain tumour.

At the 2001 Reunion, I met several Kiwi Anglo-Indians. Another instance of the "smallness" of the Anglo-Indian community in the subcontinent, came when I met Bill Barlow (1929-2004) from Calcutta, then living in Christchurch, who had attended Victoria School in Kurseong. My father's brothers had attended the same school, and Bill had been in the same class as my youngest uncle. My grandmother had been the dormitory matron at the same school, so Bill also remembered her. It's a long way from Kurseong to Christchurch, New Zealand, but another family connection unfurled here 50 years on.

Of course, the Reunion in Auckland meant meeting many more Anglo-Indians from the Diaspora and, subsequently, I attended the first Anglo-Indian Conference in Melbourne and the Reunion there in 2004. In ever-decreasing circles (or increasing circles, whichever way one chooses to look at the expansion of contacts and the discovery of the closeness of the community), I have met more and more Anglo-Indians, especially the older generation who were the first to leave the Indian subcontinent.

One of the salient features of this generation, wherever they migrated, was their independence, self-reliance, and ability to knuckle down and learn to adapt and fit into their new homes with few complaints. Significantly, not one of the people I have interviewed ever resorted to going on the dole at any time in their working lives. Family members, if necessary, supported one another through times of financial hardship. Fifty years or so later, most of the octogenarians I know reside in their own homes, or a few have bought retirement villas, rather than enter rest homes for the aged. Strong family ties and support have enabled them to retain their independence. Perhaps their mental agility and strength gives support to recent medical research that turmeric is good for the prevention of Alzheimer's disease and dementia. The people I interviewed have crystal clear memories, excellent health, and enjoy cooking their favourite Anglo-Indian recipes containing generous amounts of *haldi*.

The closeness of Anglo-Indian family ties have resisted the intrusion and breakdown of family bonds engendered by a reliance upon the state and social welfare systems in Western societies, which has resulted in younger generations ceasing to tend and care for the elderly in the manner of the age-old reciprocal cycle. Anglo-Indians have held fast to their old entrenched values, which they consider founded in Christianity. But possibly this trait stems also from living in India, where there has never been a welfare system, and everyone has to rely on family members and the goodwill of others. This proud, independent trait underlies the Anglo-Indian community, whose members not only support their own families but, increasingly, offer help to the not-so-well-off among their wider community.

The success of Anglo-Indians, as I see it, is that they have integrated so well into their new home countries. In New Zealand, they have integrated to the extent that they are almost unidentifiable unless paths actually cross and a conversation ensues. Then some of the old traits are recognizable—especially how well we speak English—as commented upon endlessly by others. Of the 40 people from India I have interviewed in New Zealand, all have achieved good success in their working lives. Two have been awarded an MBE (Member of the British Empire), and one an OBE (Order of the British Empire), in recognition of outstanding services.

Since I began my search to ferret out Kiwi Anglo-Indians, some have voiced an interest to meet one another. Like myself, encounters with other Anglo-Indians were few, if any, during their years living in New Zealand. The cooler climate and remoteness must have posed a deterrent to migrants, because even now the country's total population is only just over four million. We have a group of about 24 Anglo-Indians living in Christchurch who meet regularly; although, sadly, some have now passed on. Most members of the group are 70 years or older, because my research has focused on those old enough to remember the working and living conditions prior to and following Independence and Partition in 1947.

At least two or three times each year, we get together for lunch to enjoy one another's company, exchange stories about the good old days, and talk about the escapades of younger family members. The stories are shared over homemade treats, such as curry puffs and whitebait patties (a New Zealand delicacy). Some of the younger members have had wonderful holidays back in India. But the reality is, their youth harks back to the bygone age of a wonderful and special era. However, everyone appreciates their New Zealand nationality, which has given them a full life and holds open a world of opportunity.

In March of 2007, in a celebration to recognize the growing diversity of the many communities now living in New Zealand, an exhibition was held at Canterbury Museum in Christchurch named, "Around the World in 30 Lounges". Thirty different groups were invited to exhibit family items, creating a small living room that would reflect their past heritage. We put together an "Anglo-Indian lounge", which one entered through a rolled-up chick, furnished with some cane chairs, cushions, and a Persian rug. Old family photographs adorned the walls and sideboard, alongside a whisky decanter and a *chota/burra* peg measure, copper Indian ashtrays, beautifully carved Kashmiri cigar boxes, china, and other memorabilia. A tea trolley was laid ready with a tiered cake stand. However, the show stealer was a tiger-skin of an old man-eating tigress that had killed more than 100 people, displayed with a copy of the newspaper cutting from the *Hindustan Times* of 1934, showing Captain Bruce Abbott, who had shot the tiger not far from Kumaon.

Our lounge provoked a great deal of interest, enjoyment, and positive comment. The "long stories" reflected by the exhibits, I was told, created an atmosphere that evoked nostalgia and constant fascination for the world of Anglo-India, one of the many exotic and romantic encounters between East and West.

I Say, Men

by Ralph N. Moore

Voices from the verandah whispered about the way we were, and when the echoes returned from within the empty rooms they ricocheted off suitcases packed with our worldly goods and ready to go. We were weighed down with our mental baggage as well; the oft-repeated mantras of our forebears about our British paternal lineage, with nary a word spoken about poor old Mum's Indian maternal line of descent.

We left behind in India, where we were barely tolerated, a diversity of people, languages and religions, and in our arrogance we increased our alienation by strutting the stage to prove our difference and Caucasian heritage. And when, with a sigh of relief, we arrived in the land of our choice, inhabited by people whom we and our ancestors had aped for generations, there came finally the realization that in some subtle way we were still different. The heady mixture of mixed blood that coursed through our veins produced a cast of features that was as varied as it was attractive but, due to the misleading range of skin tones and accents, it was especially difficult to establish our origins.

Many who identified with the new citizenry on the basis of colour quickly suffered a lapse of memory and forgot from whence they had come, while those of a darker shade of pale hastily claimed a line of descent from the Iberian Peninsula. While admittedly survival is the name of the game, a degree of honesty would not have gone amiss. To deny one's heritage is an insult to the parents who lovingly nurtured us, and who now lie forgotten in some weed-overgrown cemetery on a dusty Indian plain, having spent a lifetime trying to instil in us a sense of values.

Inexplicably, in our new surrounds, the latent Indianness within us has begun to surface. Hindi movies, once considered a joke, are now essential viewing at home. We devour large quantities of spicy food because we've lost the taste for European "side-dishes". Our conversation is peppered, for effect, with words from many an Indian language, and our homes are overflowing with Indian artefacts and paintings. We cling to casual acquaintances of like background as if we are members of some secret society, and with whom we celebrate on the slightest pretext, while excluding the native-born of our adopted country. Wallowing in a miasma of pungent food odours and giddy with wine, we relive the past as if it was some golden age—forgetting, in our nostalgia, the contempt with which some of us were held.

Every few years, hundreds of us circle the globe at great expense to rehash old memories with other ageing émigrés and exchange horror stories of our last visit to the land of our birth.

"It was soooo d-i-r-t-y, Beryl, yuk! With huge cockroaches everywhere!"

"Not to mention the crowds of people, the traffic, the pollution, and garbage piled sky-high in the streets that smells to high heaven. Nothing seemed to work. It was unbelievable."

We forget that it was always thus: the very atmosphere in which we were weaned.

There's little mention of those who were left behind, some unable to escape a miserable existence. These poor people go unnoticed by our smug travellers, who clutch the passports of their adopted countries grimly as they scurry back, brimful with after-dinner conversations.

"I couldn't believe my eyes, men. Some of our girls out there are actually wearing *saris* and *churidar-kameez*—really, it's such a shame."

And we will never change—for that's The Way We Are.

Raking Through the Ashes of that Bonfire of the Vanities

by Peter Moss

I've just had Liam Fitzpatrick over to lunch. Like me, he is Eurasian, and was born in Hong Kong in 1965, the year I arrived here. The difference is that in him the mixture is compounded of an Irish father and a Chinese mother, whereas my father was a London Cockney and my mother a product of the great Anglo-Indian community that formed the backbone of the Indian Railways.

Like many of our kind, we're both in the writing business, Liam on the staff of Time Magazine's Asia edition, and I freelancing and writing the occasional novel, biography, travel guide, or treatise on diverse Asian topics ranging from architecture to the social ethos of our times.

Once Liam and I might have more consciously thought of ourselves as Eurasian, in the days when being Eurasian and bold enough to testify to the fact carried a certain cachet, a suggestion of "otherness" that might intrigue those of more conventional origins. But today that "otherness" is fading, and blending into the prevailing "all-togetherness" that constitutes our progressively miscegenated society.

We are unquestionably losing our distinction, which could be a good or a bad thing, depending on how one might look at it. Though aware I am deprived of that little frisson of curiosity that once greeted my declarations of Anglo-Indian provenance, I personally find it a good thing that the world is melding into a sort of *caffè latte* blend. How can divisions arise once there are no demarcations to identify?

The only bad thing I can see about this ethnic adulteration and homogenization, to which we are increasingly subjected, is the loss of racial identity and culture; the frail and delicate strands and fibres of our source materials that don't always carry safely and securely down through our successive generations.

I look through very early family photograph albums, dating way back before I was born, and spot those in the group photographs that look that shade darker, wondering what cultural and spiritual continuities they carried in them that would not be passed on to their successors.

In their generation, being identified as Eurasian was less a source of pride than a cause for shame, for they had the misfortune to live when the British Raj was at its flaming apogee, reigning supreme over its own superimposed caste system based exclusively on the purity of its bloodline.

The merest suspicion of "a touch of the tar brush" would drive women to their dressing tables to apply skin conditioners and face powders. The last thing to be encouraged was any suggestion of "Indianness", which had to be bleached out of us. And of course this meant, to our shame as a community, that we Anglo-Indians adopted our own scale of colour-coded social acceptability.

What an incalculable loss we forfeited when we consigned that native inheritance to our eagerly torched "Bonfire of the Vanities". We volunteered to dam one stream of our heritage to give fuller flow to the other, effectively turning our backs on the accumulated wealth and wisdom of one of the world's oldest civilizations to reinforce our bonds with one of the world's newest (albeit fastest growing and most rapacious).

We lacked even the impartial detachment of the genuinely British, who could at least safely indulge their curiosity concerning native customs and festivals without fear of censure to the effect that they were in danger of "going native". For us, all things native were taboo; not to be indulged on any other than the rare occasions such as Diwali, when it would have been unpardonably cruel to have kept the children from a celebration more important to us than Christmas and Easter combined.

Today, the sins of our forefathers are coming home to roost, for I find that my nephews and nieces, and their heirs, are awakening to a genuine interest in their "roots", only to court frustration at the lack of a complete and balanced record of whence we came.

How lopsided our family trees begin to look when the branches are so thick on the one side and so sparse on the other. I feel I'm cast in the final edited version of a family saga that has left much of its riches on the cutting room floor.

I am reminded of an eminent fourth-generation U.S. surgeon of Filipino extraction who was asked by his children what he knew of the Philippines. Being all those generations removed, he of course knew next to nothing, but was eventually coerced by his progeny into tracking down distant relatives who had remained behind in the family's original heartland, which happened to be Davao City, in Mindanao.

To his amazement he learned of a distant cousin in Davao practising his own specialty of kidney transplants, although in his case using techniques predating the "keyhole" method perfected in America. So he wrote to this cousin, proposing that he would bring a highly trained medical team to Davao so that, together, they could embark on a two-week campaign to provide free surgery to as many patients as they could manage in that space of time.

In the course of this mission, the cousin and his associates learnt the latest Western surgical methods, while the thoroughly Americanized Filipino and his children were given the opportunity to regain a heritage long lost to them.

A similar voyage of rediscovery occurred a couple of years ago when one of my cousins, born in India a few years after me, was induced by a younger sibling, who had been denied that claim, to accompany her to India. They embarked on a journey that, in the one case, amounted to an extensive re-familiarization and, in the other, to a completely new experience. So fulfilling was the result that both undertook a second, longer and even more rewarding tour of India last year.

Roots can be retraced, however arduously and tenuously, but they can seldom if ever be wholly regenerated after sustaining the massive damage inflicted so long ago. We rake through the ashes of that "Bonfire of the Vanities", seeking reconnection with the native stock our forebears worked so assiduously to eradicate. But too often we end up resigning ourselves to the fact that, after so long a hiatus, the trail has grown cold.

And so I find myself envying Liam Fitzpatrick, for the more balanced scales that have maintained his family equilibrium. Here in Hong Kong, Eurasians of his generation were spared the aspersions cast upon those of my place and time. Here the intensely proud Chinese heritage would never have allowed itself to be suppressed, subjugated, or overshadowed by the European admixture.

The resulting progeny, such as Liam, are enriched and enlarged by their dual inheritance, enabling them to draw from two deep and bountiful wells. Would that the same were true of us, born in that forsaken land of Anglo-India, where we had to choose between those wells.

One thing I have no cause to envy Liam is the fact that we have both elected to live on in Hong Kong—he because he was born here, and I because I have resided here just as long as he has. After 41 years, I cannot countenance the thought of living anywhere else.

By sheer good fortune I elected to cast my lot with the one fragment of Empire that would serve the entire colonial epic as its valediction, and indeed as the best argument for its ever having been. For not in India, that much-vaunted "Jewel in the Crown", but here in Hong Kong did the whole colonial experiment achieve its greatest triumph; leaving a legacy so illustrious that the Chinese have reclaimed this tiny prodigal, this immensely powerful, culturally laundered returnee, with a promise not to interfere or change a scintilla of its diadem for the next half-century.

And so far that promise has been faithfully observed.

Furthermore I live, with Liam as my neighbour, in the jewel of Hong Kong's own particular crown, the island of Ma Wan, which lies beneath the immense and spectacular bridge to the new international airport.

Following her visit to my home in October 2005, Jan Morris, author of the *Pox Britannica* trilogy, described in an article for *The Guardian* this prospect from my rooftop:

"I think of Ma Wan (now known as Park Island) as Hong Kong in miniature. History is absorbing it into Hong Kong just as history is fusing Hong Kong with China. Behind my friend's house there is still a little grassy hillock, to remind me that only a few years ago this was just a rural islet of the South China Sea, but to the south the huge bridge rushes its traffic to the airport, cars on the upper deck, trains in a tube below. The island has become quite pleasantly suburban, and from its balconies gleeful children can watch the firework displays of Disneyland."

I derive particular pleasure from the fact that Ma Wan obstructed British attempts to colonize the South China coast for very nearly 50 years. In 1794, when Lord Macartney stopped off in neighbouring Macau on his return from an ignominiously futile embassy to Beijing, he commissioned Lieutenant H.W. Parrish of the Royal Artillery to conduct a survey of Ma Wan, with a view to fulfilling King George III's wish for "a grant of a small tract of ground or detached island" as a depot for the hoped-for exchange of Sino-British merchandise.

It was not to be. Parrish reported that Ma Wan failed to meet the requirements of a satisfactory harbour for trading ships owing, among other things, to the rapidity of its offshore currents, which even today swirl past the old Ma Wan pier at six knots on the ebb-tide.

Forty-seven years after Parrish packed up his theodolite and departed, the tide surged in an entirely different direction when Captain Charles Elliott planted the British flag on that other, larger island of Hong Kong just nine kilometres due southwest. And sleepy old Ma Wan continued its uninterrupted slumber.

In another respect, too, Ma Wan fulfils my expectations of an ideal world. For here, amidst this predominantly Chinese community that makes up the bulk of Hong Kong, we have accidentally created another microcosm of inter-communal tolerance, admixture and—yes, let's use that once fatal word—miscegenation. I have neighbours of all races, producing gloriously Technicoloured variegations of progeny.

I only hope that they will instil in their children the thorough understanding and love of both streams of their inheritance that I was denied in my childhood.

A Long Journey in Search of an Identity

by Gerald Platel

I was 15 years old when India gained its independence from Britain and split into two brand new countries. My family found itself in a new country called Pakistan. With some two-and-a-half years left of my schooling, I spent little time in reflecting on what this change might mean, and how it might affect me. I now know that a 15-year-old thinks about what he has planned for that night or the weekend. Ten years down the road is far, far into the future. I did notice changes, like the immediate departure of many friends and relatives. The British Government had offered all Crown employees free repatriation to any part of the Commonwealth, and many accepted this offer. My father, who was in Government service, decided to stay put. Old friends left, but new friends arrived to take their place. There were still enough of us left to continue on as if nothing vital had happened.

But things had changed. Anglo-Indians were steeped in British culture and traditions, and were finding it difficult to abandon a lifestyle which sometimes conflicted with the values of their new homeland. The exodus continued and, eventually, there were so few left behind, that social institutions had to shut down for lack of members. An older brother was the first of my family to leave, in 1948, and others left in dribs and drabs, until finally I was the last one left.

I suppose the new reality really hit home when an electronics course I was enrolled in changed the medium of instruction from English to Urdu. My Urdu was just not good enough for me to survive technical instruction. I should point out that there was a very good reason for this. Prior to 1947, the city of Karachi was very cosmopolitan, and many languages and dialects were commonly spoken in the streets. What we had learned was a sort of hodge-podge of all these elements, which was perfectly adequate for getting by on a daily basis, but not good enough to absorb complex teaching and, even more important, to write an exam in Urdu. Reluctantly, I left the school and made the decision that I would also have to leave the country of my birth, to which I had such a strong attachment, and make a new start elsewhere.

In 1961, I arrived in London, England, full of hope. Well, I had reasoned, since I cannot be the Indian part of Anglo-Indian, let me see if I can be the Anglo part.

It was very easy to adapt to my new country. Many things were familiar and comfortable, and I had many friends in England to lend support. Meanwhile, my pioneering brother, the first to leave for England, was now making plans to move to Canada. Not me—I was too eager to taste the England of my school history books: the England of King Arthur, Julius Caesar, Boadicea, the Norman Conquest, Shakespeare, Christopher Wren, Elizabeth I, and Raleigh. The list could go on and on.

Life did improve in many ways. I was able to pursue further education, get a reasonable job, buy a house, and generally improve my standard of living. But as the years went on, and I married an English girl, I found that I was really missing some aspects of life in the India that I grew up in. I missed the food, the comfortable social life, the dances, the picnics, the household employees to cater to your every whim, and even the weather. My semi-formal tuxedo, which I had so optimistically packed on leaving, lay unused in a suitcase. A germ of an idea was born in my mind. I had always had a great attachment to England, but I had some difficulty in casting myself as British. Could it be that once an Anglo-Indian, always an Anglo-Indian?

My brother from Canada would make periodic visits to London and was full of glowing praise for Canada. It was a new country, still developing, with boundless opportunities for advancement. Many Anglo-Indians had emigrated to Canada, and most were doing extremely well. Since we were stagnating in Britain, and were in the throes of a recession, my wife and I decided to make the move. Maybe there was hope for me yet. If I could not be an Indian or an Anglo, perhaps I could be a Canadian. It was certainly worth a try.

We arrived in Toronto in the spring of 1974. Whereas England had been cool, green, and cluttered, Canada was cold, brown, and spacious. Not a very good first impression. However, summer soon arrived, and Canada became green and hot, though it still remained spacious. I found my first job; we bought a house and started a family. I was too busy with raising a family, augmenting my education, and getting established to give any thought to who or what I was. Having made major lifestyle changes in England, there were not that many changes required for adapting to life in Canada. True, Canadians were different, but they were strongly linked to Britain, which was a giant plus for me. We often socialized with other Anglo-Indians, and inevitably the conversation would turn to our old life, how good it had been, and how much we missed it. There was a lot of nostalgic talk. It frequently annoyed my wife, who is English, and felt a bit left out, but she good-naturedly accepted that this is the way Anglo-Indians are—she's since become quite an authority on them.

The old "identity bug" still lurked in my brain. My children were a bit confused. If I was from India, and mommy was English, what did that make them? To me the answer was quite straightforward—there would be no identity crisis for them. I told them that they were born in Canada, raised in Canada, educated in Canada, and that made them Canadians, which they were quite happy to accept.

So now here I am in 2007, still living in Canada, and still reflecting on the long journey I have made in search of my identity. I have made a bit of a compromise. Canada is my country and has my allegiance, but deep, deep in my heart I know that I will always be an Anglo-Indian. I have lived longer in Canada than I have in India, Pakistan, or Britain, and am quite comfortable here. Recently, a registry was started for my alma mater, and it has simply been flooded with the nostalgic recollections of many Anglo-Indians and non-Anglo-Indians from around the globe, which confirmed that many emigrants from Pakistan feel the same way I do. Unlike some other nationals, we cannot go back to, say, Poland or Brazil, and find the place more or less as we left it.

There never was a country called Anglo-India to which we can return. That magical place and time we yearn for was real enough, but the conditions which enabled that reality no longer exist. We had created a self-contained little world of our own, with our own traditions, culture, and even a bit of history. True, we had borrowed heavily from the British, and not quite so heavily from the Indians, but we had enough of our very own to distinguish us from either of them, and to grow and thrive as a proud, separate community. That is why we talk about it and write about it such a lot—just to keep those wonderful memories alive.

Ah, well. Better to have loved and lost, than never to have loved at all.

The Way We Are At Pondicherry

by Cheryl-Ann Shivan

Pondicherry, a town south of Chennai (the former Madras), is small in size but large in terms of its past history. Since the beginning of the 16th century, the Portuguese, the Dutch, the French, and the British have wrestled over this enclave on India's east coast. In the battle for dominance, the French and the British proved more successful than the others, and took turns ruling it until the French, in 1815, took control and governed the enclave into the mid-20th century. It wasn't until 1954 that France voluntarily ceded the territory to the new Indian nation.

As in other colonies the world over, these ruling powers left behind a visible legacy, evidenced in Pondy—as the town is more commonly referred to—in the layout of the town, the architecture of the buildings, the monuments, the French language and, most important of all, a mixed-race people who go under the nomenclature of Creole. Even now, 54 years after Pondicherry's independence from French rule, the Union Territory still has people who call themselves Creoles. By Creole they mean French-Indian origins; they speak French in their homes and cook a range of food found only in Pondicherry. But take a closer look at their roots, and a different truth emerges.

While defining who an Anglo-Indian is, Mr. Frank Anthony, in his book *Britain's Betrayal in India* (1969), has this to say about a request he received from Pondicherry to open a branch there of the All-India Anglo-Indian Association:

> *Thus with the de facto transfer of Pondicherry to India, the leader of the persons of French descent there had addressed me for permission to open a branch of the All-India Anglo-Indian Association. I replied that while culturally his community perhaps had much in common with the Anglo-Indians, the Association regretted that it could not have a branch there because a* sine qua non *of membership of the Community was the mother-tongue, English. (p.8)*

The identity of the leader of "French" descent has not been determined, nor does it bear much relevance here; but what is relevant is the fact that a branch of the association was not started in Pondicherry then—nor is there one even today—because of the assumption that Pondicherry has a mixed-race population of only the French variety.

Because Pondy was a mere 162 km from Madras and a free port, it was a great attraction for many of the British and Anglo-Indians residing in Fort St. George and the surrounding areas. Villupuram, a famous railway junction 40 km from Pondy, and which was home to a large Anglo-Indian community, was another town from which Pondy drew frequent visitors. On retirement, many Anglo-Indian families settled in the French colony, where living was cheaper and the way of life very European, especially in the White quarter of the town, which extended from the seashore to the Grand Canal. Hence Pondicherry, long before Independence, has been home to families such as the Dartnells, Sandles, Olivers, Straceys, Thomases, Josephs, and Quintals, to name just a few. Testimony to their residence is to be found in the Protestant cemetery, located opposite the Roman Catholic one.

For the families who moved to Pondicherry there were two options regarding an education for their children. The first was to send them to the vernacular schools and the other to educate them in the French schools run by the missionaries and the French government. Though English was taught as the second language in these schools, English-language schools made a late entry onto the educational scene. The missionary-established English schools that exist even today were initially French-medium schools. Given the limited choices available in earlier days, the French schools were the unanimous choice, and so the English-speaking children from Anglo-Indian families were taught in the French medium, and came to speak it as fluently as they did their mother tongue. Gradually, both English and French came to be spoken at home.

When Pondicherry was ceded to the newly independent nation, the French, unlike their British counterparts, offered every citizen the option of taking French nationality, thus ensuring that they could not only reside in France, if they so desired, but could also avail of facilities on par with the French. Many thousands of Indians took advantage of this provision, as did a majority of the Anglo-Indian families. At the end of their schooling in Pondy, the younger generation of Anglo-Indians, Creoles, and Franco-Indians left for France to continue their studies, or to do two years of compulsory military service before finding jobs, marrying among the French, and settling down in their new homeland—and were gradually lost to the community. This group constituted the first generation of Anglo-Indian migrants from Pondicherry.

While a few from the older generation accompanied their children abroad, a good number remained behind and were visited infrequently by their children, given the state of transport in those years. Those who did not make the choice of opting for French nationality or migrating found employment in the local government and private sectors.

To the older generation of Anglo-Indians with French nationality, France was the promised land. It was not uncommon to find framed photographs of General Charles de Gaulle in their drawing rooms, just as some others in the community proudly displayed English royalty in theirs. Through living in a more French-oriented environment, and having reaped a rich financial harvest from French munificence, many were drawn into calling themselves Creoles. This was in all probability a show of allegiance to their generous benefactor. The absence of a formal Anglo-Indian association, which might have drawn community members together, and the lure of life in Europe—which was more easily secured if one possessed French nationality—combined to cause defection to the French camp. Even today there functions a Creole society whose members are Anglo-Indian, or who have at least one Anglo-Indian parent. They are quite fluent in English but speak French when conversing among themselves.

Those Anglo-Indians who did not opt for French citizenship stayed on and made their lives in Pondy. In later years, a few migrated to England and Australia, or to larger cities in India, with the result that through the 1960s the number of those calling themselves Anglo-Indians started falling. The 1970s saw an influx of Anglo-Indians from other states, but most especially from Villupuram. With reservations[13] for Anglo-Indians in the Railways and other services coming to an end, many youngsters of working age moved to Pondicherry. A great many of them found jobs in various government departments, helped by the absence in those days of regulations enforcing registration with the local employment exchange. It is these young men and women who are today senior citizens, or approaching retirement, who helped restore an Anglo-Indian population in the former French territory, and whose lives constitute "The Way We Are" in this little town.

At the time of writing, Pondicherry has become Puducherry, and is home to 191 Anglo-Indians belonging to 50 families. This is a reasonably accurate estimate because the community here is small, making it easier to verify its numbers. Earlier, the families were concentrated in the heart of the territory. But with suburbs opening up with new housing, the community is now spread out, with 23 families owning their own homes in the limits just outside the main town. Given the smallness of Pondy, no family is further than 15 minutes away from another.

The social life of the community is restricted to an annual Christmas dance, a Christmas Tree party for the children, a few "pound" socials, and weddings. As there is no association, the functions are conducted by a few individuals using funds generated by way of sponsorship and entrance fees. Some of the families still belong to the Villupuram branch of the All-India Anglo-Indian Association, and their experience benefits what is organized in Pondicherry. Weddings are looked forward to with a great deal of excitement because they give folks the opportunity to party Anglo-Indian style.

As is the case in other cities, the community in Pondy is no longer endogamous. Anglo-Indian girls outnumber the Anglo-Indian boys here. This imbalance has resulted in quite a few of the girls marrying non-Anglo-Indian boys with good educational and financial backgrounds, and making good marriages across cultural and linguistic divides. Lionel Caplan, commenting on these successful Anglo-Indian/Indian marriages in his book, *Children of Colonialism*, states,

> Not uncommonly, their non-Anglo-Indian husbands have attended Anglo-Indian schools, grown up alongside Anglo-Indians and established close friendships in the community, and are at home in its "culture", including the speech forms and humour of Anglo-India. (p.81)

This is also true of such marriages in Pondicherry. In cases where both the partners are Anglo-Indian, the girls are from Pondicherry while the boys are often from neighbouring states, and of late from abroad. After marriage, many couples move to the big cities, which offer better job opportunities than laidback Pondy.

The quality of life led by the Anglo-Indians in Pondicherry is very fortunately quite high. Most of the households belong to the middle or upper middle classes. Poverty is not a problem here, and neither is unemployment. Many members of the community work in government jobs, and others in private business houses, hospitals, schools, and colleges. The members of the community are respected and in demand, especially as teachers and secretaries, based on their solid reputation for providing sincere and efficient services. The principal of a local college, commenting on the efficiency of one of his staff, stated matter-of-factly, "It's not surprising that she does her work so well, it is in their (Anglo-Indian) blood." The younger generation is educated in English-medium schools (there are no Anglo-Indian schools in the Union Territory), and after schooling all but one or two go on to obtain graduate, postgraduate, and professional degrees. Education is viewed with great respect and seen as a means of scaling the economic ladder.

The Anglo-Indians of Pondicherry have a strong sense of their distinct culture and have not assimilated into Indian society. But it can be said they have integrated into the local milieu, in matters of clothing, food habits, and friendships. Some of the women regularly wear *saris* or *salwar-kameez*, others have a mixed European-Indian wardrobe, but generally sport Western clothing when it comes to celebrations such as dances and weddings. The younger generation changes clothing as the occasion demands. Since Pondicherry has long been a cosmopolitan town, the Western clothing and social life of the community does not draw negative attention. The food habits are South Indian but with an Anglo-Indian flavour. A bit of Pondicherry Creole cooking has also crept into their menus. Because the community is so small, most friendships are forged with people from other communities. Indeed, because Anglo-Indians are a casteless community, they are viewed as "neutral"—a group that does not judge others based on caste. Hence, friendships with non-Anglo-Indians are strong and lasting, and large numbers from outside the community join in its celebrations, both private and public.

Anglo-Indian life in Pondicherry may not be as active or as bonding as that led by those who live in the big cities or in Anglo-Indian enclaves, but it is nevertheless an Anglo-Indian way of life, celebrated daily through a common language, quality of work, and social interactions. Although no formal association exists to endorse the authenticity of the Anglo Indian existence in Pondicherry, the community here has survived such doubts and is quite comfortable with its identity. *We are what we are* is the maxim that endorses their lives and will carry them forward, as it has done all these many years.

As the Bough Is Bent...

by Sylvia W. Staub

The girl in the photo is tiny, wearing a frilly white dress made of organdy, which, from the limp look of it, has been laundered more than once. The way she's standing in her white cotton socks and patent-leather shoes, with one knee slightly bent, suggests shyness. She's looking down, her hands covering her mouth, shy about having her picture taken. She'd much rather not be there, already at age five a most private person. "Stop being *jungli*," her mother says, as Anglo-Indian mothers were wont to say when, as children, we acted gauche in an India as faded today as the yellowing black-and-white photo of the small girl. She could have been the poster child for her community, half a century ago.

The photo, modestly framed, stands on a shelf just above my computer table in my home in America. I keep it there less from self-love than to remind me of who I was, a kind of yardstick of who I have become. Studying it now, I realize that I am still shy, though less so than all those years ago when I stood so awkwardly posed in my grandmother's garden, painfully self-conscious as I waited for my mother to press the button on the Kodak black box camera. And that makes me wonder, as I often do, about pre-ordination, which thumbs its nose at free will, pushing and pulling us in appropriate directions from the moment of birth, in its demand that we become the best that we can be.

How well have I met the many challenges of that mysterious dictator? Is shyness a characteristic I was meant to overcome, like my fear of swimming, and driving a car? In the West Bengal town I grew up in, only the European elite had access to a swimming pool, and cars were as rare as unicorns; I could make excuses for my ineptitude in pursuits that seemed to come naturally to others. But by the time I was 40, I knew that life's challenges have an annoying way of repeating, until the lessons they imply are learned, the required degree of maturity reached. So I have, willy-nilly, become the kind of person who, by dint of trial and error, has learned to take the road less travelled, the less cautious route that I ignored in younger years—largely, I suspect, because of my Anglo-Indian roots, which rendered me uncertain about my identity and self-worth.

Born into a family of people with powerful personalities, as its youngest member, it was fitting, in terms of this mysterious life-shaping factor, that I should have come to live in America, which touts itself as "the most powerful nation on Earth", a nation in which the cult of personality dominates. Early on in my life here, I grasped its symbolism as a substitute for my talented, strong-willed family, scattered abroad on three different continents—which, of course, presented me afresh with the concomitant challenge of acquiring an identity all my own. I believe, in the course of my life here, that I have accomplished that goal, preserving the best of my Anglo-Indian self while adding to it the best of what the New World has taught me.

America, unlike the pre-Partition India I grew up in, an era in which Britannia ruled the waves and made mincemeat of those of its colonial subjects who were not *pukka*, meaning, in an Anglo-Indian sense, not born-in-Britain, was welcoming—a relief from the strictures of what had gone before. For the first time scanning the New Jersey cliffs from the deck of the cargo vessel that brought me from Britain, I felt I could breathe again, deeply, as I had in my home in India. America and India, both vast, with room for all, or so I imagined as I stood watching those cliffs and the skyscrapers of New York's Manhattan emerge out of the early morning mist. The cliffs were broad, the skyscrapers tall; they represented the new dimension I was going to have to deal with. And after the initial trials of displacement, my new home began to reward me, making me feel special and privileged, someone of worth—a veritable princess. It took work—and luck.

Instrumental in this transformation of self is a crucial lesson I learned, while yet in my teens, from an important diplomat at the United Nations in Geneva and Paris. This was Appa Sahib of Aundh, the son of the *maharaja* of one of the smaller, but more noteworthy, states in Old India. Appa Sahib's father lived far in advance of his time, working for the common good, bringing electricity to villages, and establishing free education for Untouchables in his state. Appa Sahib, as I recall him, was a tall, handsome man, a member of Moral Re-Armament (MRA[14]), well-schooled in the give-give-give of humanism. Not infrequently, he'd greet me from an upside-down yogic position as I came through the door of his suite in Paris's Hotel Palais d'Orsay, responding to a call for note-taking. He once told me that if you want to turn the world upside-down, you must first learn to do it yourself! He hired me as his secretarial assistant because, as he said, "You are talented, yes, but, more importantly, you are humble. Humility is a great quality; don't ever lose it." I believe I never have.

America, so important a part of who I have become, has been an enormously different experience from the tight, restricted, British environment of my Anglo-Indian youth. In the main, it has been an experience of higher-education in the school of life, forcing me to adapt from my ingrained soft-sell self to something less gentle than soft-sell but, at the same time, less harsh than the hard-sell of this predominantly materialistic society. It has afforded me opportunity and reward beyond anything I might have dreamed would come my way. I love that I have retained the lightness common to my community: its propensity for fun, for easy laughter, for the camaraderie we knew and know, still, every time we get together in lands far spread from where we hailed. And beyond lightness, the generosity and hospitality that I believe is part of our Indian endowment, as is India's "sweetness," secured forever in the poetry of Rabindranath Tagore, *russagoolas* and *gulab jamuns*, and the extravagant perfume of India's flowers.

In starker context, each time I come to a difficult and painful turn in the road, I recall—and take heart from—our doggedness, our courage in the face of severe odds, and the compassion to self and others for which we, as a community, are well known. The values of my Anglo-Indian family, as well, are undiminished by time. They are essentially Judeo-Christian, now broadened by aspects of other religions and ideologies that I have come to respect and admire. Those root values also express the best of what British ethos used to be, explicit in the words of the hymnist, "Where duty calls, or danger, be never wanting there;" and in the team spirit we learned from athletics, implicit in the motto of the high school that was local to my hometown, "Play up, play up, and play the game." The motto is an extract from *Vitaï Lampada*, a poem by Sir Edward Newbolt, which expresses a concept central to England's public schools: The game itself is more important than the winning of it. I am sentimental about my Indian roots to an almost maudlin degree, and deeply grateful to America for the opportunities it has put in my path, but at heart I am a world citizen. That, too, that strong sense of the global, of the brotherhood of man, comes from my Anglo-Indian heritage.

Having left our homes in India to venture forth like so many Pancho Sanzas, armed with carrom boards instead of swords, we became displaced persons, much the same as people forced to leave their homes because of war. Meeting the repeating challenges of displacement became a major pattern in our lives. No room in the West, or Down Under, for *jungli* (read "shy and timid")! We, from early waves of the Anglo-Indian Diaspora, have dared to investigate and develop whatever in the way of talent we were born with. We have survived gracefully, successful, in spite of discouraging odds, in a variety of professions. We became doctors, dentists, lawyers, financial advisers, accountants, scientists, writers and editors, movie directors, famous pop singers, athletic stars, as well as coaches—you name it! And now, in later life, with our children in their forties and fifties, and our grandchildren young adults, we are called upon to give back to our fellow beings—and all of life on earth—much of the good fortune granted us. That is part of what we *should* be doing.

I've no doubt that we, graduates from who we were to who we are, are meeting that challenge head-on.

Becoming Myself

by Deborah Van Veldhuizen

I have never been to India. I have only heard the recounting of tales about the India of long ago, from 1812, when our first English ancestor stepped ashore from the *Broxbournebury*, until 1963, when my family left India for England. I know some of the stories of my family's past by heart: the tragedy and the humour. I know the food, songs, and places well, some smatterings of Hindi, the stories of everyday lives lived, of heroes and villains, of grandeur and poverty, of the bravery, and of the clash of cultures and faiths. I understand the dissonance that exists between an historical entity such as the British Raj and the reality of Ottawa, Ontario, where we now live.

The stories of my family's time in India have taken on a dreamlike quality to me: as when you read a good novel that you cannot put down, and then you can recount the details for ages afterwards because it was so good. These recollections are separated by time and space from the events themselves, and also by lives that in one way have nothing to do with me and, in another, everything.

It took me a long time to become proud of my Anglo-Indian heritage. In the first place, I was too young to truly understand its intricacies. As a child in England, I self-identified with being English. The India that my parents and grandparents spoke of, with all of its charms and trappings, seemed like a faraway, exotic locale. The food, the servants, the beauty of the land itself, as well as the horrors of Partition, the prejudice they witnessed, the danger: all of these conjured up a fairytale land. It was not my family's homeland, I believed, even though they had been born there, because we were English.

Once we moved to Canada and became Canadian citizens, it was easy to proclaim, "I am Canadian," as others did all around me. There were people of every skin colour, religion, and culture imaginable in the multicultural atmosphere of Toronto in the 1970s. If anyone asked about my background, I indicated that I was born in England, or that I was British, and so were my parents, which was, after all, true. If anyone pressed for more information, I responded that my parents were born in India. End of story.

In high school, I remember telling a classmate about my

background—a kind, intelligent young man who nonetheless wasn't buying what I said. He found it hard to believe that both my parents were Anglo-Indian, had met in India, moved to England, and immigrated to Canada, and that this was, in fact, representative of a fairly large group of people, especially in Toronto.

To my amusement, a couple of months later he approached me, and in an excited voice said: "You won't believe this, but I met someone the other day who is Anglo-Indian, and so are his parents!"

In my early twenties, I became more interested in my cultural background, at the same time that I realized the answers I had given to people were inadequate, even if technically correct. I then started to proclaim to anyone who asked that I was Anglo-Indian. This led to much confusion. People invariably thought that I meant any of the following: (1) One of my parents was English, and one was East Indian (2) I was East Indian (3) I was English, or (4) I didn't really know what I was. I tried explaining that my ancestry was the result of inter-marriage many generations earlier, which led either to much speculation or pure flummox on the part of listeners. I found it incredible that even people of greater than average intelligence and education couldn't understand.

From this was born the yearning to learn everything I could about being Anglo-Indian and to be better informed so that I could inform others, a desire that continues to this day. From this also started to emerge, albeit slowly, a sense of pride and positive self-esteem about who and what I am.

I must have been 30-something when I made the conscious decision to embrace my heritage, no matter what the result. I researched specific areas of both sides of my family tree—unfinished and definitely a life's work!

At some point, it dawned on me that the closest parallel here in Canada was the Métis people. I would mention this, explaining that Anglo-Indians were a mixed-race people, just like the Métis, with their Aboriginal and French blood. They and their descendants are recognized as a nation. In this sense, they bear a strong parallel with Anglo-Indians, who also have a culture and traditions distinct from both the British and Indians. Amazingly, this explanation doesn't seem to result in further understanding about Anglo-Indians. In order of frequency, it has been suggested by others that I must be Italian, Spanish, Portuguese, East Indian, or Native Canadian.

I suspect that my background—with ancestors living on the margin of mainstream society— has influenced my choice of career. I teach English at the college level to Aboriginal Studies students, most of whom are Cree from Quebec. I also teach English at the high school level to adult students who want to enter college; many of these are second-language learners.

Now in my early forties, having spent most of my life in Canada, I find myself rejoicing in my Anglo-Indian background and happily explaining it to others, even though they just don't get it. The difference is that this no longer bothers me.

So who is this "me" that I have become? I am a Canadian, a daughter and a sister, a wife and a mother. I am a Christian and a teacher. I am a supporter of diversity who enjoys meeting people of all races and cultures. And yes, I am Anglo-Indian.

My Irish Grandfather

by John Walke

It was not uncommon when I was growing up in the Pakistan of the 1950s to view the Irish with disdain. Such acquired prejudices still persisted within certain communities of the former British Empire. We didn't know any full-blooded Irishmen, but there seemed to be one hidden in every Anglo-Indian's family closet. With their enthusiasm for a song, a dance, a drink, a fight, and then a story to regale you with, the Irish were passionate, social creatures. This heritage seemed prevalent in many Anglo-Indian families, and ours was no exception. My grandfather, whom I never met, was Irish.

As a child, I was dimly aware of my father's weakness for liquor, though in Moslem Pakistan such activity was always concealed. I was more aware of his passion for the piano and song that broke out at our Anglo-Indian "pound-and-pint" parties, private affairs held in our homes, where each woman brought a pound of her favourite sweet or savoury dish, and each man a pint of his favourite liquor—well hidden. And I had heard of my father's reputation for sweeping women off their feet at the Anglo-Indian dances in Delhi, in the 1930s, before my parents married. But I had never thought of ours as a fighting family, until I understood that fighting also meant a general contrariness, revelling in verbal repartee, tongue lashings, and being argumentative at the drop of a hat.

My mother said of her father-in-law, whom she never met, "Your grandfather, you ask about? Well, he was Irish, nothing more, son of a Dublin tram-conductor who ran away from home and joined the Welsh Regiment as a fife-and-drum-boy! Then to hear *your almighty* father say he was saving *me* from the gutters of Calcutta," she added, as if being Irish were a curse.

For years, that was all I knew about my grandfather, William Francis Walke. He had fled Dublin to shape his future on some distant, foreign shore. Looking homeward had never been an option, and he also maintained a distant relationship with his own Anglo-Indian family: he travelled around India with the Corps of Engineers, while his wife remained with her kin in the Punjab, and my father and uncle were sent off to boarding school. He only saw his sons on holidays and, when he died, he hadn't seen them for 15 years.

The most memorable incident my father could recall happened when he was 10. He entered his father's bedroom one morning. His father, in a moment of awkward familiarity as is the wont of fathers who are strangers to their sons, reached for the service revolver that he slept with beneath his pillow and jokingly pointed it at him. "Don't look so terrified, Basil, it's empty," he said. Perhaps my father had seen him load it the night before, and I've always wondered why he didn't protest more vigorously as he flinched, but how could he contradict this stranger who was posing as his father? My grandfather pulled the trigger, the bullet grazed my father's heart. My grandfather leapt from his bed. With his son on his bicycle crossbar, he frantically pedalled off to the military hospital. En route they hit a bullock cart, and broke my father's nose!

William Francis Walke was our only European-born grandparent. Although he lived into the mid-20th century, there was no surviving photo or sample of handwriting. I assumed that my father, fair-haired and light-skinned for someone born and bred in India, must have resembled him. I was wrong, I should have paid greater attention to my parents' wedding photo. It included my grandfather's other son, my uncle Derek. I didn't notice him at first because I was distracted by my mother's bewildered expression beneath her bridal veil, like a caged animal. When I finally sought my uncle out in that photo, I noticed a short, darker man, with jet black hair that shot up on edge, as if he'd been struck by lightning. But that was a black-and-white photo. His hair was maroon. That's what William Francis looked like, a short Celtic man, with dark maroon hair.

When 40 years later, across a kitchen table in Boston, I first learned of my birthright to Irish citizenship, it was as if an awkward, newly met and poor relative had knocked at my door. I wasn't sure what to make of it. To a family that had come within a hair's breadth of possessing four different passports, spread across the world, what would a fifth matter? Hadn't we done enough globetrotting for one lifetime?

I thought the idea of obtaining Irish citizenship implausible and far-fetched. There had been other ill-fated ventures into the past, including attempts to secure my father's and grandfather's pensions from India and Pakistan. I didn't take on ambitious tasks lightly. But my young American sons urged me on. Over time, the lure of our Anglo-Indian Irishness swelled. I wanted to revive my family's lost past for my children by becoming an Irish citizen. The documents we needed spanned three continents and 120 years. We possessed both the first and the last, like bookends: my grandfather's Irish birth certificate of 1873, and my father's California death certificate of 1994. That gave shape to my search, and all that remained, it seemed, was to flesh out the middle. But only government records would do, and in those days European births, marriages, and deaths in India were recorded only by the family's church.

Much was known but two mysteries persisted: my grandparents' marriage and my grandfather's death—though how death could prove lineage puzzled me; no doubt some bureaucrat's inspiration. I began my search casually but soon learned that after 50 years as the law, impending changes in the Irish statutes made speed imperative.

We had no contacts in India. Professional investigators were no help. My project was not lucrative. I had heard that help might be found at the British Library in London. With nowhere else to turn, I took a stab at it and left an inquiry in the Library's general Internet mailbox. An anonymous staffer responded almost immediately. Within a day we struck gold! Like a starved man stumbling upon a feast, I immediately pounced upon every document the library could offer. I casually inquired what legitimacy these documents possessed, careful not to hint at what I was seeking. I feared that anything Irish might put me back at the end of the line, but document followed document, each engraved with the red seal of the Secretary of State for Foreign and Commonwealth Affairs.

Despite the flood of documents, my search began unravelling. The 18-year spread between my grandparents' ages had been shaved down to 16 on their marriage certificate, presumably a ploy to win the hand of Iris May Wächsel—surely no surprise to the consulate, considering a passionate Irish nature was involved. Another problem: my grandmother's maiden name had been inherited by my father, Basil William Wächsel-Walke, as part of his hyphenated surname. As the informant at the time of his death in California, I had misspelled it. Now I would have to explain. Finally, only my birth and my grandfather's death remained to be established. Neither could be documented by the British because both occurred after the British left India in 1947.

My baptism certificate could not be vouched for by any government. I was born soon after the Partition of India when confusion reigned, with mass migration and the massacre of millions of refugees. The fledgling Pakistani government of those dark days faced more urgent tasks than services handled by the church. I would have to convince the Irish of this; their experience with British rule would surely come to my aid.

My grandfather died in Bangalore in the early 1950s. Anglo-Indian investigators asked if he'd been Catholic or Protestant, to determine where he was buried. Though Irish, there was never a hint of any Catholic upbringing. His recently acquired marriage record revealed a ceremony within the Church of England in Simla (now Shimla), where his sons would later attend the Anglican Bishop Cotton School. He was probably not a churchgoer. His military records would be more difficult to locate. Time was running short. I was ready to give up.

Word of my quest spread through my family. Via a casual phone call, I learned that my brother in New Jersey had something that might help. I called him. It was William Francis Walke's will of 1944 and correspondence from the estate trustee, the Imperial Bank of India, none of which had seen the light of day in 50 years. I asked my brother to read the letter.

"9th, Feb. 1950," he began. "Your father passed away at St. Martha's Hospital, Bangalore, 24th ultimo."

"24th ultimo, meaning…?"

"Latin for previous—24th of the previous month, Jan. 24."

He kept reading the stilted, awkwardly written letter, but I said, "Just overnight it."

I got on the Internet. The hospital still existed, a Catholic charity run by the Good Shepherd nuns. I tracked down a street address but no Internet link. A hospital death was more conclusive than any cemetery search would have been. I wrote to them with my e-mail address, just in case.

As I anxiously awaited a reply I tried teasing details out of the papers my brother had sent. I carefully spread out the fragile 18" x 24" carbon-copied documents, trying to imagine the oversized typewriters on which they had been prepared. The letter to my father announcing my grandfather's death read, "With reference to your inquiry without date, we confirm that..."

"Without date?" That was not my father; he was precise in matters of time and date. The only prized possession of his I recall was a Swiss-made Omega wrist watch, with date screen. Was he so distraught he had overlooked that? Perhaps my mother hadn't been exaggerating when she'd said that, upon news of my grandfather's death, my father had hardly spoken for weeks.

The will continued: "Subject to certain specific bequests of his motor car and a few pieces of furniture, etc.,... Personal effects are of negligible value, for he was living in a room at Langford Gardens." Despite being a major in the Corps of Engineers, constructing dams and bridges, my grandfather never planted roots. He could have returned to the British Isles, as many did at Independence, but he belonged to a class of old soldiers who stayed on in boarding rooms—accustomed to the privileged, seductive life of the East; their pensions amounted to a king's ransom in India but a pittance in post-war Europe. He'd lived in India for 50 years, it was the life he'd made.

Then there was the statement of accounts and assets and, almost as an afterthought, a copy of his will. From his trust accounting I could reconstruct:

- "Personal effects, nominally valued at R400/-, and entrusted for sale to Frank Abraham & Co., auctioneers; the firm has closed their doors, the proprietor is absconding. There is no prospect of recovery." [What little he had, had been stolen. I like to imagine that he was intentionally a man of few attachments, and that he'd planned to deny any thieves their bounty. One item escaped theft, however, found on his person at the hospital—an expensive wristwatch, reminiscent of my father's.]
- Cash on his person at the hospital: R45/-.
- Tailor's Bill: R15/- .
- Bowring Institute bill, Jan. 1950: R6/- [a prestigious private club founded in 1860. For a man without property, boarding at Langford Gardens, there was one extravagance]:
- An Austin touring car appraised at R3000/-, for which he paid R25/- mo. to garage and R117/- year to insure.

A tailor's bill, an insured, garaged touring car, the Bowring

Club dues, an expensive wristwatch. Another image began to emerge.

Further in his will certain specific bequests came to light: "The Austin car, one combined chest of drawers and dressing table, and two cane chairs with blue cushions, left to Mrs. Ramakrishna Rao, wife of Mr. S.M. Ramakrishna Rao, and daughter of the late Balasundram Iyer." A woman defined only through her husband and father. It was still 1944.

Something jarring, a splash of colour bled into his dry, parched will and overflowed: blue cushions! Two cane chairs with blue cushions. Were the cushions woven into the cane, or attached by ties to the frame, or merely loose and removable? And who was this woman written into his will, when he was 70? Had she been his caretaker, or something else? How many meetings had those cane chairs and blue cushions hosted?

Then lightning struck! The hospital e-mailed me promptly, detailing their records—but the unravelling resumed. They showed my grandfather to be a widower, though his wife, Iris Wächsel—the only grandparent I ever met and who had emigrated to England—would survive him by 20 years while collecting his pension. She was mis-identified as his mother. The date of death was 25th January but the bank letter had 24th ultimo.

No wonder death records mattered, discrepancies arose even from the grave. I suspected the informant had been Mrs. Rao. She may have had her reasons for providing false information, or had my grandfather misled her? I thought better than to pry. Instead, I sent copies of my records to the hospital. I had become what a few days earlier I had been seeking, the gatekeeper of records. I wanted to correct records 50 years old. In my haste, I referred to the birth certificate I was sending them as the certificate that I was seeking; wishful thinking—no doubt they chuckled at my expense.

Thelma [from the hospital's medical records office, last name withheld], apologizing for the delay, replied, "As you may know our airmails are always screened in your country [it was post-9/11, several envelopes and contents had arrived separately], and I was on leave on 21st October, my birthday." How sweet and personal! I should wish her a happy birthday.

I was also in touch with an Anglo-Indian researcher who had contacts throughout the community. I forwarded him a copy of

Thelma's e-mail, and he must have got right down to work because, soon after, Thelma wrote again:

"Dear Sir...A Good Shepherd nun I know [at the hospital] contacted me with a copy of the e-mail I sent you, and asked me to expedite matters. I assured her I had. I don't know how you happened to know her [if meant as a question I never answered it, I was learning to be discreet], but my mind was put to rest that I am helping someone in good standing; such information is not normally given once a death certificate is issued. I impressed on our staff [the need] to help you as a fellow Christian, but the records cannot be corrected and I was warned not to take any personal interest. I'm unable to help you further. Please delete my e-mail."

Warned not to take any personal interest? Please delete my e-mail? Was I implicated in something conspiratorial? What an awkward development. Yes, St. Martha's was a charity hospital. Charity was to be dispensed at arm's length; personal interest led to an expectation of some acknowledgement. Thank God I hadn't wished Thelma happy birthday!

To obtain the state death certificate I had to appear in person. But my Anglo-Indian researcher saved me the trip.

"They couldn't find it at first," he wrote, "but, sadly, with more than a little greasing it was found." I had sent him $100, a small fortune to some in India. Perhaps to earn their fee they had simply reconstructed it from the evidence I'd provided. "But the date of death was one day off the hospital record," he added, "a common mistake over here. People take the date of burial as the date of death." Intriguing, this mistake of dates, until I recalled my mother's stories of her father's death in Calcutta. In oppressive heat, burials were prompt.

A damp Dublin summer morning a year later, and the proud possessor of a brand-new Irish passport, I was having breakfast with my sons—true to the Anglo-Indian Irish blood coursing through their veins, both pursued their passions in music and theatre. That morning, they marvelled at how my grandfather had led such a singular life with hardly a trace left behind: he'd fled home as an adolescent; had lied about his age to marry a woman he could have fathered, and who was later identified as his mother; he'd barely known his sons, yet shot one and broke his nose; he could have afforded a substantial retirement, but spent it in a negligible yet stylish fashion; he was robbed and misrepresented in death; and all of that was only what we could uncover by cutting through protocol and red tape.

"That was long ago, far away, in a very different world," I said to my sons. "Perhaps if we visit India we might understand. Interested?"

A joint visit to India might yet happen, but that morning we set out on foot for 43 Lower Cranbrassil St. I'd read that the neighbourhood had been gentrified. As we approached we noticed derelict buildings and old kosher slaughterhouses, from a time when East European Jewish refugees thrived there. Within a mile stood the birthplace of George Bernard Shaw, one of my father's favourite authors.

The two-storey, Victorian-era tenement building where my grandfather was born still stood, though many surrounding it had been torn down. Upstairs, a family home, a window open, a potted plant on the sill, the curtain fluttering in the breeze; below, at street level, a worn corrugated-iron storefront.

Thinking of my grandfather, who'd lived and died in India, I had to smile at the irony—the potted plant was a perennial blue Gentian, a reminder of those blue cushions my grandfather left in his will, and the store an Indian sweet-and-spice shop, in a setting not very different from a roadside stall in Bangalore. The world had come full circle. I lingered a few moments longer in the rain, then turned away and went home.

Traditions

Maxwell Piers—One Who Stayed On

by Quentine Acharya

My cousin Maxwell Piers, known affectionately to the family as Maxie, belongs to that rare group of Anglo-Indians who never left India but went on to make a great success of their lives. Maxie is an authority on the grading and pricing of mica. One of only a handful of specialists in the world, he continues—at the age of 76—to travel each month from his home base in Bangalore, southern India, to the northern state of Bihar, where he works as a consultant to the few remaining mica-producing mine owners and their managers. His work entails sourcing for mica supplies, sending samples to potential buyers all over the world, arranging for shipment of supplies, and performing the critical and crucial mica inspections and certifications for every shipment.

Though now banned in the United States for use in toasters, hair-dryers, and other home appliances, mica is still a valuable and sought-after mineral, with many industrial applications. India is one of the few places in the world where it is still produced. In the '60s, when the bulk of the mineral exported was called Bridge mica (for radios and televisions), mica sold for roughly Rs. 10,000 a kilogram, and companies such as GE, Westinghouse, and Phillips were among the large corporate buyers. In 2001, it sold for Rs. 25,000 a kilogram.

Maxie has logged numerous hours journeying from Bangalore to Calcutta, and from there by train to Bihar via the Coalfield Express or Black Diamond Express, trains which snake through India's industrial heartland of coal mines and steel plants. An avid reader, life-long learner, and a man of many interests, he uses his travel time to catch up on his reading and correspondence.

"Mica was my life for 50 years," recalls Maxie. He says he has never once regretted his choice of profession, which not only provided him with a comfortable life, but also has given him tremendous personal and professional satisfaction. Buyers as well as sellers have come to rely on his solid reputation for accuracy and honesty. He has many buyers and business contacts in the UK and Australia.

Maxie relates an interesting and serendipitous experience

he had in the '60s, when he was establishing himself as a mica expert. He left his home early one morning, taking his family and a visiting nephew on a much-anticipated picnic trip to a scenic spot called Telaiya Dam, in Bihar. Barely 20 km from home, his usually trusty Ambassador car broke down, and the family returned disappointed to the house. Five minutes later, a taxi drove up, and an Australian jumped out. He turned out to be a mica buyer who had been given Maxie's name. His telegram from Melbourne hadn't yet reached Maxie. Had the Ambassador not broken down, Maxie would have lost the opportunity of his life. The Australian, Brian Royston, owned a company called Royston Electronics in Melbourne and became a valuable contact, inviting Maxie on an all-expenses-paid trip to Australia, and passing on his name to two other businessmen. Maxie reaped the benefits over many years of doing business with this unexpected guest. And through his contacts in Australia and the UK, Maxie has been able to link together various businessmen in Bihar and Calcutta with buyers abroad.

Because he's been in the business for so many decades, Maxie says he now deals with the grandsons and nephews of people with whom he started out working. He is known to them, simply and affectionately, as "Uncle".

Although I term him a cousin, Maxwell Piers is not really related to me: he married my cousin, Gabrielle Pinto, in 1960. They have had a long, happy, and successful marriage, based on mutual love and understanding, faith in God, and a strong desire on both their parts to give back to the community. Both Maxie and Gabrielle are devout Catholics who engage themselves in works of charity, helping in various homes for the aged, and church-affiliated community improvement projects, in and around Bangalore.

Maxie had a very strict upbringing as a child, and his mother instilled in him a solid code of conduct and personal behaviour. He begins each morning with a brisk walk to the chapel of the Sisters of Mary Immaculate to attend the 6:30 Mass, and he kneels down to say the rosary every night, even after a late-night party. He has brought up his four sons with a strong sense of discipline and insists that his children live a life of moral responsibility.

Born in Coonoor, in the scenic Nilgiris (Blue Mountains) of southern India, his maternal grandfather was a Scotsman named John Chapman Walker, who worked on a coffee plantation; his grandmother, Sabina Coelho, worked as a nanny to an English family. His father, Joseph Anthony Piers, whose grandparents had come to India from Burma in the 1850s and settled in Telicherry, South India, was a Gazetted Officer and served for 35 years in the Military Engineering Services (MES). An uncle, John Piers, served as a judge in the Small Causes Court of Madras. His mother, Cecilia Walker, a strong influence in his life, was an excellent homemaker who was famous for her cakes, pastries, and pickles. Maxie fondly recalls her specialty, an Anglo-Indian sweet called "Matrimony", which, he says, "was made of ground cashews and almonds and coloured pink with cochineal"; she was also famous for her Christmas cake.

"From the age of seven, she used to take me to mass every morning, and she was very happy when I became an altar boy at St. Xavier's Church in Pune," he recalls. Maxie had his early education in Pune, graduated from St. Vincent's High School, and went on to Wadia College in Pune. As a young boy, he played cricket and hockey and represented his school and college in both these sports. In 1954, he started work as a young apprentice in Gudur, in Nellore District of Andhra Pradesh, learning hands-on about the mica business from his employer and mentor, an Anglo-Indian gentleman named Mr. K.M. Kirkpatrick. He and his wife Marie, who was British, took the young apprentice under their wings and showed him a lot of kindness. Maxie soon displayed a keen acumen and a great desire to learn. Perseverance and hard work were the hallmarks of his character.

In 1961 he was asked to leave for Giridih, in Bihar, to take over the mica business from another Anglo-Indian, Mr. Douglas E. Rosair, who was getting ready to retire and move to England. With his bride of two months, Maxie settled into a beautiful, old bungalow, which he acquired "lock, stock and barrel" from the Rosairs, and where he lived and worked for the next 40 years. Known as Mathidih Bungalow, after the village of Mathidih, 5 km away, the bungalow once belonged to the manager of the Eastern Coalfields, a British-owned coal-mining operation that had closed down. Built in 1886, it was a huge, gracious, verandah-wrapped bungalow, with flowering trees and shrubs tended by numerous servants and gardeners.

Maxie credits Douglas Rosair and his wife, Margaret, with offering a great deal of help so the young couple could adjust to their new home in an outpost hundreds of miles away from their families in Bangalore.

"They were a lovely, old-fashioned couple, with a wealth of experience of living and working in Giridih," he says.

The house and grounds were an idyllic place for children to grow up in, with abundant fruit trees and a well on the property that was known as a source of good, potable water year-round. In fact, the locals believed that drinking the well water guaranteed that one would have sons, and, to prove the point, Maxie and Gabrielle were blessed with four robust, healthy boys while they lived at Mathidih. Their driver Edward, a Bihari of the local Santhal tribals, also lived on the property and had three sons of his own, so the children had a wonderful childhood filled with many happy hours of play. A Santhal tribal woman named Martha, who had been raised in a local convent and trained by the nuns, became a faithful and constant companion to the children and travelled with the family on trips and vacations. The local people loved and revered Maxie, who they referred to as "Maxie-Sahib". Being a fair, handsome Anglo-Indian, witty and urbane, he made a huge impression on the locals, who considered him to be a Britisher.

My sister Anna and I once spent a memorable summer in Giridih with Maxie and Gabrielle, and fondly recall long, lazy summer days punctuated by feasting on the luscious, local *langra* mangoes and delicious vegetarian and "non-veg" fare prepared by their cook. Every morning at five o'clock we were awakened with trays of "bed tea", after which we would lapse back into slumber until it was time to rise and wash up for an 8 a.m. breakfast with the family. Our days were spent reading James Hadley Chase novels, and our evenings playing snooker or card games, and sipping rum-and-cokes or shandy at the local club. When Anna woke up one morning with a bad toothache, an old Chinese dentist with a portable, wooden, hand-operated drill was summoned from the nearby town. With all of us in attendance on the front verandah, he had her tooth fixed in no time. Similarly, the tailor and other vendors would periodically visit the house to sew clothes for the children or reproduce fashionable dresses from the imported dress design catalogues, which we mulled over for hours. Many a leisurely afternoon was spent with the tailor, drawing and sketching and being measured for the outfits we would order for a special occasion, such as a dance at the club.

It was a life in India, now almost vanished, that was peaceful, languid, gracious, and away from the noisy hubbub of a crowded city—a life that could only be enjoyed by the fortunate few who could live in comfort and work in places like the tea gardens or coffee plantations, or outposts such as Mathidih Bungalow in Giridih, Bihar.

Although Maxie never joined the immigration queues to the UK, Canada, or Australia, his two brothers left India years ago and never returned. His older brother settled in the UK and is since deceased, and his younger brother, Claude, lives and works in Melbourne, Australia. His parents lived out their retirement years in Bangalore. Of his four sons, two have settled in Australia. Sunil, the eldest, is a physician and works for the Department of Public Health in Melbourne. Andrew, the youngest, is a former model and now works as a business development manager for a Melbourne bank. The other two, David and Michael, have established careers for themselves in Bangalore. David runs a popular cold storage shop and deli called The Market Basket, selling roasted chicken, ham, prepared foods, homemade pickles, etc., for which there is great demand in the emerging and affluent middle-class of India. For special times of the year, such as Christmas and New Year's, David prepares dozens of roasted, stuffed turkeys and chickens, and takes orders for all sorts of specialty food items. Michael and his wife, Smitha, design and sell high-end bed linen, furnishings, household wares, and clothing through their businesses in Bangalore and Bangladesh.

A breezy, friendly, and outgoing personality has always helped Maxwell Piers make friends wherever he goes. A modern-day senior who is very savvy about using the Internet, he is known for keeping in touch via e-mail with a wide group of friends, colleagues, and relatives all over the world.

People come to rely on his good sense of judgment and his readiness to help anyone who needs a leg-up. There are numerous young men and women who have been nudged along with a word of timely advice or a job referral from him. Maxie has educated the children of Kabir, his faithful retainer who has worked for him for the past 40 years, and given them a head-start in life. He and Gabrielle also look after their cook, Radha, having employed her for more than 30 years, feeding and educating her children as well. Their home on Spencer Road, in the Cleveland Park area of

Bangalore, is a favourite gathering place for family and friends. The Piers are always ready and willing to entertain friends and cousins, such as me, on our visits from abroad.

Maxie is proud of his heritage and the fact that he is an Anglo-Indian. He describes Anglo-Indians as "a virile race", and believes that the particular circumstances that led to their Diaspora have also in many ways contributed to a reawakening, renaissance, and revival of the unique culture and qualities of this community. He himself speaks Hindi fluently and is comfortable doing business with the largely Hindi-speaking businessmen of Bihar, as well as the Bengali-speaking merchants of Calcutta, who are his clientele.

Maxie is able to navigate successfully in both societies. He is truly a magical blend of a British-centred education and upbringing, and a native son of the soil. His exemplary life is an example and inspiration to the younger generation. And proof that one did not have to leave India to find one's self.

A Day at St. Joseph's Hostel, Melbourne

by Robyn Andrews

As part of my new research, I've stayed the night in a vacant room in St. Joseph's Hostel: the low-care facility for Melbourne's elderly Anglo-Indians.[15] Without any personal effects, the room is spacious, utilitarian: painted, pale walls, a single bed, two white dressing tables, a wall heater with stains or scorch marks above it, and a door leading into an en suite "wet-area" bathroom. The buzzer call-buttons in the bathroom and above the bed, and the push-in timer button for the bathroom lights, add an institutionalized feel to the room. This is in contrast with residents' rooms, which are crammed full of their lives: family photos, holy pictures, greeting cards, wall clocks, calendars, TVs, comfortable armchairs, mats on the floor, ornaments on dressing tables, pretty bedcovers, and in one room a huge portrait of Elvis Presley. The corridors and public spaces also have a homely feel, and are redolent of India's Anglo-India: Stations of the Cross line the corridor walls; in the dining room there's a picture of The Last Supper, a statue of St. Joseph, and a plastic banana tree, complete with monkey, in one corner.

6 a.m.: It's still dark. There's someone shuffling down the corridor from my room. I haven't slept well in the unfamiliar, narrow bed. What sleep I've had has been punctuated by thoughts of the room's previous resident: an always well-groomed (her hair was tinted and set once a week by the visiting hairdresser), and sweet-natured woman, who died a couple of months ago after a brief time in hospital. Losses such as this come with research into this age group. Each time I come from New Zealand to visit I worry about who might be gone from the home. I try to sleep some more…

6:30 a.m.: The sound of cups knocking on the bench, the radio is switched on—probably playing songs from the '50s. I think of David[16] telling me that he gets up early, makes a cup of tea, and watches evangelist/gospel services on TV—using his headphones so he doesn't wake anyone. I give up on sleep, knowing the first of the residents will be heading to the dining room soon.

7 a.m.: Dressed but not showered (there's still plenty of time for that), I go down to the dining room. Denzil is there and dressed already: tidy, winter-weight trousers with a thin, black leather belt, light-coloured shirt collar showing at the neck of a warm jumper, socks, and slippers. He sits at his usual place, drinking a cup of coffee out of his metal mug. He's opened his side of the room's curtains already, respecting the fact that Edward will open the others when he comes in—as long as he hasn't gone off for another early morning walk (5 a.m. yesterday).

Laura, a younger (relatively, because most of the residents are in their eighties and nineties) Anglo-Indian woman who is employed to stay overnight for three nights of the week, is blearily making porridge and checking the list of who has what for breakfast:
- Mary—a bowl of sweet, very milky porridge, and jam sandwich, quartered.
- Zena—porridge with milk, no sugar, and two slices of bread with butter.
- Denzil—a large bowl of porridge with milk and sugar, and two slices of toast and marmalade.

Laura's mixed up the spreads on Zena and Mary's bread, giving Zena jam when her diabetes necessitates just a thin spread of butter. They won't tell her, though; neither likes to make a fuss. One after another they come out for breakfast, most of the women in pretty pink, blue, or lilac dressing gowns. I sit down at "my" place and Denzil tells me who will come in next, and what they like to eat for breakfast. Most have a blister-pack of pills to take with breakfast. Kate has her only "medicine" in a glass just before her evening meal. By 7:30 a.m., they're all in the dining room but for Patsy; and she won't come until after 8:30, I'm told. I can relate to that. With so much time in the day, why get up any earlier? As the places at my table are filled, they ask after my plans for the day, and I ask about theirs. Kate and Mavis have their Southern Cross helpers coming to change their bedding, do their washing, then take them out to post mail and get some provisions; Patsy's daughter will be visiting—to bring news of Patsy's great-grandchild, who has just been born; Kath says, "There's nothing happening today, as usual;" Laura has some messages to run and, when her niece comes, will be off for the day with her. My plans: I want to record a couple more interviews. I have two volunteers—one of whom (Mary) the day before questioned me about whether or not it's compulsory, and Denzil. The day stretches before us. I set up interview times with Denzil and Mary, and after most have gone back to their rooms, and as the late one, Patsy, hasn't yet appeared, I go back to my room to settle it and shower.

9 a.m.: While sitting on the bed to write up my field notes, I wonder how I'm going to present the material I'm collecting—interviews, observations, and experiences. After I get back from Calcutta at the end of the year, I should be in a position to make some comparisons between the homes for Anglo-Indians there, and this one in Australia. Food for one thing: I was always told in Calcutta that their food preferences were Western (I read just recently, "An Anglo-Indian will always prefer a Continental dinner"), but what Anglo-Indians say they love most of all about this Melbourne home is the food—particularly the curries, rice, and *dāl* that they have every day. So in India they like Western food, but here they like Indian. It's an interesting reversal.

I'd also like to write up a set of life stories, but I have concerns about preserving their anonymity. After a while, I head back to the dining room and see that Patsy has arrived; but everyone else is in his or her room. Brian will be reading his paper—he's the only one to get a local morning paper, which he reads before giving the crossword page to Zena. Denzil will be reading the Bible, as he does every day. Most of the women will be showering and settling their rooms, as I've just done. Patsy takes tiny bites of the bread that's been left for her. She forgets to take her breakfast pills.

9:30 a.m.: Denzil comes out of his room, wheeling his walker. He reminds me that we're off to feed the birds. It's barely 5° C outside. And foggy. He has a hat for me, he says, and bags of bread—hidden inside our hats. We wander down to the meandering, litter-surrounded stream that runs behind the hostel, where he tells me he has gone every day of his six years here. He shows me where the Chinese neighbours feed the cats with their meal leftovers. We stop once we get a clear view of where the stream widens and ponds, and Denzil begins to break bread and toss it down the bank. One by one ducks make their way towards us, but hesitate to come too close—because I'm here, I'm told. For the next 20 minutes Denzil tells me about the different birds that usually come, and of the ducklings, and the rats (one of whom makes a brief appearance), and the water level at different times. As we walk back, he tells me that, yes, there's not much going on in his life now, but he's learnt to make the most of it. We make arrangements to meet again at 10:45 for an interview.

10 a.m.: The Anglo-Indian Anglican minister arrives; Dot has been waiting in the entrance to let him in—as Denzil said she would. Over the time I've been carrying out this research, Denzil has slipped into the role of informal research assistant. It's he who points out the patterns of the place: he tells me who comes into the dining room and when, who gets on with whom, and who eats what. He also checks up on who I'm interviewing, and suggests that some people would be better to talk to than others.

10:45 a.m.: I settle down in the "Anglican" lounge (of the hostel's two lounges, one is used by the Anglican group for their prayer meetings, the other by the Catholics for their rosary sessions) with my digital voice recorder ready to interview Denzil. I begin ...

There's two things I'd like to ask you about; one is your life, where you were born in India and when you came out here, and that sort of thing; and the other is just about living here...what do you think makes it an Anglo-Indian home?
Okay.
Like we were talking about at the table the other day—the food that you like and things like that...
That what I came here...nat [Denzil's pronunciation] for anything else, but I only came for the sake of the food. I told you that before, too.
Yes, you did, yes you did.
Because I couldn't eat Australian food.
Yeah...
When I go to the hospital I used to suffer.
Oh did you? Why, how did you suffer?
I couldn't eat the food they gave me... it's very good food but the prip-peratins [his pronunciation] and all these things I couldn't stomach.

Too bland?
The only thing I ate was my breakfast in the morning.
Toast?
Yeah, toast, porridge, and some juices like orange juice, ahh... apple juice, something like that, make up a coffee, saficcient [pronounced this way] for me.
I see, because that's what you have here as well.
Yes, ha ha ha.
But the other meals you'd like to be a bit spicier, or a bit...just what you're used to...rice?
I'd like the rice, I eat the rice, I like the rice, of course I eat. After my going to hospital and coming out, I eat bread and all at night.
When were you in hospital?
Oh, I went in about three or four times. I go in according to my diabetes, it suddenly attacks me. I don't know how I got it. When the doctors told me I was so surprised. They sent me to Corfield, they've got a good hospital there in Corfield, a diabetic hospital.
Yeah, oh, Caulfield.
Yes, the diabetic hospital. And I have a very good doctor, we are friends now.
Oh yes.
I mean between a patient and a doctor they must be friends first, then a doctor, that is how I take it...

12:30 p.m.: We'd spent longer on the interview than I'd expected. The rest of the interview was about his time in India: about railway bogeys and the job of a station manager, and what it was like to send his young children to boarding school. I'd asked about his coming to Australia with his family, and learned that they had migrated more than 30 years ago. They'd arrived in Sydney via Singapore, then had to wait around in Sydney on the coldest day of that year, for a flight to Melbourne. They didn't seem to have struck any problems with their luggage and customs—even though they'd come laden with garlic and ginger, and chillies that they'd had ground at the local mill before they left India.

Lunchtime: By the time we come into the dining room some are already sitting at the tables with their lunch. Today it's sausage curry, *kofta* curry with potatoes, *dāl* and rice, a salad of grated carrot and red onion, turmeric cabbage, and a *brinjal* pickle. There are glasses of water on the tables, along with serviettes, hanging sets of cutlery, plastic flowers, and packs of cards. Dessert is always fresh fruit: today it's mangoes—my contribution. Earlier I'd given the tray of mangoes to Phyllis, the Anglo-Indian cook, but she said I would have to distribute them, and find out how the residents wanted to eat them. I was puzzled—how many ways are there of eating a mango? So I asked each in turn. David asked for Phyllis to cut his—and wanted only the cheeks. Gerry wanted to do his own, so I got a plate and knife for him. Mary wanted her cheeks diced. Ken's snuff-box cut didn't work. He ended up with something more like mashed mango. Some took theirs back to their rooms—"for later". I heard a story of a trip David had made as a school boy, travelling with his father in the cabin of a freight truck to Salem—"where the best mangoes come from". Denzil repeated an oft-told refrain, that nothing tastes as good as it did in India. Astonishingly, most could tell me when they'd eaten their last mango.

1:30 p.m.: I interview Mary. She doesn't play Bingo, and said she could have a lie down later. Before we begin, she rubs her skinny stomach and tells me how good it feels to have a mango in her tummy again. She tells me a little about her school-teaching days in railway towns in India. She says she didn't notice the effects of Indian independence—"things carried on as usual"—and apologizes before and after the interview for not being able to remember much. It's hard to keep the momentum of the interview going. We finish after a while, and I reassure her that I am happy with the interview. She collects her stick and goes off to her room for a rest.

3 p.m.: The room is filling up with visitors. Mary's niece and nephew always come this day of the week. They first play Bingo, then visit her in her room. Residents of St. Mary's, the retirement village next door, come too. Daughters and friends of others also arrive. One of the office assistants makes it a point to arrive on time—this is her first job of the day. It's just after 3 p.m., so someone checks that all the "regulars" are out of their rooms and set up. It's $2 for a single set of five games, $4 for two sets. I'm sitting at Zena's table, hoping her year-long lucky streak will rub off on me. We play through five games, with numbers called as "two little ducks, 22, legs 11, on its own, number 9, Christmas day, 25, top of the house,

90, all the sixes, 66, two fat ladies, 88…". I'm pipped each time by Zena, and others, as they beat me to "*jeldi* five", ice-cream cone, four corners, marching soldiers, and Bingo!

4:15 p.m.: After tea and lamingtons, visitors leave, and the residents go to their rooms to watch TV. I'm at a loose end. More than two hours until dinner…I head out for a walk, out of the cul-de-sac and along a road that runs parallel to the railway track. I've talked with Rodney about the reasons for the location of the hostel, so I check out the local amenities: medical centre one corner along, train station five minutes' walk away, and a short strip of mainly food retailers across the railway line. There's an interesting mix of people living around here. It might have been an Anglo-Indian enclave 12 years ago, when the hostel was built, but it's "Aussies", Somalians, and Eastern Europeans I see as I walk up to Noble Park. This is the closest well-serviced shopping centre: there's a post office, banks, chemists, a flower shop, real estate agents, shoe shops, and a multitude of bakeries—selling more iced cakes and pastries than bread.

5:30 p.m.: It's becoming dark outside, and the dining room is cosy when I return. I make a cup of tea and sit down near Patsy and Kath, who are half-heartedly flicking through magazines. Kate comes in eating a jam sandwich, and sits beside them. Kath asks her, "Did you make that yourself?" She did, and offers to make one for Kath. Just the response Kath was after. Getting up, Kate notices my tea, goes to the jug, taps the switch on, goes to the fridge, gets some milk and makes a cup of tea, and sits down again. Kath asks, "What about the jam sandwich?" Kate is confused, and surreptitiously takes chocolates out of her pocket and gives one to Kath and one to Patsy. Kath mumbles, "You've got a very poor memory," while accepting the chocolate ungraciously.

6:30 p.m.: It's dinnertime, and everyone's out of their rooms again and checking what's on offer: spiced vegetable soup with bread or toast, followed by chicken pieces, cooked carrots, and a dessert of jelly with chopped fruit in it.

7:30 p.m.: One by one, as they finish dinner, they say goodnight and head to their rooms. A few come out again with their Thermoses to fill with hot water, to make a hot drink later—Horlicks? Four of the five at my table remain behind. Dorothy, from another table, also stays up, and she waits until a particular seat is vacated at my table to re-possess the spot for the rest of the evening. They tell me that this is what happens every night: all the others go to their rooms early, but this group stays and chats until 8:30. They say, "We're the sociable ones." So it wasn't by chance that I ended up sitting at this table. Initially, I'd sat at different tables every mealtime—with mixed results in terms of being able to chat and start to get to know people. In the end, it was mainly this group, plus one or two other individuals, with whom I felt comfortable enough to intermittently impose upon, so this had become "my" place when I visited.

Just before 8:30, Denzil walks to the notice board, takes a red felt pen to the large calendar, and puts a tick through tomorrow's date. And bids us goodnight.

February

by Pat Brown

Mechanically reciting her morning prayers, Thelma shoved her feet into warm, fur-lined slippers and slowly, achingly, moved towards the bathroom. She heard the clock strike eight as she entered the kitchen, filled the kettle, and plugged it in for her morning coffee. Gazing out the window at the snow lying in monstrous drifts, she sighed—it was mid-February, and there was going to be no let-up. She had heard on the radio that temperatures were not expected to nudge much above two degrees as the mind-numbing cold persisted—all around resembled an Arctic icescape.

The kind of day I would generally have spent in bed with a good book, she thought, but of course this was impossible because Charlie was coming to fetch her at two o'clock, to take her over to the Smith-Pandell Funeral Home, where Olga was laid out. Her eyes misted at the thought of her dear dead friend. For the past two days, she had refused to face the fact that Olga was gone. She was not away on a holiday, she was not visiting her son, Freddie—she was very definitely gone. Hastily wiping away the tears that slipped unchecked down her cheeks, Thelma collapsed on the easy chair beside the electric fireplace. The kettle whistled noisily. Rising, she shuffled back into the kitchen, prepared her coffee, and made her way to the dining table with two slices of buttered toast.

Each year, the freezing cold snatched a body from her circle of friends. She often wondered, Will I be the next to go? But in spite of her many aches and pains, good health persisted, while those around her slipped away. "We are nearly all past 70 now, and time has taken its toll," she muttered. "February is a test which many of us fail." But it was no use grumbling; the screeching storms and endless days without sunshine were inevitable.

The shortest month of the year, too; if one could only stay focused and look beyond the 28th day, there was the promise of daffodils and spring. Unfortunately, old age and pessimism often combined to dull the imagination. Why, even those born and bred in these northern climes often lost the battle, she mused. One needed an armada of strength to ward off cancer and heart disease, let alone wrestle February to the ground.

"Olga," she cried out, "dear, dear friend, I will miss you. What on earth will I do without you? Leaving like this in your sleep without so much as a goodbye. How could you?"

They had known each other in Poona (now Pune), in the halcyon days of youth. Thelma's mind raced back to that place in time—both of them free as the breeze, riding bicycles down side streets and alleyways, swerving to avoid the great humped bulls chewing the cud in the centre of the road. Picnics at the Botanical Gardens in the winter months, with family and friends seated beneath the giant trees. Hampers spread out—potato cutlets, hard-boiled egg sandwiches, and over-ripe bananas. It seemed like heaven. Screeching at the top of their voices, filled with the exuberance of youth, they had circled the colossal trunks of the banyan trees, singing childish songs:

> *"Four partridge pies with season made,*
> *Whipsee diddle dee dandy dee,*
> *Two potted larks and marmalade,*
> *Whipsee diddle dee dandy dee.*
> *With a harum scarum diddle dum darum,*
> *Whipsee diddledee dandy dee."*

Dear God, where had the time gone? In this very room, huddled under heavy blankets and sipping rum toddies, she and Olga had spent many winter evenings giggling like schoolgirls, as they leafed through old photo albums, and tried to recall the long-dead faces and distant places, captured in ancient sepia prints. Thelma suddenly felt very cold and tired, filled with inertia, not wanting to leave the safety of the house, or the armchair, to go with Charlie to the funeral parlour where Olga lay embalmed, and no doubt immaculately attired. Freddie would have seen to that; he was all about making an impression. She on the other hand wanted to stay put, and remember her friend in the living years.

Leaning back into the chair, overcome with feelings of extreme solitude, Thelma closed her eyes and was once again flooded by memories of warm golden days: she and Olga, like a pair of painted birds, had lived what seemed a charmed life. Their worlds were entwined, and yet separate. Both resided in trellised bungalows on the same dusty street. Both saw the light of day beneath the Indian sun, and took their first faltering steps in the ragged garden with the broken swings, where goats often grazed. They both went to the same convent; after graduation, they took Pitman's stenography course together, and became typists. Nurtured in an atmosphere of watchful *ayahs* and protective families, they suddenly blossomed into womanhood and discovered men—everywhere. Not the troublesome boys of adolescence who mocked and teased, but real men. Beneath the Chinese lanterns strung overhead at open-air functions, behind the high hedges; the men watched with sly eyes as the girls crossed their legs under poodle skirts. The men came courting, with neatly pressed clothes and slicked-back hair, and sat mute upon the sofas in stuffy sitting rooms. There were long, lazy afternoons, and lingering looks beneath the covered porches that shaded them from the summer sun. For a while it was magic—she and her girlfriends exchanged hot, breathy secrets, shrieking with giddy laughter in the shaded corners of the old crumbling bungalows.

Most families on the street were large, and often there was less to go around than they needed, but they made do. They ran up skirts on Mummy's Singer sewing machine; attended parties, arriving fashionably late with ten pounds of sweet watermelon as a contribution. They drank spiked punch, smoked fags, and sashayed all over town on the pillions of motorcycles. Imitating celluloid heroines, they lived on the edge.

Time passed and things changed, however, when they slipped into wedlock. With the onset of motherhood, the carefree life disappeared on a swallow's wing. The sun was always there, sweltering hot, taxing their bodies as they lumbered down the road, each heavy with child. The old ones retired, and some of them died, energy sucked from brittle bones by the torrid heat.

Suddenly, contentment vanished, as their menfolk shared big dreams and even bigger ambitions, which drew them to explore the endless possibilities waiting beyond the horizon. The West had much to offer, and they left the subcontinent. Both of them, with husbands and children in tow, arrived in Toronto, penniless. They came with a bagful of dreams and a willingness to work; the future looked rosy, and nothing seemed impossible. It was September 1960, 47 years ago; Thelma shuddered in disbelief. Both she and Olga celebrated their 30th birthdays in their newly adopted country. Discovering others of their community already settled in the sprawling metropolis, they took comfort in knowing some measure of the past was still with them. Olga fitted in right away; she went to work as a secretary for a steel mill executive. Her husband Harold found a job, and their only son, Freddie, attended school.

Thelma never had it so easy. Hugh was employed, but she had to stay home with two children in school, and one on the way. Her thoughts often wandered back to India, and she felt homesick, making unfair comparisons in her despondency. Everything seemed cold, and new, like the plate glass windows and shimmering shops she passed on her way to the grocery store. She often found herself wandering needlessly through the aisles, searching high and low for "curry stuff", ingredients to make her mother's special chicken recipe. Much of her new life seemed like drudgery: wringing out laundry, cooking Hugh's dinner. The dream had been rosier than the reality. One morning she shared her sorrow with Olga, but her friend showed scant sympathy.

"Get a-hold of yourself!" she chided. "Soon the kids will be grown, and we'll be able to travel. And as for Poona, it will still be there. We can never forget it; it was all we knew before we came to this place. Thelma, old girl, trust me, will you?" Olga reached across the table and squeezed her hand. "You can always go for a visit when the kids are off your hands; you'll have the money then. Harold and I are planning a trip. Why not come along? It's no good fretting about such things; you can't turn back the clock. Besides, your plate is full as it is, with Hugh and all the children to care for."

"I wonder what it would be like to go back and settle," she had whispered, betraying her longing.

"Have you gone daft?" Olga inquired harshly. "Return and settle, where? It's not the same as in your dreams, believe me. There have been some brave souls, I hear, who have ventured back, only to return broken and disappointed. 'You can't go home again,' just like the writer said."

She abandoned her dream. In any case, Hugh would have none of it. He proved to be a good husband, and a kindly father to their brood. God bless him. He, too, had left her suddenly, expiring one night as she snored in the bed beside him. Just 55 years old, 10 years from retirement, and not a thing wrong with him. After he died, she was forced to take a job. Olga and Harold, good friends, visited often. Freddie, a smart lad, was studying to become a lawyer.

He didn't come around much, though, and she sensed this made Olga sad. I had too many children, she mused, but no matter; I love them all dearly, and am not a bit sorry. When the last one left home, and after Harold died, it was Thelma and Olga again; they found comfort in each other's company.

"We spent a lot of time together," Thelma spoke aloud, her words echoing through the empty room. "Gallivanting all over town, joining old friends for lunch, or a bit of Bingo." Most of them were now living on pensions—supplementing their fixed incomes with what little they had saved. Life was good for a while. That was before they began to die, one by one. It's the natural order of things, she reasoned, bound to happen. But their deaths followed a pattern—nearly all of them passed on in February. She began to dread the month.

"It seems like I will be the last to go. They are dropping like flies all around me," she declared to herself one morning, uneasily, as opening the paper she read of another friend's death in the obituary page. "At this rate, rather not hang around. I would hate to be a solitary sentinel waving goodbye, sending them on their way."

"What an imagination you have," Olga had laughed out loud, when Thelma shared her thoughts. "Solitary sentinel, indeed! Not you my dear. Why, there are many in our age group who show no signs of turning up their toes. It could be one of them. Anyway, no more gloomy thoughts from you today. Let's go have a bite to eat." Olga had grown quite plump in the last few years, and Thelma smiled, contemplating her friend's ample derrière. "Yes, let's," she agreed.

Swallowing the last bit of toast, she drained the cup of cold coffee, and decided to shower and change. She would wear her burgundy outfit with the grey silk blouse for Olga. Besides, dressing warmly in her best suit would make all the difference to her frame of mind.

Charlie carefully negotiated a bend on the icy road, and the Smith-Pandell Funeral Home came into view. Coming to a halt on the gravelled driveway, they walked up the wide, marble stairs, and were ushered in through imposing mahogany doors by a pair of funeral attendants. The place was familiar; so many friends had taken their leave from these premises in the last little while. Organ music soared to the vaulted ceiling of the chapel, and the air was heavy with the scent of flowers. Evidence of Freddie's success was everywhere; he had spared no expense. Olga's son had achieved his goal, and was now partner in a prominent law firm. Many of his associates could be seen milling around in the throng. Ignoring the other mourners, Thelma walked directly to the platform where her friend lay in a showy wooden casket, draped in satin and smothered with roses.

Peering in, she beheld Olga in her final resting place. "You're all made up for the journey, old girl," she said, speaking softly. "Lips painted in a perfect bow with scarlet lipstick, powdered and rouged, with your spectacles perched on your nose, and your hands neatly folded, holding a rosary—for appearances' sake, I guess. He didn't know you very well, did he?"

Olga's last birthday had passed, forgotten. She recalled the hurt in her friend's slate-grey eyes, and the gruff way she dismissed her son's oversight. "It doesn't matter, just another year here and gone." Later that week she came for a visit, carrying a monstrous bouquet of roses, a belated birthday gift from Freddie. Arranging them in Thelma's best crystal vase, she stood back and exclaimed: "There, that brightens up the place, doesn't it?"

Leaning into the coffin, she lightly brushed the cold, dead face with her lips. "Goodbye, my dearest," she whispered.

Father Murray gently touched her on the shoulder, and she turned to face him. "Dear Thelma," he said, pressing her hand, "I knew you were great friends with the deceased. I am so sorry for your loss. God give you strength."

"Thank you, Father," she replied.

"How long did you and Olga know each other?"

"It seems like forever, Father. We were childhood friends, in India."

"Umm," he squinted at her through steel-rimmed glasses. "What was she really like? I didn't know her very well you see, but would like to make some mention in the church paper. Her son Freddie wanted it."

"I guess you'd say she was all right," was her brusque reply. Thelma bristled, full of hurt and indignation. If they were really interested in knowing about Olga, they should have asked her to write the eulogy. Or did they think a wizened, grey-haired old woman was incapable of delivering a fitting tribute? As it is, not even Freddie, but his son, a mere lad of 17, had stepped up to the podium and mumbled a few honeyed words about his "Gramma".

The service over, Freddie came towards her, and nearly lifted her off her feet with a huge hug. "Aunt Thelma!" he exclaimed, enthusiastically. "I'm so glad you could come."

"Where else could I possibly be on such a day?" she replied. "Your mother and I were like sisters."

"True, true, " he said, mopping a florid brow.

She quickly sized him up; he had been drinking. She wondered how the shy, scrawny boy had turned into this big lug. A pale, young woman stood by his side, with a frozen smile plastered on her face. He didn't introduce them. Thelma knew he was divorced.

"Have you a ride home?" he inquired dutifully. "Just let me know when you're ready to leave, and I'll arrange a ride for you." Before she could reply, he turned and was gone, the pale young woman hanging on to his arm.

So much for that, thought Thelma, and went in search of Charlie. She found him sitting at a table with a group of old friends. "Ready?" he asked.

"When you are," she replied.

Seated glumly beside him on the ride home, Thelma contemplated the dull, grey, February afternoon with a feeling of quiet hopelessness. What now? she wondered, staring moodily out at the thick, soft flurries coming down, enveloping the earth like an Arctic shroud.

"What's up, old girl?" Charlie inquired. "You seem bothered. Let me tell you there's no need to worry; Olga's at rest, and she went in her sleep. What could be better?"

"Nothing."

"She had a good send-off; everybody thought so."

"Did they? Then who am I to think differently?" She gave him a dour look.

He leaned over and squeezed her arm. "Come now, cheer up. We old-timers live too much in the past. Look to the future."

"What for? Everything I know that is worthwhile is in the past. There's nothing to look forward to."

"Nothing, you say?" he asked lightheartedly, a merry twinkle in his bright, blue eyes. "Come now, you can't be serious."

Feeling the friendly warmth of Charlie, she gave him a weak smile. They were at her driveway. He helped her out of the car and up the steps to her front door. Impulsively, she turned to him: "Care to step in for a coffee?"

"Don't mind if I do."

He followed her in, and Thelma's spirits suddenly lifted. The mere presence of another body cheered the place.

Five Flags

by Joy Chase

This was our first Christmas together in 25 years. We were celebrating my mother Isabel's 80th birthday—it's actually in February, but no one in the family except my sister could be there on the day, so we decided to have a reunion at Christmas to honour her. Our beloved dad, Stephen Chase, had gone to his glory almost 10 years earlier.

The family flies five flags now. My sister immigrated to Australia to be with my parents many years earlier, but her son was born in Toronto, Canada. Her first husband, Gaston, had died there but not before their son, Timmy, was born and carried a Canadian passport at the tender age of three months. Margo was now married to a great guy called Sam, from Northern Ireland. My brother, Eric, had immigrated to Australia with my parents when he was just 10, but had now moved to New Zealand with his Australian wife and their daughters—Holly, Jemma, and Miranda.

I was the first to leave India after graduating from Queen Mary's College, Madras (now Chennai), in 1963, travelling alone to the United States of America. There I remained alone even after my sister, Jen, came to California. I was in Madison, Wisconsin, working on a Master's degree, and it was six years before I was able to get a job in California and live closer to her, though still some distance away. I still often feel alone in America.

This Christmas, however, we were all gathered in Brisbane, Australia—the four adult children of my mother, Isabel. Either by domicile or citizenship, in our minds we were flying the flags of five countries: Australia, the USA, New Zealand, India (once an Indian always an Indian), and the Union Jack. My mother had revoked her long-held British citizenship for Australian, but the Raj was still alive in her. All her siblings but one had left India to live in England in the late 1940s. And, of course, there was Sam from Northern Ireland.

It was important that we were all together, and now the cooking had to start. We also had to have what I call "face time"—talking, chatting, and catching up face-to-face—so much better than e-mail, instant messaging, or even Skype. We had most of our children with us: my daughters, Natala, Sheila, Jasmine, and

Joslyn, are Americans. Holly, Jemma, Miranda, Sam's son Sammy, and my brother's older daughter, Jasmine, were born in Australia. We all had different Christmas traditions by now, but the festive tree was a common link. For dinner, we had a succulent Australian ham and a roast turkey, with stuffing made by Mother, but we added some curries for old times' sake. My American husband, Bill, carved the turkey.

During the week or so we were together, we each made sure our favourite dishes came to the table: crab curry—hot and spicy; vegetable *kormas*; yellow rice—made in a cooker; cabbage *foogath*—my mother's specialty (among many); and dark fruitcake. There were other Anglo-Indian Christmas foods that we may have added—*kul-kuls, halvas, dol-dol, rosa cuikees, OT* (a teetotaler's drink made mostly from chilies and ginger), Xmas pudding (with coins in it), and other items dimly remembered from times long past. Our children remembered none of these but were intrigued by our memories all the same. Some of us had tried to keep them alive, but none of us had married Anglo-Indians, and so often had to eat them alone. Yes, I have eaten a whole dark fruitcake myself over the holidays, though I refuse to do it any longer. Mincemeat is ground meat to Americans, not the fragrant chopped delight of preserved fruit that the British put in pies or cakes, and that we loved in India. In larger pieces, with the addition of a few good mango chunks, it made great chutney.

Back to our Five Flags Christmas. Summer in Australia, especially in Queensland, is hot. Hot as a winter in India. Christmas in December in India was always warm unless you happened to live up in the hills somewhere, or in the north. Pine trees were hard to come by in India and I remembered we used a croton once. Its brightly coloured leaves hardly needed any decorations. Another time, we had the *mali* cut a huge branch from way up high off a casuarina, on the beach in front of our house when we lived in Cochin, Kerala. There was no Christmas tree lot to visit way back then, but we still enjoyed the childhood excitement of finding a suitable tree. In other years, we would drive miles to a casuarina farm, cut down a small tree, and take it home on the roof of the car, carefully secured with jute twine. A friend told me a story of how he had inadvertently stolen a tree off the grounds of a *maharaja's* estate and been reprimanded by the ruler himself. Good thing for him that he was a classmate of the *maharaja's* son.

My brother decided to give a crab curry feast for his friends in Brisbane, and we all helped out. He had it at a friend's place that looked like it was in the Australian bush, with lots of verdant greenery around, although it wasn't that far from the centre of town. He rented cookers and bought at least 50 large crabs, which he cracked, cleaned, and sautéed with bottles of *vindaloo* paste and cans of unsweetened coconut milk. Can you taste it now? It was delicious, and his Australian friends loved it, too. We made aromatic *basmati* rice to go with it, and side dishes galore. It really was a feast, but the best part was yet to come. Eric's friend, Virgil, a vendor of high quality vegetables and fruit, provided us with cases of the best mangoes we'd ever tasted. I still have visions of all those delicious mangoes that we sliced and ate with ice cream. Naughty me, I hid a case for Mum to eat and savour slowly over the next few days. All of this, in true Raj style, went well with the inimitable, and unavailable anywhere else, Bundaberg Rum. For the teetotalers like my mother, there was the non-alcoholic but just-as-good Bundaberg ginger.

Many of us were not used to Brisbane's debilitating heat, but we still enjoyed our Christmas with some traditional help. My adult daughters brought gifts—Natala put together a CD of favourite songs, garnered via interviews with all of us. "It's a Long Way to Tipperary" for Mum; "Love Me Tender", by Elvis, for me; "Hit the Road, Jack", for my brother; "Waltzing Matilda" for the Aussies; "God Save the Queen"—well, that was a bit over the top! "California Girl", by David Lee Roth, for the California girls, who stood up and sang it with actions; "We Are a Family", for all of us; Holly, Jemma, and Miranda, real Kiwis now, did the *Haka* for us—the New Zealand Maori war cry that the All Blacks rugby team does before each game; and, of course, the Indian national anthem, *Jana Gana Mana*. My sisters, Margo and Jenny, and I stood up and sang it by heart, having memorized it when India became independent in 1947.

Jana gana mana adhināyaka jaya hē
Bhārata bhāgya Vidhātā...

We ended with a triumphant and victorious...

Jaya hē jaya hē jaya hē
Jaya jaya jaya jaya hē

... finishing on the high note because to go down after that would be to show defeat, or so they said. My brother in law, Sam, was very impressed. "I always wondered if you were true Indians," he said, "but now I know you are!" We chorused back at him: "Anglo-Indians!" (That brought back a memory: my father told me as a child, when we were taunted with songs mocking our mixed heritage—"*Missey, Missey Lul*" they sang, as we rode by high in our rickshaws to school. Dad said: "Remember, we have the best of the British and the best of the Indian in us.")

My daughter, Sheila, a professional photographer, gave us calendars of photos she had taken in India. Jasmine (Jenny's daughter) told us of her world travels as a student, including visiting cousins in Madras. My brother and his wife, Marg, did a skit my parents had performed for years, and read a poem that Dad had written. Margo rendered a song that I had found after much research for my mother, one that my father had sung to her in 1939 called, "My Little Persian Rose". We already had nary a dry eye when Jenny sang, in her beautiful alto voice, pleading that we all spend just one more Christmas together. "This is the time for hoping and dreaming, wishing, and scheming," she sang. "But, what if all the wishes were through, and I had to choose one wish, just one wish for you?"

> I'd wish for one more Merry Christmas,
> A fond forever with my friends,
> And if I get my wish this Christmas
> I'd wish it never ends!

We didn't know if this would ever happen again, and it hasn't yet. None of us was really home but, then again, all of us were. Peter Ustinov, the famous multi-talented star, said of his own varied background and travels that he was "at home nowhere and absolutely at home everywhere". I think that many an Anglo-Indian can say that, too.

I once heard a Native American, an elder, tell the story of six generations of her female ancestors. Americans with ancestry in India are referred to as Indian Americans. I suppose that would make me an Anglo-Indian American. Anyway, the idea of six generations intrigued me, so I researched six generations in my own female line. This is a difficult thing to do, if you are an

Anglo-Indian. The male line is usually clear, and once you can authenticate the British connection, which is not hard for most of us, the rest is easily researched online through the Mormon records or the British Library.

My own maternal grandfather, Harry Shepherd, was born in Norfolk, England. My maternal grandmother, on the other hand, Florence Grace Shepherd née Lilywhite, was born in India. Her mother, Florence Lillian Lilywhite née Clapham, was also born in India, as was her mother, Jane DeBeaux Clapham. Jane's mother, Julia Honey, was born in Kamptee, Maharashtra, in 1829. I found Jane's record of marriage to Mathew Clapham, in 1865, at the Scots Kirk, St. Andrew's, in Madras. I found her grave in Bangalore when I was with a cousin, Ruth, from England, whom I had met on the Internet, and whose great-great-grandmother was also my Jane. Anglo-Indians are connected all over the world. Our flag, whatever that might be, is always aloft, and the sun never sets on it.

I enacted the stories at the Christmas reunion. Generation One was Jane DeBeaux; we don't know much about her, but my newfound cousin, Ruth, had a picture of her sister. I wore a similar outfit and talked about her, as much as I could find. Generation Two was my great-grandmother Florence Lillian, called Lulu. Her father, a sidenote that has special implications of pleasure for me, also called her Joy. She was the one who was abandoned by her husband and lost her precious son to him; she had to go to work (unheard of in those days). She loved to read the classics and would spend her Sundays reading. Generation Three was Florence Grace; unfortunately, she was a smoker, very *avant-garde* in those days. She died of cancer in England, after giving birth to nine children, of whom my mother was the second.

Generation Four was my mother, Isabel, and it was especially good for her grandchildren to hear her tell her life story herself. A devout Christian, she gave credit to the Lord Jesus for all the triumphs and victories in life. She had started her own business in Australia after the age of 50, and made a huge success of it, selling handmade lace from India on the "party plan". At one stage, before she retired and sold the business to my sister, Margo, she had 100 women holding the parties and selling lace for her all over Australia. My sister has created *The Lace Place* now, and incorporated lace crafts into her products. My mother spends her time completing a dream both she and Dad had, to found a Christian retreat centre in India. *Elim* in Whitefield, a suburb of Bangalore, is the fulfilment of this dream. She raises money to support many indigenous missionaries in India and, when the great tsunami hit, she raised funds to rebuild a church on the Andaman Islands. At 86, she pursues these interests with the help of her computer and the Internet.

Then it came time for me to stand up for Generation Five. I am a faculty member at a community college, in the San Francisco Bay Area of California. I love California, but it is a rare thing for me to meet another Anglo-Indian. However, thanks to the ubiquitous Indian restaurants here, we can enjoy a South Indian *dosa* every week, if we want. I cook my favourites, which are now my husband Bill's favourites, too: ground turkey *keema*, *dâl* mash, chicken curry, *masala* fish fry, or chilli omelettes. For Generation Six, my daughter Sheila wrote a lovely poem that pulled it all together. A seventh generation, Jasmine's children, sat taking it all in.

We cheated a bit. We could have gone back to the first male on my maternal side, George Honey, who came to India about 200 years ago on the sailing vessel *Minerva*. He was from Kent. But, what do you know? He came to India and married Charlotte Young, who was already there! She was Indo-European, they said. Perhaps some Portuguese, perhaps more Indian. We don't really know her genetic makeup and now, so far into the future, it does not matter. In California, when my daughters were in the elementary grades, they were asked to fill out forms stating their race. This is a pretty ridiculous question to ask a child, unless they've been carefully schooled by their parents to recognize one race from another. They looked to one side at their Japanese friend and to the other at an African American, and all checked Hawaiian. That seemed like a good race to be.

I could have enacted my paternal Chase family history going back to Georgiana Francis Cherry, who married Morgan Charles Chase. He was born in Madras in 1790. She, too, was from Madras. Although we have an unbroken thread of oral history, given to me by my father, some of the links have been difficult to authenticate. Early deaths, large families, and subsequent marriages make this a never-ending genealogical puzzle of love. The most illustrious female in this line was my great-grand aunt, Esther Chase, who went to England in the 1930s to become a doctor, then returned to work in India and the Andaman Islands, in the *zenana* missions among women. She bought a large house with a compound and a lake in Madras. It is now home to the YWCA.

So that's the saga that unfolded that Christmas: almost 300 years of Anglo-Indian history. Our children listened, rapt, though it was hard to tell how much they absorbed. Their eyes are set on the future. They have to grapple with acculturation, assimilation, and national identities. But their children, our grandchildren, will ask questions. Their grandchildren will want answers. So we must write it all down, every word of it.

When we are gone, there will be few like us ever again. Three hundred years of inter-marriage and intra-marriage have almost disappeared, like it never happened. But it is written in our hearts, and it can continue to exist if those of us who remember write it down, say it aloud, and honour the memory of those who have gone before.

It is who we are, wherever we live now, whatever we think we are now, whichever country's passport we carry. That, too, is us. Anglo-Indians.

At the end of our reunion, our imaginary flags came down, and those of us from faraway lands began the long journey back. Our new homes are the homes of our choosing—or, perhaps, in my case, it chose me. When my Dad died in Brisbane, Australia, I thought: "Poor Dad, he's buried so far from home." But my sister said, "No, he loved the Brisbane Broncos rugby league team and they practise not far from here, so he'll feel at home."

Home is always just where you are—Australia, America, Ireland, Canada, New Zealand, England, or India—wherever Anglo-Indians are. Let them raise the flag! Because...

>I'll be home for Christmas.
>If only in my dreams.

My Bow Barracks

by Esther Lyons

Mrs. Hazel White has lived most her life in the 90-year-old Calcutta Improvement Trust (CIT) housing complex known as Bow Barracks, in central Calcutta. In fact, she is only 15 years younger than the Barracks, which lie just behind Bow Bazaar police station, off Chittaranjan Avenue.

Her flat has a neat garden in front, with a henna hedge separating her home from the neighbours, Mr. and Mrs. Jones on one side, and the elderly Miss Gonzalves on the other. Bougainvillea and roses adorn the front wooden balcony and the verandah, on which are placed two old chairs. In the small backyard are a guava tree and a clothesline. Another henna hedge partitions the backyard from the neighbours.

The three-bedroom flat is old, with paint peeling off the walls, in which cracks are all too visible. But it is very neatly kept. All the windows have clean floral curtains, as do the doors leading to large, airy rooms. The front door opens directly into the drawing room; on its walls are many photos that tell something of the history of her family over more than a century. In the centre of the far wall is an altar with a picture of the Sacred Heart, a candle, and a vase full of fresh roses. In one corner is a venerable Singer sewing machine, with foot paddles.

On this day, Mrs. Hazel White sits in her rickety old rocking chair, sleeping, with a rosary in her left hand. Her daughter, Esther, sits on the sofa with her friend Dolores Evans, while Durga, the cleaner, swabs the floors. Esther's son, Robert, is in the kitchen making himself a cup of tea. Rani, the *ayah*, is slicing onions for that afternoon's curry.

Dolores takes a sip of her tea and says: "Have you heard the worrying news? You may have to move—all 1,500 of you living in Bow Barracks. And why? Well, our West Bengal Minister of Urban Development, Asok Bhattacharya, has declared that Bow Barracks is in such a dilapidated state that the seven buildings cannot be renovated. He says they have plans to demolish the buildings and build new apartments."

Dolores lives a few blocks away, and, since it's a Sunday, she has dropped in to sympathize with Esther, who she's known for many years because they taught at the same school.

Esther says, "Yes, I heard that. This means, of course, that we have to move from this place where we have spent our childhood and brought up our own children."

Robert calls out from the kitchen: "That's a bloody shame. I grew up here—I love the old place." Robert has spoken loudly enough to wake up his grandmother.

"Who is saying that we have to move from Bow Barracks?" asks Grandma Hazel. "Why should we move from Bow Barracks? It is my home. I have lived here since I married Henry. My children and grandchildren were all born here."

Grandma Hazel struggled out of her rickety chair and walked towards the side window with the help of an old walking stick. She suffers from severe pain in her legs and needs knee replacements but cannot afford the surgery. She is dependent on her daughter, Esther, and the small old-age pension she receives from the CTR Fund organized by Blair Williams of the USA.

"I still remember the days when your grandfather used to drive me down that road," she says, pointing with her stick out of the window. "We had a black English car and drove around all the time. Those were good days; we attended parties and dances, and had great fun. This house was always full of friends, relatives, and guests enjoying lavish diners and parties." Grandma adds, with a twinkle in her eyes.

"Yes, Mama, you had a great time but saved nothing for us," says Esther, her 60-year-old daughter.

"How could I?" replies Grandma, "We had no time to think about the future. Besides, we never dreamed that India would get its independence, or that the British would leave us without any means or resources."

She walks towards Esther and, face glowing with the memory, says: "Esther, I cannot forget the day you were born—your father was so happy to have a daughter. He named you after the famous swimming film star, Esther Williams. We never missed any of her movies."

Grandma looks towards the other room, and her mood turns sombre. "Your father died in that room. He had a massive heart attack soon after India got its independence, on August 15th, 1947."

She turns back to Esther. "I can still hear Henry playing that old piano in the corner. He loved music and his Triple XXX Rum and pegs of whisky. But he never quite recovered from the shock when your elder brother, James, met with an accident saving a wretched dog on Park Street. James became crippled in one leg. My Henry died soon after, and I had to sell the car and go back to working as a secretary to support all of you children."

Grandma makes a helpless gesture. "My two sisters and brother emigrated to the UK and Australia with their families, but we couldn't do that, not with a crippled son. I couldn't leave James behind."

Suddenly, she bursts into floods of tears and collapses in her rocking chair again. "Poor James. He finally died of tuberculosis in the back bedroom—I still have his gramophone and stacks of records he loved. Unfortunately, by then I was too old to emigrate. In any case, how could I have left this house, and Bow Barracks?"

Grandma wipes away her tears with a small handkerchief. "There are so many memories here—this is my Bow Barracks. I would rather die here than leave! The memories of my husband and my son are everywhere; they live with me every minute of the day and night. Every family in Bow Barracks has its own stories to tell. They all have fond and sad memories, which they treasure behind the four walls of their homes."

"Stop crying, Grandma," says Robert, walking towards her from the kitchen. "No one can get us out of this house. I promise you—I shall see to it."

Robert left school when he was 12 and started working as an assistant in shops and people's homes in the neighbourhood. He loves cooking and is now working with a catering service, graduating from a steward to a cook. Many of his friends and acquaintances in the Bow Barracks buildings also work in restaurants, hotels, and clubs as cooks, barmen, and waiters.

"Mum," says Esther, "we will do our best not to leave this place. Don't cry." She came to live with her mother when her husband, John, deserted her and went to live in the Middle East. He left Esther with three small children. Her eldest daughter, now grown up and married, lives in the neighbourhood. Both she and her husband work at a call centre, as do many others in Bow Barracks because of their fluency in English. Esther's only son, David, has emigrated to Melbourne, Australia, while her younger daughter, Mary, is aiming to become an air stewardess. Many of Mary's friends from Bow Barracks have joined the leading airlines as air stewardesses.

"*Memsahib*," Rani the *ayah* calls from the kitchen, speaking in Hindi, "the yellow rice and the sausage curry are ready. If you would like to eat now, I can set the table up for lunch."

"Set the table and go home, Rani, we'll eat a bit later," replies Grandma. "When you come back again at four in the afternoon, bring some pork meat for the *vindaloo* this evening." Turning to Robert, she says, "Son, please take some money out of my handbag and give it to her for the meat."

Esther turns to her friend Dolores, smiles, and says: "It's so nice that we Anglo-Indian residents of Bow Barracks still feast on traditional Anglo-Indian delicacies like *vindaloo*, beef or chicken *bhuna*, sausage curry, and *tahari*, listen to Engelbert Humperdinck on the few remaining turntables, and swap tales on lazy afternoons while sitting on our verandahs. The young play hockey or soccer, the older ones take a stroll in nearby Nalanda Park.. Some prefer staying at home and watching television news and documentaries in English."

"Yes," says Dolores, "and young children play rounders, hopscotch, or cricket on Barracks street, with soft-drink crates doing duty as wickets. You are going to miss all this if you have to move away from here."

Esther takes a sip of tea. "So many traditions. Families here have made their own wine from old recipes, passed down from generation to generation, for a long time. Wine from grapes, apples, beetroot, and even ginger. Of course, it's mostly downed at our annual Christmas Eve bash. You know what a colourful gala it is, with live music, a benevolent Santa, homemade goodies, and lots of cheer."

Robert nods. "All this will be forgotten once we move out and get separated in new housing. What a loss for the community!"

Esther goes on, with a note of pride in her voice: "While the Anglo-Indians in other parts of India are slowly assimilating, and starting to wear regional clothes like *saris* or *salwar-kameez*, and celebrate the feasts of the other religions of India, the Anglo-Indians of Bow Barracks enjoy preserving their age-old culture and traditional values. We love our own heritage and culture, partly because so many of us have grown up together here. We want to hang on to our traditions."

Grandma Hazel has been listening quietly, but now she interjects: "My grandson David, who emigrated to Australia, and my sister's children from the USA, come out here every year to celebrate Christmas. These days the Christmas celebrations in Calcutta are largely confined to hotels, pubs, and nightclubs, and there just isn't the same atmosphere. But here in Bow Barracks we know how to bring on the old Anglo-Indian style. And there is a difference. David says he has spent Christmas in Sydney, in Times Square in New York, in London, and in Paris, but he has not found the warmth that one gets in Bow Barracks."

Grandma smiles now, obviously moved with pleasure at recalling good times. "The warmth and liveliness of Bow Barracks draws youngsters living abroad to India every year. It's hard to find a gathering of so many Anglo-Indian families in one place, and the best thing is that it all takes place on the street—something you won't find anywhere else. Anglo-Indians, young and old, get together to dance the night away. And even if there are no big artists to draw a crowd, who cares? We make the best of the home-bred talent we have."

Grandma is so animated now she pauses to pick up a hand-fan with which to cool herself. This gives Esther a chance to say: "Anjali Dutt, a local film director, has made a film called *Bow Barracks Forever*. It is about the Anglo-Indians living here, people like us. She's promised to use some of the money from the film to help repair and improve Bow Barracks."

"Yes, that is true," says Robert. "Unfortunately, she has portrayed Anglo-Indians in a stereotypical way. Our community all over India has protested and called for a ban on the film. Sixty years after Independence, Anglo-Indians everywhere are redefining themselves. They are taking advantage of the country's economic boom in services, moving to jobs where proficiency in English is a bonus, and out of ghettos into mixed neighbourhoods. They are gyrating to Bollywood pop, celebrating Hindu festivals, and dating outside the community. Today, in Calcutta, Anglo-Indians own restaurants, beauty salons, and property firms. They work for call centres, newspapers, airline companies, and hotels. They are moving beyond the old-type jobs—secretaries, teachers, telephone operators, and typists. All Anglo-Indian men are not alcoholics and unemployed. They own publishing companies, like Harry MacLure, who lives in Chennai and publishes a community magazine. Many are educators and principals of their own schools. Some also hold important positions in the Government departments. Many are authors—Ruskin Bond, for instance—or celebrities like cricketer Roger Binny."

Robert names a few more well-known Anglo-Indians, among them world billiards champion Wilson Jones and quiz master Derek O'Brien, and then he adds: "We are a hardworking community that started with little, and many of us have made successes of our lives. Why make a film about the few that might not be doing well in the new India? Why not show the good and progressive ones, too?"

Hearing this, Grandma bursts into a flood of tears again. "Oh, Robby, I don't want to leave Bow Barracks. I want to die here amongst all the memories of the past. This is my Bow Barracks, and I love this place!"

Both Esther and Robert go over to Grandma Hazel and try and to console her.

"Grandma, no bloody man will get you out of this place," Robert says. "I shall see to it, now stop crying please. Bow Barracks to some may mean just another heritage building housing Anglo-Indians in Calcutta, but to us it is life itself! In every home there is a story, a handful of money, and hearts tipsy on dreams; we shall fight for it."

"Yes, Mum," Esther says, "the families here have already approached Gilian Rosemary Hart, who represents the Anglo-Indian community, and the Minority Commission for help. This is our Bow Barracks and will always remain ours."

In the meantime, Rani has laid the table for four and quietly left. Robert, Esther, and Dolores help Grandma to the table. They start to eat their lunch, and the younger ones try to cheer Grandma with amusing tales and memories of happy days.

Ginger Wine

by Joyce Mitchell

Ginger wine brings back memories of the happy times we spent celebrating birthdays, anniversaries, weddings, Christmas, and New Year. I close my eyes and can hear the laughter and the clinking of glasses as we sip this spicy-sweet-tangy golden liquid.

Mummy is at the piano, accompanying Uncle Dickie, my father's brother, as he sings a sentimental ballad; there are homemade fruit cake, chutney sandwiches, and potato chips on the tables; and the rest of our family and friends are clustered around in small groups, enjoying light chatter, and tapping their feet to the music while sharing a story or a joke.

This winter, when I was on my annual visit to my sister Daphne in Ratlam, an important railway colony located halfway between Bombay and Delhi, we talked about the "good old days" and remembered how much fun it was to participate in the daylong process of making ginger wine.

Actually, all we did was hover around the kitchen and watch Mummy weigh all the ingredients: fresh, peeled ginger, crushed cloves, cardamoms, and cinnamon, coarsely ground peppercorns, sugar, fresh lime juice, water, and a bottle of Ratlam Rum, courtesy of our friend, whose father owned the rum factory.

Enaus, our cook, and his assistant were the stars for the day, as they mixed the spices and ginger in carefully measured amounts of water and boiled this concoction in a huge *dekchi* for at least an hour. The whole house would fill with the aroma of the spices. This mixture had to cool completely before being strained through a fine muslin cloth. Sugar and lime juice were added, and the whole mixture brought back to the boil and cooked until the sugar melted. Then followed lots of tasting, and adding a little more of this and a little more of that, until Mummy pronounced it just right. The mixture was cooled again. The following day, the rum was added, with more vigorous stirring. Finally, the wine was bottled and stored in a cool, dark place until the sediment settled, leaving the golden liquid we called ginger wine ready to drink.

This winter, we decided it would be a good idea to invite Twinkle and Philo to join us for a ginger wine-making spree, and agreed to double the quantity and share the wine. Twinkle said she would bring the recipe and all the ingredients since we were planning to use our kitchen, and Philo offered to bring the invaluable Maria to help out in the kitchen because both Annapurna, our cook, and Chipu, the supervisor[17], are teetotalers and have never tasted any liquor.

We planned to start at nine in the morning but Twinkle was late and, when she arrived, she was empty-handed.

"Where are the ingredients?" I asked.

"What ingredients? Was I supposed to bring the ingredients? I thought I was to bring the recipe, and you would supply the rest. Here is the recipe. Oh dear, did I forget to put it in my handbag? Never mind. I know it by heart. I have made it many times before. I must warn you that each time it turns out different. I don't know why."

"It doesn't matter, Twinkle," I said. "Chipu will go to Chaturlal's on his motorbike, and he will buy all fresh ingredients. In the meanwhile, we will get the rest of the preparations taken care of."

Philo had never made ginger wine and was excited and delighted to be included. She came sailing in with Maria, apologizing that she could not actually stand over the stove (two gas rings embedded in a stainless steel stand and fed by bottled gas).

We sat in a semicircle near Daphne's bed, sipping tea while Twinkle—making sure everything was exactly right—inspected the large, stainless-steel *dekchis*, the strong wooden ladles for stirring, and the colander and muslin for straining the wine. She also ensured that 12 wine bottles with caps were washed and dried in the sun. Twinkle is a retired schoolteacher and a venerable 80-plus in age, so she expects her orders to be carried out exactly. Philo is our cousin, and we can trace our friendship back to our first day of kindergarten at the railway school. She is a great storyteller. She was widowed at a very early age and left to feed, educate, and nurture seven children. She interweaves her tales of hardship, faith, love, good fortune, and hard work—always hard work—with humour, saying that none of her accomplishments would have been possible without "the Grace of God".

Chipu returned with the ingredients and emptied his shopping bag onto the dining table so we could inspect everything. The first job was to peel the ginger root—a mammoth undertaking, which required " all hands on deck". Annapurna collected the spices, sat on the floor in front of the grinding stone, and began pounding them, adding small sections of ginger to make a thick paste. Chipu whispered to Maria that it would take too long to extract the juice of 50 small limes with a hand juicer, so he coaxed her into allowing him to cut them in quarters, place them in the blender and strain the juice. Mummy would never have allowed such a short cut. But I let it go, even though I was certain this would affect the taste of the wine.

When all the ingredients were ready, Twinkle presided over the procedure of mixing the paste with water and instructed them to boil this mixture for an hour. While we waited, Twinkle rambled on about recent events at the English-medium school where she retains the title of (honorary) principal. She has had a long and distinguished career as a teacher for 50 years—in England, and at the local railway school and convent. When she retired, she started a modest, one-room kindergarten in her home, which has blossomed into a bustling high school administered by her family.

Daphne listened attentively even though she has heard these stories many times before. She remains an excellent listener, and that is why she is never alone. She is always available for those who need to talk, to be reassured, to have a chance to sort out problems. Since Daphne is confined to her bed due to her illness, she is an anchor to which everyone can cling.

Chipu announced the mixture had boiled and was ready to cool. While waiting, we were served lunch: a bowl of homemade vegetable soup, cheese sandwiches, and tuna salad sandwiches (a new treat I introduced). I knew our guests loved this kind of diet, which brought back memories of our youth, and was a welcome change from the usual *dâl*, rice, and vegetable lunch. I unwrapped a chocolate bar, and each of us had two squares (the favourite dessert of all time). Chipu brought steaming cups of milky coffee to keep us awake because we were all accustomed to a nap after lunch.

After a while, Maria reported that the mixture was cool enough to strain through the muslin cloth over a colander. Everything else was ready. Just then Baby Girl, Philo's youngest sister, arrived from Mumbai (Bombay). She'd made the trip because she had heard from their brothers that we were making ginger wine.

"I had to come and see what you are doing," she said. "We never made ginger wine in our home, not like you 'la-di-dahs.' We were too poor. Mummy had to feed and clothe eight of us on Daddy's small army pension. All I remember was that we made the best of whatever we had, and we managed to stay together and support each other, just as we do now. The good times began when I married my beloved Buster. He was a good husband and a loving father, and I am so thankful that he—God rest his soul—left me comfortably off, and I can maintain two homes. Both the children are married and happy. What more do I want in life?"

We invited her to join us for coffee, and she said she had a little time so would wait to taste the wine when it was ready.

"Why don't you settle down here now that your children are married?" asked Twinkle. "You have such a good voice, and you know all the hymns—you would be a great asset to our choir. The Indian Christians are taking over everything these days; there are so few Anglo-Indians left. These Kerala priests want to replace the English Mass on Sundays with another in Hindi because, they say, the congregation is mostly Hindi-speaking now. We must stand firm and fight for our heritage, our language, our customs."

"Oh, Aunty Twinkle, things are changing these days," replied Baby Girl. "We have to move with the times. My daughter has married a Hindu boy and speaks Hindi with her in-laws. When they have children, I am sure they will be equally comfortable in Hindi and English. Even today, during the talk shows on TV, the hosts speak 'Hinglish[18]', and most people understand perfectly what is being said. Our newspapers do the same thing, and so do the films. Philo's girls have married Parsis and Iranis[19], and her grandchildren are good-looking and accomplished and have no difficulty blending into the 'new society.'"

Daphne settled down for her nap, undisturbed by the hum of conversation and the noises emanating from the dining room and the kitchen. Twinkle tasted the cooled and strained mixture, presided over the addition of the lime juice and sugar, and then watched as it was reheated to a full, rolling boil. Chipu kept stirring vigorously, and then lowered the heat to allow the liquid to continue boiling for another half hour.

Twinkle took up the thread of the conversation again. "I know things are changing, Baby Girl. But tell me why my school still has hundreds of Indian children on the waiting list? English is just as important today as it was in the days before Independence. Maybe even more so, as India is sending all her brightest and best to America to work in the high-tech industry. And what about the call centres in the major cities? I hear they have to retrain the young people to speak good English before they can give them jobs handling the telephone calls. And these are all in English, not Hindi or any other Indian language. Look at the fees they are charging at private schools in the hills, where the students are taught in English, graduate in English, and go off to foreign countries for further degrees: always English, only English."

Twinkle paused and her face grew more animated. "Do you want to hear what my dream is—I want to start a lending library so I can encourage students and housewives to read, develop their skills, and broaden their outlook on life. They have public libraries abroad, in England and Australia and America, where people can go and borrow books. Young women need to have some stimulation in their lives besides taking care of their children and families. If they have to keep up with their husbands and children in later years, they must keep on improving themselves, so they will not be forgotten and shoved into the background because they are unable to cope with entertaining and joining in conversations. What about you, Philo? What do you have to say?"

Philo said: "I was widowed when I was 35, with seven children to bring up. It was impossible to manage on the meagre railway pension I received but I was fortunate to be offered the job of matron in a boys' boarding school, and I thank the Good Lord for this; also, the fact that I got the job because I was educated in English. My children were all educated in Anglo-Indian schools."

She went on: "Later, I applied for the job of governess to a wealthy family in the Middle East. I was surprised when I was chosen, and went to live with this family until their children were grown. I accompanied them to London and Paris and many places in Europe before I retired. My children all married well, own their own businesses, and I can choose to live with any one of them. I travel from one child's home to another with Maria, who takes good care of me, especially now that I have trouble walking. But like you, Twinkle, I have a dream: I dream of a simple little house of my own, right here in Ratlam, near my brothers, near my sweet Daphne. I want to return to this place of my birth, to the only real home I have ever known."

It was time to remove the boiling liquid and allow it to cool completely. Twinkle said it should rest quietly overnight, and then we would add the bottle of rum. It was also time for tea and Mhow Baker's Biscuits. We moved to the front compound, where it was pleasant and cool. We were shaded by an ancient neem tree and a curry *patta* tree, and could admire the bougainvillea and poinsettias in full bloom. Chipu had arranged for Jeva—the Bhil[20] odd-job man—to sprinkle the ground with the water saved from the morning's rinse-water after our clothes had been washed. Chipu also assured us that the 12 wine bottles were dry and ready to be filled tomorrow.

I put a cassette of the Mills Brothers and the Inkspots into the tape player, and we tapped our feet and hummed along as we sipped our tea. We spotted Handsome Ricky walking home from the local court, and I invited him to join us. Ricky is as handsome at 70 as when he was a teenager—and doesn't look a day over 50—with beautiful sun-tanned skin, twinkling blue eyes, dimples, and a full head of ash-blonde hair; even his few wrinkles just serve to make him look distinguished. Age has been his friend, not an enemy. Even though none of us would ever want to admit it, his presence makes our lives lighter (and maybe even makes our hearts skip a beat or two).

Ricky retired from the Railways after a very short period of service, and became involved in many start-up businesses, which folded all too soon. A few years ago he decided to represent the poorest railwaymen, who could not afford a lawyer, and at this he proved successful, winning their insurance, accident, and pension claims. He has never had any formal legal training, but he has built up a formidable reputation and has been given a room with food for the rest of his life by one of his grateful clients. Some evenings, he drops by to read some of his briefs to us. I am convinced that the flowery, Victorian English he uses befuddles the judges, who are more comfortable with Hindi.

Ricky had his tea, tasted the lukewarm ginger wine mixture, and commented that it would taste better once we added the rum. As dusk approached, I reluctantly asked Chipu to arrange for auto rickshaws to take our guests home. We said our goodbyes, and I told them I would supervise the addition of the rum and the bottling tomorrow; then we would distribute the wine, which they should take home but allow to mature.

After our guests departed, Daphne and I sat quietly and watched the birds as they flew hither and thither, finally selecting the tree where they would spend the night. I thought of us and our family and friends, in so many ways like the birds, going from one home to the other, hoping to find the most comfortable place to roost. Soon it would be dusk and time to go indoors, before the mosquitoes and other insects took over the night.

The following morning, Twinkle sent the handwritten recipe, copied from her well-used recipe book.

GINGER WINE - 6 bottles
INGREDIENTS
1 *tola*[21] cloves
1 *tola* green cardamoms
50 2-inch cinnamon sticks
4 tablespoons nutmeg, grated
$1/4$-kilo fresh ginger root, ground
Juice of 25 limes
5 bottles water
$3/4$-kilo sugar
1 bottle rum
1 bottle orange juice—make with 1 pkt. *rasna*, for colour

DIRECTIONS
Boil 5 bottles water
Add ground ginger and spices, and simmer for 1 hour
(Boil fast for a few minutes, then very slowly, but it must boil)
Take off the fire, cool, and strain
To this mixture, add the juice of 25 limes and $3/4$-kilo sugar
 and boil again for 30 minutes
Cool and add *rasna* (optional)
Cool for 12 hours
When quite cold, add 1 bottle rum
(If not sweet enough add one cup sugar.)

A week later we met again for the official wine tasting. The sediment had settled and the wine was the colour of light beer. We agreed it was different, not like it was in the past. Too much spice masala? Had our Ratlam water changed over the years? Had we added the rum with too heavy a hand? It also had a slightly bitter aftertaste (those wretched lime skins, I thought). We refilled our glasses several times and drank a number of toasts, and soon the years disappeared and we were re-living our memories with misty eyes.

When Two Worlds Collide

by Lesley-Anne Raymer

Melinda and Morgan were excited. This was the day their Grandmother Naylor was due to arrive from India. They had never met her. They were told their grandmother had visited when they were babies, but they did not remember her at all. All they knew was that she was a "Tartar" when their dad referred to her, and that she was "living in the past" when their mum talked about her. She was their paternal grandmother.

The visit had been intended for years, but what with one thing and another, it had never happened. This year, the 7th World Anglo-Indian Reunion was being held in Toronto, and some of their grandmother's friends were travelling from different parts of the world to attend. This would be her opportunity to see her grandchildren again, as well as meet up with many girlhood friends who had left India all those years ago when the British Raj had come to an end. Many Anglo-Indians, being of mixed European and Indian ancestry, felt forced to choose between remaining in India or moving to Britain, or to Commonwealth countries like Canada and Australia when India became independent. At the age of 75, their grandmother felt that it would be her last chance to see some of her friends.

Melinda was 10 years old and her brother, Morgan, 12. Since their parents had immigrated to Canada before they were born, they had never really known any of their grandparents. They had often speculated on what it would be like to have a grandparent around—someone who would definitely spoil them, and to whom they could turn with complaints about their parents. However, when they voiced these opinions to their parents, their father told them that his mother was as stern and strict as when he was a boy, and even advancing age had not caused her to abandon the high principles she had always possessed. A nurse by training, when she was younger she had worked in a boarding school as the matron, or school nurse.

The time came for them to leave for the airport to meet their grandmother. They travelled to Toronto's Pearson International Airport dressed in their Sunday best. Their mother said Nana would not countenance anything less. At the airport, they waited anxiously. Grandmother Naylor finally walked through the Arrivals door, and they had their first glimpse of her. There she was: plump smiling face, large blue eyes, iron-grey hair, dressed in a pale, pink pantsuit, with a matching pearl necklace and earrings. She held out her arms, their mother pushed them towards her, and she enveloped them in a big, comfy hug. This was nice, they thought, just what they imagined a grandmother would be.

When they got home, she handed out various gifts she had brought with her. One of the gifts was a black, gooey sweet, called *dol-dol*. They weren't very keen about eating the funny-looking stuff, but their parents exclaimed with delight and gobbled it up, saying that it brought back fond memories. So far, they were very happy to meet Nana. They kissed her good night as she was very tired and needed to rest.

The next morning they came down dressed for school. They were both wearing jeans. Melinda had put on her favourite hoop earrings to show off to Nana, and Morgan was decked out in his huge soccer T-shirt. Nana was downstairs drinking her first cup of tea. She looked at them and asked why they were not dressed for school. When they told her they were ready for school, a look of shock came over her face. She looked at their mum and wanted to know how they were allowed to go to school wearing big hoop earrings and "ill-fitting" sports T-shirts. In her day, children wore a starched and ironed uniform, with hair neatly tied up, and no jewellery of any kind. A scruffy appearance—implying that's what she thought of *their* appearance—would lose them marks on their report cards and for their House, which usually resulted in being pulled up before the House Captain. The blue eyes peering over her glasses were not twinkling kindly at all. Their mum said that in Canada they were allowed to dress this way for school because they did not have a uniform and, in *sotto voce*, said that some of the other kids dressed even more scruffily.

As the days went by, Nana had long chats with Melinda and Morgan. She told them about their Anglo-Indian heritage. She lamented the fact that their generation did not seem to know what it was to be Anglo-Indian—this with a sideways glance at their parents, as if somehow it was their fault. She advised them to work hard and not become "wasters" like so many of the "Byculla loafers". She told Melinda not to be giddy and to "keep her head on her shoulders". Mother was not at all happy to hear her say this, as Melinda had a spontaneous, bubbly laugh, and her mother did not believe she needed to change that. Grandmother took their father to task for not keeping a closer eye on who the children mixed with—some of their friends did not look the "right type". For example, the one who was "black as the ace of spades" and who wore those gaudy clothes.

Mother shushed Nana when she said that, telling her that in Canada people do not make such comments about other people. She explained that the friend was of Jamaican origin and in her culture it was customary to dress that way—we have to accept that Canada has different kinds of people living in it. Nana sniffed but was somewhat mollified to hear that at least the friend was Christian. One of her fears for her own daughter had been that she would get mixed up with and marry a Hindu, who would make her take a Hindu name and then look down on her because she was not a full-blooded Indian. Marrying a Mohammedan was definitely beyond the pale—he would go off and have four wives, and where would that leave her daughter? As it was, her daughter had married a Goan boy, and while that was not as good as marrying an Anglo-Indian, at least he was a good Catholic and spoke English.

The children had no idea that their grandmother felt this way about people who were not Anglo-Indian, although they later learned it was fairly typical of her generation. They continued to bring their friends home to play: friends who came from different backgrounds and different faiths, and as Nana watched them interact together, she came to like their friends because there seemed to be little difference between them and her grandchildren. Back in India, every community seemed entrenched in its customs and ways, and viewed any change as something negative or as "giving ground"; it was different here in Canada. While the children noticed the differences in each other and commented on them, they put these aside and came up with their own sets of rules on how to interact with one another. Perhaps, thought Grandmother Naylor, her daughter-in-law was right when she said that immigrating to a country like Canada allowed everyone to keep their most cherished traditions while reaching out to embrace other traditions as well. No one felt overwhelmed by one tradition because there were so many different traditions, and everyone shared a little bit of each.

However, when it came to Melinda and Morgan, Nana seemed to disapprove of almost everything they wore, said, and did. She was always telling them to stand up straight so that they did not develop a "*dhobi's* bundle". Her rules on table manners seemed rigid and unnecessary. What was the point of a table setting that included a knife and quarter plate when they did not use either? As far as the children were concerned, all that was needed was a spoon, fork, plate, and glass. Nana refused to see the logic of this and went on about maintaining certain standards. She did not approve of them "back-chatting", as she called it, when all they were doing was telling their side of the story. They began to keep out of her way.

One day their mother found them skulking in their rooms and asked what was wrong. They told her that they did not want to go downstairs as their grandmother obviously did not like them. Their mother smiled and said that it was because their grandmother loved them that she was so hard on them. They still thought it was grossly unfair that grandmother kept trying to impose her standards on them. Things came to a crisis when grandmother, mother, and father told them they would have to attend one of the events of the Reunion. They were aghast. Waste an entire precious day of their summer holidays in a room with strange people— probably all like Nana? Mother tried to explain that this was an opportunity for them to be amongst Anglo-Indians of all hues, and from different parts of the globe, but this did not allay their fears. Mother then offered the bribe of taking them shopping the next day, and only then did they reluctantly agree to go.

The day dawned, they had to dress up again, and off they all went to the symposium, which was being held at the Pavilion Royale in Mississauga. They entered a room full of people who dressed and spoke in ways very similar to their parents and grandmother. Everyone was very friendly and paid lots of attention to Melinda and Morgan, looking at them up and down, and exclaiming on how Anglo-Indian they looked, etc. Then Grandmother met her friends and dragged Melinda and Morgan off to meet them, too. Her friends kissed them, patted their heads, and told them their grandmother talked about them all the time and was very proud of them. They were astounded to hear Nana telling her friends that Melinda played the piano very well, had a voice like an angel, and was taking down all her mother's Anglo-Indian recipes. Morgan, they were told, was a whiz at mathematics, just like his grandfather, and the family hoped he would have the opportunity to go on to university.

Melinda and Morgan could not believe that this same grandmother, who was always nagging and correcting them at home, had obviously observed and was very proud of their accomplishments. They realized that she did love them very much, just like their mother had said. They felt more relaxed, and began to mingle and listen in on the conversations of their community members, and slowly they began to feel a sense of belonging— all these people knew their ways, knew their history, were proud to be different, were proud to be Anglo-Indian. They knew the shortcomings of "Anglos" but chose to focus on the strengths and achievements of the community.

The next day, Melinda and Morgan went back to wearing their usual clothes, and their usual Canadian habits of talking on the phone and e-mailing and MSN-ing their friends. But, thanks to Nana, their parents could see they now also understood a little of the world their grandmother came from, and that a little seed of appreciation was planted. Their parents hoped that as the children grew older, that seed would take root and burgeon into the trees and branches of the next generation of Anglo-Indians, who would take pride in preserving their ways, history, and culture while integrating seamlessly into the mainstream of Canadian society.

What's in a name?

by Marina Stubbs

Dad and Mum wanted me to call the woman next door Aunty. They said it was the right thing to do. I had a horrible, prickly feeling when I thought of it. I wanted to listen to Mum and Dad, but it didn't *feel* right. Dad said it would show my "respect", and it was rude not to. I was used to being reminded about respect. My world was full of real aunts and uncles, as well as Mum and Dad's friends. When talking to grown-ups, I had to make sure that I said "Hello", "Thank you", or "Goodbye", followed by their title, loudly enough for Dad to hear, or I would have to say it all over again.

The woman next door had the most amazing hair. Its soft, blue curls were so much more interesting than Nana's hair, which was a dull grey. I asked Mum if I would have hair like that when I was old, but she just laughed. Our neighbour liked to keep up with gossip and talked to anyone with the time to listen. She would chat to Dad about the best plants for the shady patch, and share seeds for the large, tall flowers she grew on the back wall. They had a really long name that sounded a bit like a posh girl. I called them Delfis. With Mum, she would discuss the comings and goings of strange men at No. 21, and the disgrace of a garden at No. 11. I had plenty of chats with her on my own. She told me about the fun she'd had in the war; how she'd learnt to drive a bus, danced the night away with American soldiers, and drawn lines on her legs when she didn't have stockings. Best of all, she listened and remembered and never asked boring questions about school.

If she saw me in the garden, she would call in her raspy voice: "Jenny! I've got something for you." She would lean over the fence, pulling sweets from a pocket of her overalls.

"Thank you," I would say, and beam at her, pretending more enthusiasm than I felt. They were always those jewel-coloured boiled ones that looked better than they tasted. They would glisten orange, yellow, and green in my hand, and were sticky in their cellophane. We had quite a collection indoors.

Every evening, the smells of her dinner drifted out; earthy smells of cabbage, boiled potato, and sometimes the sour stink of kidneys for a pie. She slammed her back door when Mum was cooking. There was always a smell of frying onions and spices coming from our house, and when Mum threw the vinegar on, it was sharp and stinging enough to choke. Not as bad as the days Mum cooked salt fish. When I was really little, I used to run upstairs and bury my head under a pillow, desperate to escape the stink, shutting my eyes tight to stop them watering. The smell burnt into you. Mum wore special clothes to cook salt-fish. She always did it in the morning so she could have a bath afterwards. Just as well no one came round: she looked very strange dressed in her cotton nightie and an old beige anorak, with the hood up. Sometimes she tucked her hair into the bright-red, velvet beret that Nana had given me one Christmas. I was a bit cross about that. Mum would let me have a piece of the salt-fish with each meal. It had to be rationed; she didn't want to cook it every day. I would pop it into my mouth and suck the juices out: salt, vinegar, tomato, onions, and fish flavours oozing over my tongue—and a big smile on my face.

I suppose calling our neighbour Aunty would be a very Indian thing to do. We're not Indian, though. We're Anglo- Indian. It's very difficult to explain. I try to avoid it because people don't want a long explanation, and I'm a bit confused myself. They always ask me: "So is it your Mum that's English or your Dad?"

I wish it was as easy as that. All I know is that I had an English great-granddad with red hair! I expect Anglo-Indian people married Anglo-Indian people, and it got a bit muddled. Anyway, I was born in England. Mum and Dad came over on a big Italian ship, all the way from India. Sounds like one of those cruises that Louise at school's Gran went on. But Mum said it was horrible. All she can remember is cornflakes, slimy spaghetti, and being so sick they had to give her an injection. When she got here, it was so cold that she had to wear all her clothes and a blanket indoors.

I don't know when Dad decided it was important for me to call her Aunty. I'd managed to avoid calling her anything for a long time, even in front of Dad. Maybe he just stood and listened one day and decided that it had gone too far. It was too familiar, too disrespectful; too "chatty" for a child. There was no point in trying to argue with Dad. He made the rules, and I wasn't allowed to break them. I didn't think that my friends called their neighbours Aunty, but if I'd have told Dad that, he'd have said that he wasn't interested in what my friends had to say.

It was all right for a while. I managed to avoid seeing her. I waited for her to go inside before I took the washing out, and hid in my room or the toilet when she was chatting to Mum and Dad. Early one morning, I heard her shopping trolley on the path. I looked out of my bedroom window. She was moving slowly, huffing and puffing across the green. The trolley, a round wicker basket on wheels, creaked behind her. We loved that trolley. Usually, if we bumped into her, she would let us take turns to pull it. Once, she even let Mark sit inside it. I knew she would be going the same way as Mark and I. But I couldn't make any excuses. We had to go to school, and I was going to have to overtake her. What harm could it do? I asked myself. I tried to ignore the sick feeling in my tummy.

Running past her wasn't an option. She might tell Dad that we ignored her, so I walked as slowly and quietly as I could behind her. Mark twisted his feet so they faced opposite directions, perfecting his silly walk. It did not slow us down as much as I would have liked. At the same time, he fired loud, fast, boring maths questions at me. I didn't want to waste time thinking about them. My head hurt. I threw him an answer to shut him up: "It's eight."

"Eight…eight…you said eight. You got it wrong!" His voice was piercing, and she heard.

"I haven't seen you for a while, dear. I miss chatting to you. Your Dad says you have such a lot of homework. Don't work too hard. You've got to have a little fun."

Somehow, I managed to smile and nod at her.

"I'm better at maths than Jenny," crowed Mark, "and she's older than me!"

"That's very nice, dear." She knew him well enough to know that this would be enough. "Wait a minute, I'm a bit out of breath today. Do you think you could pull this for me for a bit?"

Before I could say anything, Mark grabbed the trolley handle and raced along the path ahead of us. I caught her eye, and we giggled.

"Boys!" she said. "Ah, that reminds me," reaching into her pocket, "I've saved these for you." She squeezed a sticky mass of boiled sweets into my hand.

My voice came quietly at first. "Thank you…," and then the word exploded loudly, "Aunty."

Her eyes widened and then her lips twitched. "Why ever would you call me that dear?"

I could feel my face burning hot. I couldn't look at her. My voice seemed small and far away. "Dad said it was the right thing to do."

"Well, much as I'd like you to be my niece, I'm not your Aunty. You can call me Mrs. Carpenter. We'll get along just as well as we've always done."

Reflections

A Calcutta Christmas

by Robyn Andrews

This article is an adaptation of a paper I presented at the "Reaching Out" forum, which was run alongside the 7th World Anglo-Indian Reunion, held in Toronto in August, 2007. This forum aimed to highlight the plight of very poor Anglo-Indians in Calcutta[22] (now Kolkata), and the work being done by CAISS (the Calcutta Anglo-Indian Service Society) to alleviate this situation. In my view, it's imperative to include, as part of these triennial Reunions—officially or not—a forum to discuss the situation of, and some solutions for, impoverished Anglo-Indians in India. To my knowledge, this forum, and a writers' lunch organized by Blair Williams, were the only events in which these significant issues were addressed.

I was pleased to be invited to present a paper; it felt appropriate because my academic research began, in a roundabout way, as a result of the poverty of Anglo-Indians in Calcutta. I first came to know about Anglo-Indians after my family had sponsored various children at Dr. Graham's Home, in Kalimpong, for almost 20 years. I was a pretty lackadaisical sponsor. I sent money whenever it was due, in order to meet the responsibility we'd taken on, but I hardly kept in contact with the sponsored children. When I finally met one of these children, Lisa[23], and her family, I was enormously relieved to find that she came from a very loving and supportive family; all they really needed from me was the money we'd been sending. This is relevant so I'll come back to it later.

First of all, though, I'd like to share some of my experiences of poverty in Calcutta. I'll begin by focusing on Christmas Day, 2005, my first Christmas in Calcutta. My partner, Keith, and I began our day with breakfast with some local street children, followed by attending mass.

In Calcutta, poverty is endemic; it's neither the preserve of Anglo-Indians, nor non-Anglo-Indians. So on Christmas day, of all the days of the year, and with our own children a long way away, we wanted to spend a bit of time with several (non-Anglo-Indian) children who lived on the streets close to where we were staying. We'd bought them new clothes for Christmas, and they wore these for the first time (after bathing in the local rainwater tank) for our breakfast together. We hardly recognized them: we'd seen them in the same set of clothes, day after day, so they looked quite different; they seemed happy that we thought so. After breakfast, they came to mass with us—not as part of any deal we made with them. Perhaps they came in case they could get something else out of us—and who can criticize them for that?

Later, after making phone calls home to our children, we took a taxi to an Anglo-Indian friend's home to celebrate with Christmas lunch. Other guests were also invited, including two writers, a photographer, and several other well-educated and modestly successful local Anglo-Indians. We enjoyed a very convivial lunch, with great food: roast meat and vegetables, followed by plum pudding and brandy sauce, and a bit of wine. Afterwards, we sat around and relaxed before going out to visit. Just before we were to leave, there was a knock on the door. A young woman and her two well-turned-out children entered. The woman had come to wish our hostess a happy Christmas. It was obviously going to be a short visit, and after a quick cup of tea the trio left, each with a bag of Christmas treats. I was then told her story.

This woman was Anglo-Indian. She was wearing a sari because of where she lives: an hour's bus trip away, in a Muslim-dominated *bustee* or slum, with the Anglo-Indian father of her children. He, an alcoholic with no regular employment and with the likelihood of dying soon of an alcohol-related illness, was refusing to marry her. Because he wouldn't marry her (and make his relationship to the children unambiguous), these children are not recognized as Anglo-Indian under the Indian Constitution. Things are bad for them now, but as long as he's alive there's the chance he will do the right thing by them all. But what will happen to his family when he dies if he hasn't married this woman? They will be in the same boat as millions of other impoverished families in India without a breadwinner. But it needn't be this way, for her or for her children, if the Indian Constitution would recognize her children as Anglo-Indian. The definition of an Anglo-Indian, as stated in the Constitution reads:

> An Anglo-Indian means a person whose father or any of whose other male progenitors in the male line is or was of European descent but who is domiciled within the territory of India and is or was born within such

territory of parents habitually resident therein and not established there for temporary purposes only.
(Section 366 (2) of 1935 Government of India Act)

Were it not for the gender bias of the Constitutional definition, these two children would qualify for all the usual benefits which may be awarded to (Constitution-defined) Anglo-Indians, such as admission to Anglo-Indian schools, scholarships for education, and grants of various kinds—in other words, the difference between a life of poverty, and the chance to live a respectable life with some choices and dignity. For me, the frustrating aspect of this story was that it's because of an out-of-date piece of man-made legislation that these (and how many other?) Anglo-Indian children are being denied the chances they should be entitled to by birthright[23].

At the time the definition was drafted, it reflected the history of the community, and because of the marriage patterns of the time it didn't disadvantage anyone—but the situation has changed. Many Anglo-Indians are now marrying outside of the community, whereas in the past, the marriage pattern was endogamous. When an Anglo-Indian man marries a non-Anglo-Indian woman, any children they have are Anglo-Indian, regardless of the ways in which they are brought up. But the children of an Anglo-Indian woman married to a non-Anglo-Indian man are not. If the definition of Anglo-Indians in the Indian Constitution is changed, so that children born of Anglo-Indian mothers can share the same advantages as those born of Anglo-Indian fathers, children such as those I met on this Christmas day would stand some chance. Their future would be a lot more hopeful.

It seems to me that Anglo-Indians are impoverishing themselves by continuing with this outdated definition. As well as the sorts of consequences that I've illustrated, there is another type of poverty here too: that of being denied one's identity.

Turning back to what we did that Christmas day: After this woman's visit, we went out with our hostess with some food parcels of roast meat sandwiches, Rosa cookies, *kul kuls*, and other traditional Anglo-Indian Christmas treats. We walked down narrow alleys and up dusty staircases, and over the course of the next few hours visited several Anglo-Indian women, as well as the CAISS-run night shelter. I'll describe a couple of these visits to give you some idea of the reality of the poverty we saw.

One woman we visited that afternoon was paralysed and completely bedridden. She was probably in her early seventies and in poor physical and emotional shape. She couldn't do much for herself but is lucky enough to be looked after, on a day-to-day basis, by her Muslim neighbours. But she said she'd had no visits or messages from her family on this day, Christmas day, and that she was ready to die. She seemed to have cheered up a bit by the time we left—especially after our hostess gently joked with her, without negating her plight, and gave her a hug.

Another woman we visited had advanced emphysema. She was not quite 70 years old but was so emaciated she looked closer to 90. In soft light, she looked elegant, in fact quite beautiful, but we sat on chairs with springs poking out of the fabric, dirt and squalor everywhere, with a kitchen we didn't want to examine too closely. She was embarrassed that she didn't have the makings for a cup of tea to offer us. We sat and talked with her for a while, and she spoke of her time in London, before she came back to Calcutta to nurse her dying father, leaving a fiancé behind (she never married). She spoke in an educated, refined manner, illustrating so well that she had seen better days. For me, this was a very distressing visit. The contrast between the way she spoke and held herself, and the conditions in which she lived, were so marked. It was a most devastating essay in poverty to witness someone, who obviously deserved better, living the life she was now.

Another stop we made was at the night shelter. This was set up by CAISS for homeless, elderly Anglo-Indians living on the streets. There might be other options for them, such as moving into an Anglo-Indian seniors' home, but for one reason or another they chose to spend their days independently (a choice many in the West would make, too), and their nights in the safety of the shelter. They arrive before nightfall, are given a good evening meal, have the use of a bathroom, have a clean bed to sleep in, and are given breakfast before they leave for the day. To stay here, they have to be drug- and alcohol-free. The reason I mention the details of this place is to make the point that there is a shelter for homeless because there *are* homeless Anglo-Indians, and that has to be about poverty.

While I had seen the living conditions of very poor Anglo-Indians before, which I'll discuss further shortly, because this was Christmas day the plight of these people seemed particularly poignant.

One response from the community in Calcutta to this type of poverty is CAISS, and it's an outstanding response, directed by an outstanding woman and her very active and capable team. They are more than just a dispersal point for the money sent by overseas sponsors through organizations such as CTR; they also provide caring, supportive, human contact. Over the years I've been involved with Calcutta's Anglo-Indian community, I've had a bit to do with CAISS: whenever I visit Calcutta, I catch up with Philomena Eaton, their convener, and attend various events. I have observed (and helped out a bit) on days when CAISS distributes rations and pensions, and at their Christmas party, which more than 900 Anglo-Indians attended. I've also accompanied CAISS members when they've visited Anglo-Indians living in Tiljallah, a Muslim-dominated *bustee*. In this quarter, people are forced to make do with the most minimal of amenities. In many of the homes, there are five or six people living in one room—sometimes three generations of the same family. Most have no running water but instead share a single toilet and cramped washing facilities with a number of other families, which poses real risks, for young girls especially.

One of the striking differences between the lonely, elderly women we visited on Christmas day, and the families I've visited and come to know in Tiljallah, was that those in Tiljallah were mostly pretty hopeful; not necessarily for themselves but at least for their children. And in my view, they have reason to hope—I saw children studying hard (in cramped, noisy conditions, with few resources). I met one young girl, for example, who's determined to be a doctor. She currently receives a sponsored education, which includes full board for the nine months of each year when she's at school—thus providing for her physical safety as well as her education. She has every chance of doing what she dreams of; she's bright, and her family fully supports her. As well as looking after the day-to-day wellbeing of elderly Anglo-Indians, CAISS keeps an eye on children and young adults such as this young woman, and ensures that they get any break that becomes available.

What so many Anglo-Indians lack are the financial resources to be educated, to gain credentials, to obtain a profession; that is, to make a positive difference to their future and that of others. This is where Anglo-Indians abroad (and non-Anglo-Indians) can help—by sending money to CAISS. A few dollars a week, or even a month, from Western currencies still goes a long way in India. In the same way that I was relieved that Lisa, the girl I sponsored, had a loving and supportive family to provide the non-material essentials, people who send money to help poor Anglo-Indians through CAISS can rest assured that it will be distributed in a fair and caring way, and that the recipients will be treated with dignity.

Along with rations, pensions, scholarships, medical care, and everything else that they do, CAISS members distribute the non-material necessities of warmth and humour, and as anyone who has seen them at work will tell you, always in God's name.

Close Families in Chennai

by Lionel Caplan

PROLOGUE   During the 1990s, I made three trips to Chennai (then still called Madras) for social anthropological research. In the course of these visits—which lasted between two and four months each—I met representatives of several hundred families, some of them more than once. In what follows, I present excerpts from conversations with members of two of these domestic groups occupying very different positions on the socio-economic spectrum. While our talks ranged over a variety of issues, one which kept recurring—and which I want to focus on here—was a concern with the responsibility close kin feel (or should feel) for each other. Since these conversations were recorded and transcribed, they provide a brief glimpse into the ways in which the value of family bonds is expressed and demonstrated among Anglo-Indians in contemporary Chennai. Their remarks have been edited only to eliminate repetition and digressions, in order to preserve the authentic voice and unique phraseology of the speakers. Names have been changed to protect the families' identities. My own comments are italicized.

Elvin and Teresa Martin
In 1992, when I was first introduced to the Martins, they were in their seventies. I learned that Elvin, after completing four years' schooling, became an apprentice mechanic, then joined the army during World War II, and afterwards became a lorry driver. But he only ever had irregular work. Teresa had a similar amount of education but never had a job. She was unwell when we met, so I interviewed Elvin on his own. They were living in a residential home for elderly and mainly indigent Anglo-Indians. They have seven children (four boys and three girls). Only two managed to complete high school and live comfortable lives. The rest struggle to make ends meet.

Elvin: My father had a small job with the Madras Corporation and we lived in his quarters. We were five brothers and sisters, all in one room. When he died, we had to leave the quarters and we shifted to a hut near my sister, Sandra, who was already married. That's how I got in contact with my wife [Teresa]; she was living with her brother, who was Sandra's husband. We married and had our children. But trying to maintain a house is hard without steady income. After coming here [to the residential home], I find it much better. I have a little rest here. Duncan [his eldest son] and his wife [Brenda] worried [urged] us to come and stay with them, but I refused. We don't like staying with anybody; we always lived an independent life. Here we move about freely, or we sit and chat. When we go out, we visit our children. Our daughter, Lorraine, in Australia, keeps in touch with us [by] letter. Now and again she phones us here or sends help. She keeps close to us.

Elvin's sister Sandra, who is 80, lives in a tiny hut with mud and stone walls and a thatched roof, without a toilet or running water. Her granddaughter, Audrey, cooks and cares for her.

Audrey: My mother left my father to live with another man but didn't take me with her. So Sandra, my father's mother, brought me up, even though she had children of her own. She had 10 children, but only four came big [survived to adulthood]. She was like a mother to me, so I come here every day, bringing food, and help her any way I can.

I knew many Anglo-Indians in Chennai who had been brought up by grandparents, and it would have been frowned on if the recipients of such care in childhood had neglected the older caregivers when they themselves became adults.

The Martin Children
All but two of Elvin and Teresa's seven children have irregular work or none at all, and lead lives of extreme hardship alongside the poor of other communities in Chennai's many slum colonies. One son, Ronald, a cycle-rickshaw driver, lives with his [non-Anglo-Indian] wife and two children in a small hut, consisting of a single room, which they rent for Rs.30 a month. He gave lack of education as the reason for his own and his siblings' difficult circumstances.

Ronald: Till second standard I studied. I didn't fail. Simply, I was not interested in going to school. I was eight years old. They'll send me to school, but I don't go. I go roaming about. Soon as I see my daddy or my older brother [Duncan], I'll run off, because they see me, they'll hit [punish] me. [Also] We never listened to our mummy, and spoiled our life. If we had listened to her, we would be nice now. My sisters [Andrea and Debbie], too, they won't study. Only Duncan and Lorraine [his sister abroad] studied nicely, and they have a good life. Not the rest of us. We didn't stay in the house, won't go to school, only rounded [went] about.

I left home when I was 10 years old. From then, I'm starting to drive a rickshaw. Until last year, I was paying rent for the cycle; I'll drive and pay the rent [to the owner]. I can't say how much I earn. One day Rs. 5, one day Rs. 50. Last year my sister Lorraine came down to Madras and bought one cycle [-rickshaw] for me and one for my [younger] brother Earl, so now we don't pay rent. Rs. 1500 for each she paid. Why she gave? She's our sister, *na*? When she comes to Madras, she comes to see us. She may send something at Christmas.

My brother Duncan used to help us before he got married, but after getting children he doesn't help so much. [But] if he comes here to see us, he'll give us anything [something].

Ronald's older sister, Andrea, lives in a nearby slum colony, in a hut with only part of a roof. She is a widow now, but was married for 27 years to a Hindu Adi-Dravida (AD).[25] She survives, like many women in the area, by borrowing money to purchase cinema tickets and selling them "on the black".

Andrea: My father and mother never put me in school. I don't know why. My own [three] children, I put them in Corporation school, but they joined with all the boys and girls and didn't study. A slum area, you know. My sons are good, if they have money they'll give me Rs. 5. When my father comes to see Debbie he'll come to see me too. But he won't help, how can he?

Her sister Debbie who, when I first met her, was homeless, living "on the platform"[26] with her young son, in a makeshift hut in a field among several busy roads.

Debbie: Thank God I put my daughter in the Centre[27]. She's saved.

My husband left me seven years ago with two children. He wasn't Anglo-Indian. An Anglo-Indian won't behave like that. My parents told me not to marry him. If we listen to our parents, we have a nice life.

From four years old until I was 16 I stayed in St. George's [school and orphanage for Anglo-Indians]. But I failed 8th standard, twice. And they sent me out. I played too much and didn't study. Now we're starving. If I haven't got anything, I'll go to my mummy and daddy, they'll give me some bread.

Lorraine [her sister in New Zealand] doesn't write or do anything for me. She doesn't keep in touch. When I asked her why, she said, "What's the use? If I write to you telling you my problems, and if you write to me you're telling me your problems. What's the use?" When she came down to Madras some months back, she said she isn't working over there [New Zealand], only her husband is working, so she has to ask his permission before she can help me. But he has brothers who need help, too, because they are not doing well in life, so they [Lorraine and her husband] can't help me. But Duncan [her older brother], when he gets his salary he'll come; he'll give Rs. 10 [to] me, Ronald, Earl, daddy, everybody. He'll give and go. But she [Duncan's wife] went and fought with Duncan's manager, and now she collects his salary, so he can't give it all away. They are rich, so they'll always have fights about [his generosity towards] us.

Duncan and his wife, Brenda, both employed and earning good salaries, had just purchased a flat in a suburb of Chennai popular with middle class Anglo-Indians. When I visited Duncan's family at their new home, the topic turned to raising children. Duncan was silent, but Brenda had strong views on parental responsibility for the children's upbringing.

Brenda: I am trying to make a good future for my children. If parents leave them without firm guidance they get mixed up. Everything depends on the woman of the house. She has to be very strong. That's what I'm doing in my own house. You say no, it means no. Yes means yes. The husband should also check them when they do wrong. They say abroad children do what they want. If you try to check them, they say we'll call the police! Here, the children listen to us [*laughs, obviously thinking of her husband's siblings, and adds*] sometimes.

[As for helping out less fortunate members of the family] when you're a little better and somebody's a little down, you should help out. If we have 10 [of anything], we can give them one. We can try and get them a job, and with that they can try to manage. If they come and worry us, we [tell them] we have our own families. On my side, my sisters and brothers are all middle [-income earners], so we don't go to each other [to ask for help]. On my husband's side, there are big differences, so how can he help them all? Yet he's doing it for years. He helps them because he knows I'm here to look after our children. But they should also try to move up. They don't want to work, I think they're lazy.

I returned to Chennai in 1996, by which time Teresa (Elvin's wife) had died. When I met Debbie, Ronald, and Earl, the big news was the wedding of their brother, Duncan, and Brenda's daughter. It involved, as is the custom among middle class Anglo-Indians, a church service followed by a reception in the local railway institute, which can accommodate large numbers of guests.

Debbie: Duncan came and told [invited] us. We all went. Daddy, too, was there.
Ronald: Both of us [Ronald and Earl] went. We put on pant and shirt only, no coat and suit. We didn't go with our wives. They're Indians [Hindu Adi-Dravidas]. They won't dress up nice [*i.e., they are too poor to afford good saris or frocks favoured by some Anglo-Indians*]. Then brother [Duncan] will have a bad name. They'll think bad of us. [As a gift] we gave one silver plate and a small cup. I gave one set and he [Earl] gave one set. We had lunch there, evening 6 o'clock; and after, dancing with band. I know to dance, but I won't dance there.
Debbie: I never ate anything. I came late, and not a piece of cake she [Brenda] gave.

When Debbie left us, Ronald and Earl mentioned the wedding of Debbie's daughter two years' previously. They were obviously offended at not being invited.

Earl: We didn't go; Debbie didn't call us. She didn't tell us anything. Not like Duncan, who came to tell us. So we don't know who went. We didn't see which place the wedding happened. Our own sister.

We stayed quiet [didn't mention it].

On another occasion, Debbie intimated that since the bride and groom were from equally poor families, the wedding was a very simple affair. With the death of their mother, Teresa, their father Elvin is on his own in the residential home for the elderly.

Ronald: We go see daddy sometimes; he's alone now. Duncan goes, Debbie will go, our oldest sister Andrea goes. Lorraine will phone [from abroad]. Once in a while, daddy will come to see us here. "I'm all right," he'll say, and go. None of us can afford to look after him, so he's better off in the home.

For the Martins, the majority of whom are among the poorest members of the community, living in makeshift housing and on the economic margins, close family ties are expressed through frequent visiting and cash gifts, from the few with the means to give to those who are in need. Stresses are evident where such kinds of generosity are neglected or refused, or where counter-claims on scarce resources are made by those related through marriage—most commonly, brothers- or sisters-in-law.

Marie and Clarence Fernandez

When I first met them in 1991, Marie was 65 and Clarence 10 years older. Like so many Anglo-Indians of his generation, Clarence was employed on the Railways (and has a pension), while Marie worked as a secretary before marriage, and for a time after it, in one of the largest companies in the city (Binny's). They have nine children (two boys and seven girls), all of whom are high school graduates. Three live abroad—one son and two daughters—while one son and a son-in-law work in high-paying jobs in the Gulf [28]. *By Anglo-Indian standards in Chennai, they are comfortably off.*

Marie: We are unusual because we own our own house from far back. This house and the one alongside it were purchased by my husband's father. He was a jeweller, and he used to earn well, so he bought. And because Clarence was the only son, he got the houses. I was one of 12 brothers and sisters, but Clarence was only one. We're the only ones in the family who have our own house.

Brother David: Maybe the Anglo-Indians have too many celebrations: birthdays, christenings, Christmas, anniversaries, weddings, golden weddings, parish days…So because of the money we spend on all this, and new clothes, dances, nice food, we have no money to buy property.

Brother-in-law Fred: Everybody says that the Anglo-Indians live for today, they don't worry about tomorrow. They like to be generous, and share.

We met again in 1996. David had died and Fred had emigrated to live with his daughter in the UK.

Marie: We still have our parties. Now it's our grandchildren's birthday parties or First Communions. I've got 24 grandchildren. Even [for] the ones abroad, we'll have a little birthday party over here, make a cake, sing a happy birthday song. On New Year's Eve, we had a lovely get-together; all the children who are here in Madras and their families. We like to be together, so any excuse for the family to meet. Two daughters are with me in this house, one in the front portion and one in the back portion. Another one is upstairs. My eldest son, the one in the Gulf, is in the next-door house. So we're all close by, and I see most of the grandchildren every day.

We have three children in Australia, the three youngest. One daughter went first, then she took up her sister, and together they sponsored their brother. Now this brother is sponsoring my eldest son, who wants to go. Sponsoring means taking care, accommodating, looking after. That's how our Anglo-Indian families are going. When we had the opportunity to go abroad ourselves after separation [Partition at the time of Independence], we didn't go because at the time my husband had his mother here, and he wouldn't leave her.

Our youngest daughter [in Australia] is very close. She worries if we get ill. She phones very often. [She wants to know] "How is our health?" Sometimes she sends something, for Christmas, anniversaries. "If you need anything, don't hesitate to ask," she says. Our daughter in the front portion cooks and brings here. Three meals she brings. Daughters are better to their parents than sons. But we won't force them. If they have a good heart, they do.

When I met them again in 1999, there were some signs of a strain in the relationship with their eldest son, who had returned from the Gulf for a time, and after deciding not to emigrate to Australia, returned for another spell in the Gulf.

Marie: My son is very good, but of late he's strayed off from us a little. I think it's due to his wife only. She doesn't like the son to do much for us. What else can it be? Very often it happens in the Anglo-Indian community; we are very much like you foreigners. He used to be very good to us. Like at Christmas, or when we were sick, he would help. And he would give rent [for the house he occupies next door]. Now he doesn't give. It's the daughter-in-law. She only tells him not to give. She must have dug him up [harassed]: "What do you want to give your parents, they're all right." As a matter of fact, we are all right, thank God for that. But now that we're getting old, we have to think of our future. We're self-supporting. Clarence is getting a pension from the Railways, plus the children [daughters] pay us a house rent, and that's more than enough for us. Our daughters will definitely help us when we are too old to help ourselves. Now my husband has to have a cataract operation, Rs. 10,000 in a private clinic. We cannot manage that much. The ones in Australia will send. They're very happy to help out.

Our children took us up for a holiday to Australia, arranged everything. We liked it there, very nice life. But after coming back we see that in India you have the freedom to go about, alone, any time, spend your time chatting, loafing, wandering, but not abroad. In Australia they're rushing, going to work. People don't have time for you. But here all my Anglo-Indian family and my friends have time. We are more united compared to abroad. I'm content with what I have here. We are more happy here. If the whole family was abroad, do you think we would all be so united, sitting down, joking, *na*? Abroad each one goes their own way, here in India we are more close to each other. So we feel we are better off than there. That's my opinion.

For the Fernandez family, who are in a stronger economic position than the great majority of Anglo-Indians in Chennai, close ties arise mainly from living alongside one another in a single compound, and being able to share any number of rites and celebrations. Those abroad take responsibility for helping siblings to emigrate, while children—daughters in particular—including those overseas, maintain regular links with parents and assist them in practical ways as they age.

The Boundaries of Anglo-Indian Culture

Lionel Caplan

Introduction[29]

The idea of cultures as bounded, homogeneous, and unique has, until recently, been among social science's unquestioned truths[30]. This credo formed part of my own training as a social anthropologist. So when I began my research in Chennai (then Madras) in 1991, one of my aims was to attempt to understand how a population of disparate origins—the Anglo-Indians—came to form a single ethnic community with a distinct culture. Contemporary Anglo-Indians, as we all know, are descended—on the male side—from British, Portuguese, French, Spanish, and Dutch ancestors, among others. And although we still have only a vague idea of the community's original maternal forebears, we can be certain they would have been no less varied. Yet all these different, even discordant, social elements did eventually coalesce into a unified—if occasionally fractious—ethnic community. In Chennai, Anglo-Indian leaders, notables, and very ordinary members of the community have a fairly clear idea of what constitutes the uniqueness of their culture. But, in the course of time, as I became more familiar with Anglo-Indian lifestyles, I found them to be very heterogeneous. What intrigued me was how these claims to cultural distinctiveness and uniformity could sit so easily alongside the reality of diverse cultural practices within the group.

The Creation of Community Boundaries

Since the end of the British Raj, a growing number of Anglo-Indian women from elite families, well-educated and in secure jobs, have turned increasingly to better-off, non-Anglo-Indians as marriage partners. The men they marry are mainly, but not exclusively, Indian Christians, whom they meet at work, in church, or at university. At the same time, males in less-affluent sections of the community (because of a high incidence of joblessness and casual, low-paid employment), have few prospects of marriage to better-educated and better-employed Anglo-Indian girls. Many are, therefore, compelled to seek partners among women from equally impoverished households outside the Anglo-Indian fold. Elvin and Teresa Martin's children are probably extreme, but not wholly untypical, examples of this tendency. All but two of their seven children married "out". (See *Close Families in Chennai*, in this volume.) My estimate, based on the genealogies of households I visited, is that between one-third and one-half of poor Anglo-Indian families—and probably a similar range among the well-to-do—have at least one member who is married to, or cohabits with, someone outside the community. The children of all such unions—even those where the father is not an Anglo-Indian—are now eligible for free education in Anglo-Indian schools. While some of these children are absorbed into the circles of their non-Anglo-Indian parent, others remain rooted in the community.

However, the great majority of Anglo-Indians—particularly those in the middle or artisan class—marry among themselves. This fact both reinforces and demonstrates the sense of community among Anglo-Indians. The evolution of a largely intra-marrying population—despite the "out" unions at both ends of the class spectrum—has served to create close-knit bonds within a defined social universe. Such close ties also reinforce notions of a shared past and common lifestyles. By the early 19th century, Anglo-Indians were conscious of themselves as a distinctive group with particular interests. These concerns were soon to be formally addressed through the creation of several community associations[31]. While these associations did not invariably see eye-to-eye on many matters, they represented the community's diverse interests to government and in the wider society. Even today, they are divided on a range of issues, but their quarrels seem to me to attest to active, vigorous community institutions. While often at odds in their aims and ambitions, they are equally focused on a common social group over, and within which, they struggle. This serves ultimately to reinforce the notion of a coherent, identifiable community of Anglo-Indians.

In Chennai, the principal associations have for some time now been important channels of access to state benefits. For example, they are frequently required by the authorities to attest to a person's Anglo-Indian credentials (which entitle them to free education in Anglo-Indian schools). Nowadays, the associations also have control of substantial funds to help community members in need. Indeed, these and other Anglo-Indian organizations established for charitable purposes in Chennai tend to confine their philanthropic efforts to assisting only Anglo-Indians. This can be understood as a commitment to community, a means by which mutual trust builds between donor and recipient.

Cultural Pluralism

But however strong the feeling of ethnic awareness among members of the Anglo-Indian population was, the influences encroaching on the community from all sides—European and Indian—gave rise to what social scientists would term a creolized or hybrid culture. There were and are certain lifestyles which colonial British and Indians, as well as contemporary "outsiders", regarded and still regard as quintessentially Anglo-Indian: English speech, European dress codes and food preferences, Christian religion, freedom of marriage choice, a penchant for Western music and dancing, etc. Even members of the community themselves, when asked what distinguishes them from other Indians, identify as specifically Anglo-Indian some—if not all—of these very features as emblematic of their culture.

Without denying this perception of cultural uniformity, closer examination reveals a considerable diversity of practice within the community itself. At the same time, we find a greater or lesser degree of continuity with practices found in other groups. Differences of class and status within the Anglo-Indian fold provide a rough basis for these cultural distinctions, though not the only one. The Anglo-Indian population of Chennai today consists of (i) a small elite (professionals, businessmen, civil servants); (ii) a large, struggling "middle class" of skilled technicians and artisans, formerly employed in the railways, telegraphs, and customs and, latterly, within the industrial labour force and offices in the city; and (iii) a substantial category of unskilled and poorly educated people in low-paid, part-time employment, or without any work at all.

But at all levels of the Anglo-Indian community, cultural influences from the wider society are present, just as they were during the colonial era. Take the matter of English, one of the characteristics through which Anglo-Indian distinctiveness is perceived. The majority of Anglo-Indians usually differentiate themselves from other Indians and, indeed, from other mixed race populations in the country, by insisting that only they speak English as a first language. Despite their diverse origins, English had early on become their mother tongue, the language in which they study, worship, and communicate with one another. The high quality of their English is attested to, they insist, by the demand for Anglo-Indian women as secretaries and telephonists in the top companies.

Even my own linguistically untrained ear could detect a range of abilities—largely, though not entirely, coincident with the speaker's education and class position. Among those who had been to university, and who move in business and social circles where English is the language of communication, the standard mode of expression is little different from that ordinarily found at such levels anywhere in the country. This also points, of course, to the existence for more than 150 years of an English-speaking, Westernized Indian elite outside the Anglo-Indian fold.

Anglo-Indians belonging to the artisan or middle class, with only an average amount of schooling, spoke and still speak a distinctive kind of local Anglo-Indian English, with characteristic modes of expression, inflection, slang, and humour. At the lower end of the class spectrum, where low-income Anglo-Indians live alongside the poor of other ethnic groups, opportunities for learning and speaking English are much reduced. More than 90 years ago, the magazine of the Anglo-Indian Association of Southern India (29.4.1918) commented on the poor standard of English spoken among impoverished Anglo-Indian children. I was told by several head teachers in Anglo-Indian schools in Chennai that not a few of their pupils from such homes arrive unable to speak English at all. Indeed, I have visited a number of such families and met children with popular Anglo-Indian names like Royston, Christopher, Jennifer, and Vanessa who speak only Tamil.

If other Anglo-Indian cultural practices are considered, a similar diversity of behaviour is evident among members of the community, as well as significant overlaps with those outside. Thus, for example, the stereotypical Anglo-Indian diet based, it is often claimed, on "traditional English fare", turns out in practice to be a medley of East and West—curries and custards—as it has been for some time.

In matters of dress, too, there are influences from outside the community, and varieties of practice within. Many Anglo-Indians adopted European costume during colonial times, including the pith helmet by men in the employ of government, which was of course a symbol of the British in India. On formal occasions, such as weddings and dances, men who can afford to do so still tend to wear suits and ties—I felt very under-dressed when I showed up at one wedding in a safari suit. But for everyday occasions in a modern city like Chennai, they dress no differently from anyone else: in light trousers, shirts, and sandals. At home, it is not yet common, but by no means unusual, for Anglo-Indian men to relax in a *lungi*.

Anglo-Indian women also assumed European fashions in dress; in the official company history of Binny's Ltd, one of the largest employers of Anglo-Indian women in the city, we are told that Anglo-Indian secretaries wore "long dresses or skirts...no *sari* was to be seen". Most older women in the artisan or middle class persist in wearing frocks even today, while younger women, if they are employed outside the home, now increasingly alternate between frocks at home or in church, and *saris* at work. But at both ends of the class spectrum, more permanent changes are occurring. Among the well-to-do, where women are more likely to have married out of the community, and/or to work and mix socially with non-Anglo-Indians, there is a greater tendency to adopt the *sari* as the primary mode of dress for most formal occasions. Younger women from such families follow the fashions of their school or university peers. These include the *churidhar* or *salwar-kameez*, popular in North India, or even the Western "maxi", rather than the kinds of calf-length, fitted frocks with short sleeves favoured by most older Anglo-Indian women.

Among the poorest Anglo-Indians, resident in slum colonies, the *sari* is now quite commonly worn, and I would imagine was in evidence in colonial days as well. Since they interact principally with poor Tamils—as neighbours, workmates, and domestic partners—they adopt many of the everyday cultural practices of their surroundings, including the mode of apparel. Some also mentioned, as a reason for eschewing dresses, the wish to avoid the jibes and hostile comments often directed at women whose clothes expose their legs.

The increasing influences from the wider Indian society on

Anglo-Indian lifestyles raises important questions about the "authenticity" of practices found among the least well-off sections of the community. I was frequently told that the poor "have lost their culture", that they are not able "to live like real Anglo-Indians". Anglo-Indian leaders in Chennai sometimes bemoan the lost identity of the poor. The late president of the All-India Anglo-Indian Association viewed those occupying the lowest stratum as somehow "not assimilated to the way of life and the attributes of the community". Remarks of this kind grow out of an assumption that there is an agreed set of practices forming a coherent Anglo-Indian lifestyle, which the poor somehow fail to live up to. They cannot or do not speak, dress, eat, marry, or otherwise behave in the manner regarded as appropriate for Anglo-Indians. They are, in effect, left with no culture.

Such a view seems to insist on the notion of cultural homogeneity within clearly defined ethnic units. Those who do not live up to this lifestyle are either deemed to be excluded from the group, or to be less than full members of it. It may be that the poor would aspire to a more agreeable lifestyle modelled on that of better-off Anglo-Indians if they themselves were middle class; but they are not. Nonetheless, they are themselves not without particular lifestyles, even if these are largely shaped by their poverty and influenced by their non-Anglo-Indian surroundings. In other words, we have to allow for a heterogeneous range of cultural practices within the community.

But while we have to acknowledge the impact of the wider Indian environment on Anglo-Indian practices, influences have gone—and continue to go—the other way as well. These are mainly through the medium of Anglo-Indian schools. First known as European schools, they were established for the benefit of European and Eurasian children in the 1880s. But very soon after their creation, Indian parents came to value their high standards and the benefits of an English education. But until well into the 20th century, the numbers of non-Europeans and non-Eurasians admitted were severely restricted. In time, because of the increasingly precarious financial position of these schools, a growing proportion of pupils allowed to attend were from that part of the wider Indian public able to pay fees. After Independence, these schools were only allowed to continue as a separate system if they agreed to admit up to 50 per cent of their children from other communities. In Tamil Nadu, where there are more than 40 such schools, the average enrolment of Anglo-Indian pupils (as of 1990) was only 15-22 per cent, and in some schools the proportion was as low as one to three per cent of the student body. To the dismay of many Anglo-Indian educationalists and leaders, many of these schools have, in effect, become institutions for the education of well-to-do members of the Indian public—on whom the schools' financial viability depends.

The impact of these schools on non-Anglo-Indians educated in them is not readily measurable. But the combination of English language, a Westernized ethos, instruction by Anglo-Indian teachers (at least in the lower grades), emphasis on competitive sport, etc., adds up to an educational environment which encourages a cosmopolitan outlook. Meeting and talking to former non-Anglo-Indian pupils of such schools, it is apparent that they share memories (mostly pleasant), along with certain speech habits and even kinds of humour. Many close friendships were forged across the ethnic divide, and often persist into adulthood. Members of other communities who attended such schools often describe themselves as "Anglo-Indianized", a recognition of the profound influence on their lives and lifestyles of exposure to many aspects of Anglo-Indian cultural values and practices.

Conclusion

To sum up, I have tried to indicate the complex cultural gradations to be found within the Anglo-Indian population of Chennai. To quote H.A. Stark, one of Anglo-India's most prominent historians, the difficulty is in knowing where the culture begins and where it ends. In this respect, "cultural pluralism" denotes heterogeneity of beliefs and practices within, as well as across, ethnic lines. While the imprint of the dominant British group on Anglo-Indian lifestyles was understandably important during the colonial period, cultural influences from the surrounding Indian society were never absent, and have grown even more significant since Independence. But the flow has not been only one way, as members of other communities inter-marry with Anglo-Indians, and some of the relatively affluent educated in Anglo-Indian schools declare themselves "Anglo-Indianized".

In the cities of India today, Anglo-Indians have to acknowledge that the old social demarcations are no longer closed and fixed—if, indeed, they ever were. The boundaries between disparate groups making up the urban order are more porous now than in the past, and are becoming increasingly so. This has resulted in a variety of plural cultures no one could have predicted before the end of the Raj. But alongside the actuality of permeable borders we still have some people insisting—at different times and for diverse reasons—on community exclusiveness. Such claims, which were a feature of Anglo-India from at least the early 19th century, are still heard in Chennai, though much less so now than in the past. Obviously, expressions of ethnic closure can and do exist alongside the reality of hybrid cultures. In India's urban centres, where Anglo-Indians have long resided, both processes occur simultaneously.

Coming Full Circle

by Dolores Chew

The title of the anthology—*The Way We Are*—invites introspection and reflection. Should I write a philosophical piece on Anglo-Indians today—a third-person meta-narrative that takes into account the vagaries of history and experiences that took us from our lives on the Indian subcontinent to, perhaps, every other continent on earth? Such pieces have been written ever since Anglo-Indians/Eurasians—or whatever the appropriate term at a particular historical moment happened to be—grappled with issues of identity, usually because the historic moment generated a need to make this identification. One can read pieces dealing with identity in the pages of every Anglo-Indian publication, from *The Eurasian*[32] of the 19th and 20th centuries to other community publications before and after 1947. Exponential, bombastic, didactic, reactive, defensive, inclusive—but at the same time exclusive. But I can't do that. I've always been most comfortable with the local, the personal, the mundane, and the informal. And so I've decided what would fit best would be something about me. I do feel that I'm a part of the "we", and "the way I am" is a part of "the way we are". Perhaps I am being presumptuous, yet I believe that our individual experiences make up the sum of our collective experiences; there can be no homogeneity without heterogeneity.

At this point in my life, now that I've crossed the half-century mark, I feel very comfortable with the identity "Anglo-Indian". However, depending on my location (in every sense of the word), I could also be "South Asian", "Indian", or "visible minority". The submission date for this anthology coincides with the date of my marriage, my second. Both marriage partners are Indian. When I was growing up, the Us and Them distinctions were clearly defined in my family. We (as in Anglo-Indians) didn't wear such-and-such clothes, or eat such-and-such food, or listen to such-and-such music. Dating and marrying an Indian was considered radical. I based my choice of marriage partners on shared concerns, interests, and values. India, and things Indian, is very much part of that sharing. Yet Anglo-Indian has not been essential. For my parents' generation, this was not the case.

I am part of the post-midnight's children generation. I grew up in secular India, where the ethos of secularism was inculcated at school (a convent run by nuns belonging to the Irish Loreto order). Prayers at morning assembly were ecumenical and eclectic, often the poems of Rabindranath Tagore put to music. Friends at school were for the most part Indian. When I was invited to a classmate's birthday party, and I told my parents, I would say I was going to an Indian friend's or an Anglo-Indian friend's party. I didn't say Bengali, Punjabi, Goan, Hindu, Muslim, Christian, or Jewish. And my friends would see me as Anglo-Indian, and by extension Christian. When I got to the party the food was Indian—not the sandwiches and patties that were standard fare at our parties—and the clothes my friends wore were "Indian". A few of us, including Indian friends, might wear skirts and dresses. But *churidhar-kurtas* and *salwar-kameez* were more common. As we blossomed into womanhood, *saris* began to appear, at times a little self-consciously, as though we were little girls playing dress-up.

Parties also held a special aura. Our Anglo-Indian parties were assumed to be more fun. In late adolescence, it was assumed we would have better music, mixed (as in boys and girls) parties, and a sense of the forbidden. While my childhood and adolescence were characterized by these differences we inhabited, they seemed normal, with no questions about who I was or who we were. There might be the occasional muttered "half-caste" from a classmate, who herself might have been trying to pass for "Indian", but for the most part we all inherited a heterogeneous Indian space very comfortably.

While all this was happening, emigration continued, mainly to England, Canada, Australia, New Zealand, and the USA. Those who went abroad were deemed lucky, moving to lands of opportunity. As a child and adolescent, I saw it as exciting simply to go abroad; to be able to buy chocolates galore, or trendy clothes that we saw in the British and American fashion magazines, or a wide range of pop music. Now when I think back, there was an undercurrent that Anglo-Indians were fleeing India, going "home"—an act that had overtones of betrayal, of un-Indianness. Curiously, Indians who emigrated didn't get classified in this way.

But growing up, hearing the whispered conversations of adults and reading fiction, there was another identity that lurked. For me as a girl and young woman, the presumed, highly sexualized identity of Anglo-Indian women became a somewhat ubiquitous presence. Fiction written in English, if set in India of the pre- or post-Independence period, would often portray Anglo-Indians as promiscuous, sexually available women, and indigent, shiftless men who scrounged off their women. Often the expectations Indian men had of Anglo-Indian women assumed the fiction was real life.

Following the migration patterns of many before me, I also left India and came to Canada. For me, migrating was an adventure, the opportunity to go abroad, travel the world, and then possibly return to India. This seemed to be the only way to beat the "control-Raj" India of tight travel and foreign currency restrictions. My personal trajectory, however, kept me in Montreal, where I worked, studied, married, raised my children, divorced, and re-married. It also made me feel more Indian than ever, effortlessly. Part of that was simply the immigrant experience, where those in the host country are unaware of the heterogeneous distinctions of countries of origin. And so for most people I was "Indian". For Indians, there would often be the quizzical expression that conveyed the unspoken question—what kind of Indian are you? Or, if the question was actually voiced, someone else might inquire, "Indian Christian"? Sometimes, I might get the trite comment, "My cousin married an Anglo-Indian;" or, "I had a friend in school who was Anglo-Indian." Rather like the, "I'm-not-a-racist—some-of-my-best-friends-are-black," statement.

I arrived in Canada in 1975, shortly after Indira Gandhi declared a State of Emergency in India. I was not at all political, but had a firm belief that India was a democracy. So I was appalled at the abrogation of civil liberties and the mass arrests there. I quickly got involved with expatriate groups that mobilized against the Emergency. I was new to political activism. My home town of Calcutta (now Kolkata), in the years immediately preceding my departure, had been the site of Naxalite (Maoist) activism and state repression. However, as far as my life was concerned, it might all have been happening on another planet: there were periodic newspaper reports about police raids on "dens" that rendered quantities of Mao's Little Red Book, but they didn't concern me in any way, and demonstrations were inconvenient events that delayed me as I sat in a taxi in Calcutta. Yet something about being away from home, and what I saw as Indira Gandhi's betrayal of what I had been educated to believe was the destiny of India, propelled me to become more involved in Diasporic dissidence. The people I organized with considered me Indian. This was most likely the result of their political worldview, where class was a more distinct identifier than region, ethnicity, or some sort of hyphenated identity. At the same time I felt comfortable being Anglo-Indian.

I entered academia and passionately studied the history and society of India. I immersed myself in Indian culture, especially film. I got involved in the women's movement and began to organize with like-minded people a centre[33] for South Asian women in Montreal. The identity of being Indian expanded to cover the entire subcontinent. I poured my energy and creativity into this, and we succeeded in building a vibrant and flourishing service, support, and advocacy organization for South Asian women and their families, which has become an important landmark on the map of Montreal in many ways.

My academic work continued. I was attracted to the subaltern studies school (of history from below), and the writing on orientalism of Edward Said. All that I was reading, and the communities I was helping to build, kept transforming me. I learned in a very practical way that the personal is political. Initially, my forays into writing feminist history made me feel, at times, that I was falling off the edge. However, the later work of other scholars confirmed the conclusions I found myself arriving at. It was affirmation and affirmative. But before then it had been lonely. Over time, what I had been acquiring as a consequence of my practical political engagement entered my academic work. I learned to challenge entrenched power systems and came to realize the nexus between knowledge and power. The methodological and theoretical tools I was acquiring permitted me to cut to the quick, and in terms of Anglo-Indian identity questions I came full circle.

What began as lived experience, with twinges of unease at certain moments—the whispered "half-caste", the man who wanted to date you because he thought you would be an easy lay, my personal reluctance to engage academically with Anglo-Indian topics because I thought it wouldn't count as serious research—became irrelevant. And when I came to my post-doctoral research, I plunged right in to examine gender constructions of Anglo-Indian women in works of fiction, in the late colonial and post-colonial period. I now had the tools to deconstruct these identities. There were sufficient written works that showed me how Anglo-Indians had been used and abused by the colonizer, and were also looked upon with suspicion by Indians as belonging to the colonizing race. Questions that I had not consciously been aware of, and had lain dormant, were slowly being answered. Often, the most difficult questions had simple answers.

As a woman and an immigrant, a state of marginalization seemed to be a constant part of my identity. As an Indian who challenged the status quo of both India and Canada, I occupied yet another type of marginal position. And as a student who was also involved in the community, I was never fully a student. Another marginality. Over time, I have come to realize that my experience and who I am, the choices I have made, have usually placed me outside the mainstream. My existence is on the margins. Being involved in the politics of immigration, challenging the constructs of multiculturalism that slot individuals into allotted spaces, also helped in this process. Dealing with the fear of difference encapsulated in the recent debates in Québec around "reasonable accommodation[34]", is part of this same continuum. Multiple identities, marginality, challenging the status quo of race and power—political, gender, and class—have meant that I have become accustomed to outsider status in many contexts, even as I occupy a mainstream position of college professor and researcher. And so what might have been an earlier discomfort or unease with an Anglo-Indian identity, partly because of what was projected towards me by the mainstream, has assumed normalcy.

The triennial Anglo-Indian world reunions have forced a different sort of introspection. There is the expected nostalgia and desire to reconnect with long-lost friends and neighbours, but there are also questions of identity. What is the Anglo-Indian identity in a post-colonial and globalized world? Will that identity continue? Identity, like culture, evolves and changes. It is not static. So even as older Anglo-Indians reminiscence and network, there is a need to recognize that identity issues are undergoing change.

Current and subsequent generations are not tied in the same way to a hyphenated identity. We are moving, travelling, intermarrying. Our children are being raised in different ways. In some cases—mine being a case in point—the children are aware of their origins, but they are choosing their own ways of identifying themselves. The way we are *is* who we are today. Who knows what tomorrow will bring.

What If?

By Ed Haliburn

Antecedents

Of the many spurious theories that abound, the undeniable and often unpalatable truth is that the British, like all conquerors since time began, inevitably left behind a residue of progeny, arguably by accident, by design, or by "whatever" in every part of the empire where "the sun never sets". The oft-proffered argument, that the birth pangs of the Anglo-Indian community was socially engineered to provide a standing vanguard pre-Suez Canal, may contain a grain of truth, but only just that. The myriad of squabbling minor *rajas* and *nawabs*, heavily dependent on British mercenary and military expertise, gave rise to the ubiquitous "divide and rule" strategy that was to ensure influence, survival and, ultimately, the creation and expansion of the empire throughout the subcontinent.

It is far more plausible and sustainable that, as empire building progressed, the lure of the tropics and warmer climes was a strong incentive to many not to return "home". For the ordinary man at that time, the appalling social conditions in Europe, allied with a brutal criminal justice system, was enough reason to stay. Regular soldiers opted to remain indefinitely, and the discharged saw opportunities in the expansion of government, the infrastructure, and transport. At the same time, traders fanned out across the country to export raw materials to feed the Industrial Revolution now gathering pace in Europe; and, in return, to import manufactured goods and commercial services to an expanding empire. Inevitably, nature took its course. Liaisons with local women, both Indian and Eurasian, servant and courtesan, consensual and non-consensual, took place, and very soon a substantial Eurasian populace was evident all across the land.

Contrary to popular perception, the Anglo-Indian community is in no way unique. Similar communities sprang up in the West Indies, South Africa, Malaysia, Singapore, China, and in all of the former Spanish, French, Portuguese, and Dutch colonies. In India, a "pick-and-mix", Cajun-type lifestyle, culture, and a hybrid signature cuisine—now universally known as curry—evolved over the years. Even a patois, derogatorily maligned as "chee-chee", came into being.

As with similar communities around the world, Anglo-Indians primarily associated themselves, in custom and practice, with the European, while being most circumspect about the other variables of the ethnic equation. This nurtured an overt disassociation and an inherent dislike of most things Indian. This dichotomy set the scene for a Homerian tragedy to be played out when, as a new world order took shape after World War II, the European "mother" countries divested or were forced to divest themselves of their overseas possessions, leaving behind a retinue of apolitical communities, bewildered and marginalized, to fend for themselves. The "idyll" was over. Fortunately for many, migration to "mother" and dominion countries provided a most timely way out. Over the next 25 years, and without a backward glance, we left India and with it a whole way of life.

It is in this context that very little introspection and informed discussion has taken place on what brought about the demise of the only non-demographic community that once helped shape the face of India, from the sands of Kovalum to the snows of Kashmir. Many of us today, who grew up in those turbulent times, now have the leisure and maturity to reflect on the events that, for better or for worse, turned our lives upside down; and now, in the evening of our lives, contemplate what might have been done for it not to have happened.

Transition

Migration, especially in the 1960s and after, has unfortunately been treated primarily as a cultural exodus, while the important economic element has been largely, almost deliberately, swept under the carpet. At a time of high unemployment and limited prospects, migration was a godsend, a deliverance for many from low-paid, dead-end jobs in nationalized industries, especially the Indian Railways. In all spheres of employment, both commercial and government, arbitrary obstacles were also placed to deny the better educated their rightful progression up the career ladder.

The transition years of 1949-60 brought famine, hardship, and bewilderment at the pace and dimension of change in India. Movement of food, especially rice, was restricted and hard to get. Rural poverty and migration saw village children being sold by desperate mothers on the streets of many a town in southern India. Many a railway livelihood fell foul of the law, especially guards and drivers with access to freight, as they laid their jobs on the line in the struggle to live, to make ends meet, and to maintain a standard of life in difficult and uncertain times. The cold, hard reality of life in many a household was to pay the school fees, to feed and clothe large families, and to make ends meet on a single salary. Debt was, at worst, a constant companion; at best, a regular visitor.

Now successfully ensconced in egalitarian countries of the first world, the hubris of many vaudeville historians, associated literati, glitterati, and others, tend to opine about an imaginary bourgeoisie community cocooned in colonial mansions, with a retinue of servants dancing attendance on the *"sahib"* and *"memsahib"*. In fact, the Anglo-Indian bourgeoisie was a microscopic element of the community, within which the socio-economic divisions were as disparate as any that one sees in India today.

Gilding the Lily

Unfortunately, "gilding the lily" has become rather an obsessive pantheon as evidenced in most Anglo-Indian Web sites. Inference of a common, inclusive heritage embracing famous personalities, who just happened to be born in British India, is a catch-all technique employed in order to wrap the community in a cloak of achievement-by-association. In this age of information technology, it is not difficult to dismiss these claims as utter nonsense, and an unwelcome invitation to derision and ridicule.

Rudyard Kipling, Juliet Prowse, Guy Gibson, etc., were born in British India but were not *jhat bhai* Anglo-Indian by any stretch of the imagination. Vivian Leigh's father was a wealthy English art and antiques dealer who married an Armenian heiress (Gertrude Yackjee). Children were raised and schooled in England or abroad from very young, and for reasons best described in Vyvyen Brendon's book, "Children of the Raj". They were, however, proud of their tenuous association, and many to this day appear frequently on the BBC to recall fondest memories of their brief childhood in India.

Conversely, genuine Anglo-Indians of recent and past world fame have been more than reticent about their origins. Merle Oberon, for instance, was born and raised in Calcutta as Estelle Merle O'Brien Thompson. Talented, with a fair "throw-back" complexion and good looks, coupled with wily pragmatism, she passed off her brown-skinned Anglo-Indian mother as the housekeeper. One cannot be too judgmental. In the not too distant past, a "touch of the tar brush" was fatal to any upwardly mobile or nubile aspirant.

However, no brag fest is ever complete without "bending it like Beckham". Here I refer to the achievements of our past hockey players. Hockey has always been a minority team sport, sometimes played in countries where football overshadows everything else and, therefore, needs to be seen in this perspective. The tabloid superlatives, repeatedly regurgitated, often smack of narcissism.

Likewise, in the vast kaleidoscope of the Indian subcontinent, the railways and hardwired communications were essential logistics to the maintenance of government, law, and order. It was, therefore, no coincidence that, as a homogeneous community, this placed us in a unique position to carve out a niche that was eventually and inevitably machined into a compliant, dependable, and dependent workforce: a contented insular minority.

Nostalgia

Jam sessions, Christmas cake, *kul-kuls,* chicken curry, *pagal gymkhanas,* and *the* dances were indeed iconic hallmarks of the community but, nice as they were, they were diversionary: they camouflaged the inherent deficiencies within. They were also no panacea for the hard times that touched most families. There are not many of us left today who can recall, while still a boy, picking up a sack of rice dropped off at the outer signal and lugging it home in the dead of night. And the Tom Sawyer and Huckleberry Finn flights of imagination as the Boat Mail picked up speed leaving Trichy every night at nine for the "Big Apple", Madras. As the whoosh of steam, the mournful whoop of whistle, and the clatter of wheels faded into the distance, we checked the wall clock, unfurled our mats on the bare cement floor, lay down, and went to sleep, to dream big time.

"A tryst with destiny", to recall Nehru, was inadvertently kept. That train was, one day, to take so many of us away, and most would never come back. Our very own Route 66.

Memories of small railway colonies dotted over all that vast land we loved are indelibly etched forever on the minds and hearts of countless people scattered all over the globe. Priceless!

We played our part, we pulled our weight, and we gave our all. The dedication and contribution of so many unsung Anglo-Indian heroes is beyond question. "Men of Harlech—Land of Our Fathers" would have equally befitted our granddads, uncles, dads, and brothers, but it was also to be their swansong. Like the man who, on being rescued from the wreckage of his bombed house during the London Blitz, wailed: "I only pulled the chain." In a flash and a flush it was down the pan—gone forever.

The Enigma

Unsophisticated in the ways of the world, the downside was that we were always intended to be mere cogs in the giant wheel that was eventually buffed and polished into "The Jewel In The Crown". In the miasma of the Independence movement, we were just the "gofers and wheel-tappers" who ensured that the proverbial train did not come off the rails. We contented ourselves with the systemic derogation that the Indian could never perform as well as the European or the Anglo-Indian, should know his place, and therefore was intrinsically inferior. Many of us wasted the supreme advantage of our first class schools, education, and English as our mother tongue, by our inability to grasp the opportunities of advancement in the fields of business, engineering, medicine, law, and government.

Most of all, we abandoned the political arena as irrelevant to our future, relying heavily on the benevolence of the British. When Independence came, it was too late to make any impact; the chance was lost forever. Unfettered by any privilege, our non-Anglo-Indian fellow countrymen had always understood the benefits of higher education as being fundamental to advancement and to the seats of power. We, in our mental *kraals,* were left wringing our hands, on the cusp of a cleft stick in post-Independent India, marginalized by our inability to roll with the changes and disadvantaged by the lack of representation and influence at most levels of power and in government. We had mortgaged our destiny, by default, to the benevolence of others, firstly to the British and, after Independence, to the cringing charity of the new order.

The Reality

The UK, to many of us, was a seminal awakening to the realities of a competitive world. Much was bandied about the welcome

Anglo-Indians could expect, but all that we were greeted with was anger, suspicion, and open racial hostility. *"Rooms for Rent— No Niggers, No Wogs, No Children, No Dogs"* was often the grim rejection and salutary reminder, at the end of a long trudge on a cold winter's day in a threadbare overcoat, that a brown face was a "wog", no ifs or buts, and applied to "Gujjus[35]", Punjabis, Pakistanis, and Anglo-Indians with equal contempt. Frustration was common, jobs were stop-gap, menial and, to many of us, we had simply jumped from the frying pan into the fire. It was a heart-stopping revelation. To mix metaphors, we had dished out the dirt, and now the chickens were coming home to roost, but never in India was I ever subjected to overt racial abuse, often hurled by much lesser mortals. The daily grind in often poor weather, irritating minor discriminations, the humiliation of being seen as an alien impostor living on social benefits, the cramped flats at inflated rents, the impossible dream of saving a 10 per cent down payment to buy one's own home, were indeed the "pits" of our lives. We expected better, but the reality was so much worse. It took time to settle in, but the only consolation for a long time was that we did it for our kids. Truthfully, however, we knew we had burnt our boats; there was nothing to go back to. We hung on by our fingertips for better times, and they were so slow in coming. Entry restrictions imposed in 1963-64 finally brought some sanity to a volatile issue but not without strife on the streets and fear in our hearts and homes.

Indisputably, we had a choice. Times were hard no doubt for most, but equally, most left because we felt that we no longer belonged. India was for the Indians now. The sun was setting. Here comes the big rub—the great hypothesis—**WHAT IF?**

What If?

What if the Anglo-Indian community had stood as one on August 15, 1947, hand on heart, and unequivocally taken an oath, "I pledge allegiance to the flag, the Indian Flag, one nation under God, etc." as all Americans do, new and old, wherever they come from, whatever their colour, race, or religion? Perhaps a re-invention of the term Anglo-Indian, by definition Eurasian, but no less proud to be Indian. Indira Gandhi, during the regional boundary and sectarian turmoil of the '70s, offered Frank Anthony the presidency of India. She said, expanding on her choice, that as an Anglo-Indian he was also the only true Indian, eminently qualified and free from any divided loyalties of state, caste, language, or religion. He was forced to decline the offer through ill health. We could have done with more like him. With a full measure of conjecture, perhaps the elite of the community—educated, urbane, politically astute, and blessed with vision—could well have been the Ivy League of India or, at the very least, what the Irish were to America. To be prescient is a wondrous thing and one is compelled to ask time and again, **What If?**

To our children, now grown up, well-educated, and with children of their own, those distant times are a revelation as they take, effortlessly in their stride, the trappings of the modern societies we now live in. Bengali-American Pulitzer Prize-winning writer Jhumpa Lahiri, author of *The Namesake* and *Interpreter of Maladies* describes the wrench of migration as "…a journey, no matter how ultimately rewarding, (that) is founded on separation, departure and deprivation, but it secures for subsequent generations a sense of arrival, advantage and acceptance". The agony of always being on the outside looking in, being tolerated by the host nation because it is politically correct to do so, but who would rather we were elsewhere. The denial of an unqualified sense of belonging still eludes many of us. To be an Englishman is a birthright, not acquired, one is repeatedly and painfully reminded. In spite of the affluence most of us have accrued in our adopted lands, the phrase, "man does not live by bread alone", has quite a wrenching poignancy about it.

India is indelibly branded on many an Anglo-Indian soul—the culture, the food, the friends, the good times—but I will always regret the demise of the Anglo-Indian community through lack of vision and foresight. It is so sad to see a once-proud community now reduced to Scheduled Caste status. We could have achieved so much more had we only the humility to see that, eventually, the sun would set on the British Empire and "home" was India, Mother India, pure and simple.

The Future?

Fortunately, in Britain at least, a new generation is in the making, the result of Asians either born in England or of mixed marriages, taking on the "the best of both". Many a staid British high street has been turned into a vibrant, colourful thoroughfare, a Madras Moore Market or a Calcutta New Market. "An Indian" has ousted roast beef as the nation's favourite food. A mutual respect is evident and only made possible by the sheer impact the Asian populace has made on the country as a whole. With the demise of the coal, steel, and heavy industries, the rust belt cities of Leeds, Bradford, Sheffield, and Leicester would now be ghost towns were it not for the entrepreneurial skills of the "sunshine" Asian businessmen. Asian men of substance are in all areas of academia, politics, and public service. Asian members of the House of Commons are now in double figures. The House of Lords has a significant handful of Asian Life Peers, and British high society is also fast succumbing to the infusion of mixed marriages.

Amongst the older generation, there is much self-flagellation and beating of breasts to bemoan the fact that the demise of the Anglo-Indian is predisposed in the lands where we have made our homes. Many, especially those clinging precariously on the periphery of the old British Empire, consistently bang the drum about their distinctive ethnicity and culture. The truth is now dawning on many of us that our children have moved on and have made their own world, either rejecting or acknowledging the touch of the tar brush in all of us. Inevitably, our existence and contributions will be confined to the dustbin of time, perhaps a footnote in somebody's family tree—and not much else.

Globalization and Anglo-India

by Alan Johnson

I travelled recently into the brambly, forested heart of Jharkhand State, to the sleepy town of McCluskieganj, to visit a woman named Kitty who has lived there her whole life. The town is named after its founder, an Anglo-Indian businessman called Ernest Timothy McCluskie, who in the 1930s envisioned a utopian settlement for his people. The few Anglo-Indians who continue to live there still reminisce about dances, the songs of Jim Reeves and Elvis, and club activities like Housie (Bingo). Although Kitty married a local *adivasi* and sells fruit in the tiny railway station, it is uncanny to hear her alternate with equal ease between Oxford English and the local dialect. In the 1960s, a visiting Anglo-Indian sailor had asked her to marry him and go away with him to England or Australia. She—or rather, her protective mother—refused. Kitty, I think, did not want to venture into a world that did not understand her. Here in McCluskieganj, though she is poor, she is free in a sense that would be hard to sustain elsewhere.

I think of Kitty frequently these days as I try to make sense of the rapid changes in our globalized world. It is a world that Salman Rushdie has described, in his inimitable way, as a "chutnification" of cultures and languages. The predicaments of culture and identity that Kitty has had to face offer a kind of paradigm for all of us, Anglo-Indian or not, who must contend with an increasingly hybrid world, where *paanwallahs* have their own Web sites (as I saw inscribed on a *paan* stall in New Delhi) and rickshaw drivers sway to Hindi rap. We are all familiar with garish headlines that speak of traditions colliding with postmodern reality: the Hollywood star kisses the Bollywood actress at a fund-raising gala in Mumbai, prompting calls from self-righteous lawyers for the arrest of the blasphemous pair. "Indian culture is insulted!" they scream. This prompts a chorus of outraged replies from forward-looking columnists: "The Great Indian Hypocrisy" is the cover story of the May 14, 2007, issue of *India Today*.

For many Anglo-Indians, this polarity of views is old news. For them, tradition and modernity have always been about chutnification, about balancing anglicized habits and Indian customs. In a way, then, the rest of India's old-new society has begun to appreciate the sensibility that Anglo-Indians have cultivated for so long. Today, as the larger world quarrels, sometimes quite understandably, over foreign intrusion and the decay of age-old practices, the very word "Indian" has taken on a new resonance. India is "Hinglish", jet-setting gurus, and British *Bhangra*. It is a milieu that the 19th century poet, Henry Derozio, or the late 20th century leader, Frank Anthony—or Kitty, if she had travelled—might well have understood. To further stake my claim about the ways in which 21st century India has caught on to what Anglo-Indians have always known, I want to look at some literary representations of the Anglo-Indian community before returning to India's postmodern moment.

A past writer comes to mind immediately in this connection, namely, Rudyard Kipling. He famously broadcast specific images of Anglo-Indians[36] that became fixed in the public imagination, for good and ill. Although there is no evidence that Kipling was of Eurasian blood, as some still claim, his bi-cultural, conflicted youth led him to create some marvellously ambivalent characters who face similarly split loyalties. The orphan Kim—with an Irish father and described by Kipling as "English [...though] burned as black as any native"—is the most notable of these. But Kipling populated his works with many lesser-known protagonists, whose psychological predicaments during the racially charged era of the Raj still strike a chord.

Although Kipling frequently gave in to stereotypical convention, his tales are just as often about the complexities of living in between official social categories. I am thinking, for instance, of his story "His Chance in Life", in which the Eurasian hero, Michele, must vie with a totemic "Borderline" that segments his own communitarian identity from that of Europeans and Indians. Above all, it is Kipling's signature tone of irony that we must hear if we are to make sense of this dalliance with borders. Many late 20th century readers have taken phrases like the following (from the same story) to impute an unchanging segregationist attitude to Kipling's oeuvre: "The Black and the White mix very quaintly in their ways. Sometimes the White shows in spurts of fierce, childish pride—which is Pride of Race run crooked—and sometimes the Black in still fiercer abasement and humility, half-heathenish customs and strange, unaccountable impulses to crime."[37] We bristle today at such words, even if we recall that Kipling was simply repeating the prevailing sentiment of the time. His next sentence, however, exemplifies the kind of unconventional views he habitually expressed: "One of these days, this people [. . .] will turn out a writer or a poet; and then we shall know how they live and what they feel. In the meantime, any stories about them cannot be absolutely correct in fact or inference" (59). Here, then, we have a frank acknowledgement about the limitation he faced as an outsider trying to depict the Anglo-Indian community. This example also tells us that we must read Kipling with an eye to every one of his sentences, resisting the urge to unhinge one eye-catching statement from the story as a whole. More importantly, this apparent oscillation between colonial convention and proto-liberalism proves to be a characteristic strategy of Kipling's, always catching his reader off-guard. It is his way of winking to his various audiences—English, Anglo-Indian, Indian. It compels Kipling's readers to re-read his stories' opening words in order to gauge his tone, and to find a point of reference that will help them arrive at a definitive interpretation of the text. And here's the rub: Kipling's tales possess no definitive "meaning". Their diction, structure, and personae all conspire to dodge a conclusive response. Or, in the best mode of Swiftian satire, his stories please (or, rather, *pleased*) a non-discriminating reader's palette whilst baring their critical teeth.

Above all, it is Kipling's irony that signals to us just how much he incriminates his compatriots for their trite summations about the lives of "natives" and "half-castes", and anyone who threatens to cross the borderlines that supposedly distinguished high from low, Anglo from India. This fleet-footed shift in perspective explains recent critical appraisals of Kipling's much-cited "imperialism". Here, for example, is Kipling's Oxford editor, Andrew Rutherford: "Admiration for the Raj alternates with debunking and irreverence" in *Plain Tales from the Hills*. "Compassion co-exists strangely with cynicism" (xxi). This, as I have indicated, misses the crux of Kipling's changeable attitude, which is that of a person accustomed, like his protagonists, to being misunderstood, misrepresented, and maligned.

I raise these points in order to underscore how the multiple perspectives Kipling brings to bear on "His Chance in Life" reflect the outlook of a person as socially conflicted as the protagonist Michele. In the story, a Miss Vezzis, the love-interest of Michele, scolds her juvenile charges (she is the nursemaid to an English family) "in the language of the Borderline—which is part English, part Portuguese, and part Native" (60). That she appears to the narrator to be "black as a boot" and, "to our standard of taste", "ugly", in no way detracts from his (the narrator's) recognition that Miss Vezzis "had her own life to lead" rather than "worry over" the petty concerns of her employers' shallow lives (60). Michele, for his part, is "a poor, sickly weed and very black", who "looked down on natives as only a man with seven-eighths native blood in his veins can" (60). Working as a signalman in a small telegraph sub-office, Michele is one day confronted with his life's great "chance" to prove himself worthy of his "pride of race." Local "natives" erupt in religious rioting, and the Bengali *babu* in the office (a figure whose caricature became a fixture in colonial prose) turns to Michele for orders. Thinking as much about his prospects for marriage to Miss Vezzis as about being "the only representative of English authority in the place," Michele grabs a rifle and fires, killing one of the rioters and dispersing the others (62). Rather like George Orwell's account decades later about his dreaded obligation to shoot an elephant[38] in Burma, Michele's almost instinctive reaction seems almost fated, arising as it does out of a brittle juridical milieu that brooks no challenge to its authority.

Unlike Orwell's tale, Kipling's does not find this active response problematic. Indeed, Michele, though weak-kneed from his ordeal, is applauded by the Assistant Collector, a "young Englishman" (63). The author reserves his irony, instead, for the conditions that set Michele and Miss Vezzis on their fateful journeys. Each must contend with whimsical British bosses (Michele, the text implies, is constantly being transferred purely on the basis of his employer's assumptions about racial behavior); and each must navigate the minefield of cultural, racial, and religious sentiment that imperial governance incites. The story's mix of irony and earnestness, iconoclasm and conventionality, captures the author's comparatively complex interpretation of colonial cultures. To a surprising extent, then, Kipling's tale of Anglo-India anticipates the uncertainties and prejudices that beset our globalized and increasingly hybrid world. We can all, Anglo-Indian or not, recognize in Miss Vezzis's polyglot language a version of our own ambidextrous visions.

To say, then, that India is a syncretic culture made up of a myriad of languages and customs is to note a sensibility that Anglo-Indians have long cultivated, as Kipling's fascination with the community reveals. This is by no means a plea for the uniqueness of Anglo-Indian society; Bollywood, to note an obvious example, has long thrived on the mesh of Hindu, Muslim, and Western music and mannerisms. Yet it is precisely the complicated negotiation of Anglo-Indian identity, before and after India's independence, when families pondered whether to emigrate or remain, that can shed light on today's conflicting signals. It is important at this point to recall that globalization *per se* is not new. When Vasco da Gama "discovered" a shorter spice route to Calicut in 1498, an Indian pilot hired in Arabia guided him into the city's well-plied harbour. Further north, the port city of Surat, in Gujarat State, had been trading with its Arab neighbours for centuries before Europeans arrived. The ubiquitous Indian chilli is itself an import, piggybacking to Goa on Portuguese ships to flavor the curries that spice our lives. And curry is today a staple of British cuisine. No, the art of planetary trade is old hat. We enjoy its ironies. What is new is the supersonic speeds at which it now operates, and the resulting demands upon individual aspirations.

Growing up in India in the 1960s and '70s, I was quite happy to watch, along with fresh Hindi films, scratchy old Hollywood movies. I had no idea that Humphrey Bogart was dead. Today, Spiderman is released simultaneously in Mumbai, London, and Los Angeles in order to satiate much the same hunger for popular culture in each city. Young Indians, like their American and British peers, are impatient. And their impatience demands to be fed with the Hindi rap and English slang piping through their iPods. They now aspire to enter Call Center College in Bangalore rather than IIT, the Indian Institute of Technology famous for its scientists and computer engineers. The irony—one that Kipling might have appreciated—is that whereas more and more Anglo-Indians can finally say, in their Queen's English, that they are at home in India, huge numbers of non-Anglo-Indian youth turn to these practitioners of hybridity for instruction in the ways of the postmodern world. True, this is a world characterized by the "permeation of the real world by the fictional", as Rushdie puts it.[39] But it is also a world of possibility, of the taste of chutney. Kitty, I think, would have understood.

Matters of Language

by Sanjay Sircar

An incident on a trip to Calcutta[40] in 1998 got me thinking about Anglo-Indians and language, and inspired these impressions about living people of various generations, both in India and the Diaspora.

Park Lane, behind Park Street in Calcutta, was a run-down Anglo-Indian locality even before World War II, and is now notorious for guns, drugs, prostitutes, and the sort of Anglo-Indians who live among them. The gracious building of the Women's Friendly Society showroom in Park Lane—with its lovely 19th century bungalow frontage, a tiny bit of greenery in front of the portico, and a glorious, large internal staircase—is like a jewel preserved from the past, in the middle of a crowded, run-down backstreet with little or no pavement. When I rolled up in 1998 to buy a tablecloth at the WFS, the street was more jam-packed with ugly, jerry-built buildings than before, but the WFS was there unchanged, like a fly set in amber.

Inside sat a triumvirate of Anglo-Indian ladies, with a young Anglo-Indian man in the background. The ladies' clothes were nicely symbolic. At the head of the triumvirate was short, plump Mrs. Marie Marker, wearing a *sari*—and wearing it, interestingly, in the old Indian Christian style of my paternal grandmother, with a brooch at the shoulder and the *anchal* (*sari*-end) pleated neatly, a style quite obsolete and today seen only on air stewardesses. The length of the *sari* was "Indian Christian", too, a little above the ankle, so that it did not sweep the floor. And she had a form of the Indian *khopa* (hair-bun) as well. Her younger companions were short-haired Mrs. Marcie Sims, in a frock, and hybrid-named Mrs. Shobha Lawrence, in (I think) a *kameez*-like top and pants. Mrs. Lawrence was described by Mrs. Sims as "the dark one"—and that she could be is something pleasant, given our general Indian obsession with colour.

I spoke English, as one does, and Mrs. Marker said, "This is a charity, men!" when I suggested the amount I was buying warranted a discount. But as they talked, the ladies all moved into Bengali, to me and among themselves, and a Bengali quite fluent and quite idiomatic, too—using such phrases as *kato ki* (lots of things) —with only the barest trace of an accent. Was it a result of their working with the Bengali craftswomen the society was set up to help? Or a result of the times? Or both?

I smiled.

And Mrs. Sims understood why. "At least we're trying to speak the language!" she protested.

"And there was a time when you would not have tried," I replied, and they agreed.

They gave me the society's card, and said I should write. A few years later, I sent an Internet-met Anglo-Indian friend, part of the immediate post-World War II exodus, I think, who was revisiting Calcutta, to get some old-fashioned "English Chinese" satin-stitch embroidery from the WFS. And he did.

Mesdames Marker, Sims, and Lawrence set me thinking about the community's relation to language. Sometimes in India itself, there is a laughing self-awareness that Anglo-Indian English is not "standard". In 1962, I was witness to one of the teachers at Mr. Pires's School, the famous Trivia Hall, in Ballygunge, who heard a colleague saying to a pupil, "Speak slowly."

"You mean 'speak softly', dear," she said. "*Āsté* may mean 'slowly,' but 'slowly' and 'softly' aren't the same thing!" A nice irony operated, and the four lady teachers laughed. *Āsté* is Calcutta Anglo-Indian Hindi, which substitutes the Bengali *āsté* for the correct *āhisté*, which Punjabis pronounce as *ayistā*.

"Miss Eileen", "Miss Agnes", was the conventional form of address the teachers taught the pupils (except, oddly, the older "Miss Steele", who got a surname), and the quaint "Sir Alan" for Mr. Pires Junior. "He's a dee-mun!" was stern Mrs. Pires's condemnation for pupils. And, in the convention whereby Anglo-Indian we-only-speak-English pride mangles Indian names, "Bijia" was how they rendered Bijoy—as later, at La Martinière College, Mrs. Phyllis Jobe said "Paath-er", for Partha, and Mr. Bellgarde proudly said "Cal-yunn" for Kalyan.

But Anglo-Indian English was and, indeed, is inflected with Indianness. As I was leaving for Australia in 1977, opposite the AAEI[41] Club in Ballygunge was a young Anglo-Indian man, "Bengali/Portuguese-looking" (a term I invented for want of a better one). He was cajoling a doctor to sign a heap of medical certificates for driving licences (in medical examinations so nominal as to be a joke) for a single fee. As he winked at me, he coaxed, "Whaaw-ṭ, men, doctor!" a direct translation into Anglo-Indianese of something like the Bengali "*Kı daktar-bubu!*" ("Oh why [are you being so obdurate], doctor?") The doctor ultimately signed. Anglophone Indian children were discouraged from saying "I say" and "men", separately or as a phrase. They did, though. But in 1981, in Loreto House convent, the little Indian girls were now exclusively using *yaar* to each other when, during my late-1950s nursery-schooldays, they would have said "men". (They were also addressing the *ayah* as *didi*—elder sister—where we would have said *ayah* or used her first name.) But that year, in the fruit-rows of the New Market at Christmas, a youngish Anglo-Indian man met an elderly lady and her daughter, and as they were parting the elderly lady said, "Come on, give us a kiss, men!" This warmed the cockles of my heart. And an Internet friend of mine confirmed in the 2000s that, "Yes, we still say 'men'." So it lives on.

But maybe with a difference. In Brisbane, in 1983, when young David Holford, raised in Australia, saw that I was familiar with his community's culture, as a pleasant, bonding gesture, he started to address me as "man". I had to tell David to go home and listen to what his parents actually said—"men" in the north, and "m'n" in the south. Ava Gardner makes the same mistake in the film of *Bhowani Junction* (though I believe that the mother in it looks and is and speaks like a real Anglo-Indian).

The "I say, men!" users say "us" for "me", as in, "Give us a fag, men." They often add the phrase "'n' all" to sentences: "No time for fooling around, 'n all." They favour "I got", as in: "I got no time now," or "Gotter paper?" or "Got 'ny money?" They like to end sentences with "but": "After dinner, I'd like to go to the movies, but." My ex-Middleton Row, Bankovsky sister friends (now of Canberra, circa 2000s) laughingly underline the Anglo-Indian (school-teacherly?) habit of ending sentences with "child", pronounced something like "cheild", as in, "Wait on, cheild," or "*Nei* (Hindi *nahin*, no), cheild!" That pronunciation substitutes "er" for "aa", and so can rhyme *ayah* with "higher" (as I have seen it written in Diasporic Anglo-Indian verses from Queensland). It renders the "ə" ("er") sound as a soft "i": e.g., "Morgin" for Morgan, and says "diffi-CULT" for difficult. At the lifts in the office (Canberra, circa 1995), I heard a left-over from my youth: a polite "blooming" with a short "oo" (for the standard "bloody"), from a dark-skinned Anglo-Indian lady of about my age. And my cousin, Surajit (Calcutta, 1998), said,

"They don't say Perth; they say Pert'!" Thus it is that a perceptive Canadian remarked to me in the 1990s that Anglo-Indian speech resembles a "sort of battery Irish".

Anglo-Indians, perhaps only the Diasporic generation that first left India, or even the more recent departees, often come out with culturally Indian usage. He's "of good family" is an example that I heard recently. "Come, come," (not the British English phrase, meaning, "Oh come now, you're exaggerating!") for "Come quickly!" is an example I heard at the cultural show at the Melbourne World Anglo-Indian Reunion of 2004, replicating Indian-language syntax and diction in English, with Indian-style repetition. "Take, take, no!" when offering food, is another. "Pretty pretty girls," or "Small small bits", also translate Indian forms of plurality. Diasporic Anglo-Indians remark on the automatic, respectful "Aunty" from adult juniors whom they have just met. This, too, replicates Indian cultural style.

My friend R. B.'s "Maltese" grandmother in the UK said in the 1990s she didn't want her voice taped because she had a *chee-chee* accent. That accent is one of the markers of community identity. Mr. Warren O'Rourke of Canada felicitously calls it the "*makkhan-roti-chini*" accent (after the Hindi lullaby, butter-bread-sugar). Sometimes Anglo-Indians are ashamed of it, as being "low", and Mr. O'Rourke mentioned it at one of the worldwide Anglo-Indian reunions as a source of pride, in response to the very ersatz, *pukka* British accent of a speaker before him. He told me that once, when he telephoned a friend, he expected a Canadian accent from the overseas-born son, but heard the familiar, unchanged, accent of old. I actually think there is a range of Anglo-Indian accents, not just the standard "Bombay Welsh". (I thought I counted seven variations at the Melbourne Reunion in 2004.)

Anglo-Indian schooling, and thus language, can produce a bond between Anglo-Indians and Anglophone Indians. An Anglo-Indian family I met at a railway station during the Melbourne Reunion ranged from a "passing white" gentleman, through an "Anglo-Indian fair" elderly aunt, to a medium Indian-brown lady. The gentleman said he was Anglo-Indian, schooled in India and grown up in England, and asked me, "You reckon I have the accent, too?" And the lady, seeing my name-tag, asked me, "Well, with that name, how come you're at the Reunion?" And I said, "Language same, religion same, culture very overlapping." They were quite happy to inquire no further, and to chat with me during the cruise.

The first Diasporic generation does not, on the whole, seem to lose the accent, though a "genuine Domiciled European" Calcutta girl of my generation told me (circa 1990s) of how she heard a *māhā* [great] foreign accent come from an ex-Calcutta woman, but the affectation was shattered by an equally great lapse in the pronunciation/enunciation of some particular word. Later post-Diaspora generations will lose the accent and the characteristic turns of phrase; it will be interesting to see if, thereafter, anyone seeks deliberately to recover them.

Anglo-Indians may not know that Anglophone Indians, like my family members, sometimes parodied Anglo-Indianese and took it further, partly in token of our own defensive relationship to the English language. My family's equivalent for "native" (with all its baggage) was an Anglo-Indianese-like mangling of *janata* (common people) into "jer-NAH-ter". Or, on the model of the Anglo-Indian pronunciation of *modi*, grocer, as "mow-dee", we might say, "'And us the bloody 'mow-jers' (socks, Bengali *mojā*, not a usual loan-word), men!" We say things like, "There's some 'black in the dawl', men!" translating Hindi *dāl mẽ kālā* (hanky-panky), which as far as I know is not actually Anglo-Indianese.

So much for Anglo-Indian English, now for the Anglo-Indian relationship to the Indian vernaculars.

Times have changed, and some Anglo-Indians now have Indian first names. In relation to the traditional topic of Anglo-Indian-looking-down-on-Goan, my mother remarked in the 1990s of family friends' daughters: "Of the two sisters, the one whose name is Lobo calls her children Darryl and Donnegan, and the one whose name is Robinson calls her child Priyanka and wears *salwar-kameez* and a nose-ring!"

On the vernaculars, more generally, my mother told me in 1971 to note the Anglo-Indian linguistic custom of the lady who later became my Ayesha-*mamima* (aunt) in how she talked to her infant son. She had an English grandmother, a Goan mother, and a very high-born Bengali father, wore a *sari*, and called herself "culturally Park Street!" In ungrammatical servant-Hindi, she would coo, *"Tum khayegā? Tum jayegā?"* ("Will you eat? Will you go?"); properly, either *"Tu khayegā?"* or *"Tum khāoge?"*). My mother said this, the community's equivalent of baby-talk, was an unconscious acknowledgement of its often otherwise ignored Indian maternal roots. The custom still exists in India; and might still exist in the Diaspora. And in context, at the Melbourne Reunion cultural day, David McMahon spontaneously evoked Anglo-Indian childhood + *ayah* linguistic experience when he checked that his audience was Anglo-Indian by asking, "You know what *susu* (wee-wee, not really a Hindi word) is? You know what *nanga-panga* (naked) means?"— to loud sounds of assent.

Using "*Bijia*" for Bijoy and the like are part of the stereotype that Anglo-Indians do not know, and do not want to know, Indian vernaculars, and so tended to fail the compulsory "Lower Bengali" or "Lower Hindi" for the Senior Cambridge (Indian School Certificate), and automatically get Third Division results. But exceptions might be more common than the stereotype goes. Our maths teacher at La Martiniere, Mr. Ronnie Holmes, was a quintessential Anglo-Indian, even to a quiff-puff on his forehead, and his wife, Geraldine, was an ordinary, frock-wearing, khaki-coloured Anglo-Indian. One day in 1967, I knocked at the door of his quarters, and it was opened by an elderly Bengali lady. "*Ami* Mr. Holmes-*er sange dekha korte eschechhi*" ("I've come to see Mr. Holmes,") I said. "*Aar ami* Mr. Holmes-*er Ma!*" ("And I am his mother!"), came the answer, as the lady beamed in delight to see how I would take the unexpected news. Her wedding photograph, too, showed her in a *sari*. Her daughter-in-law called her Mum, rather than Ma, I think; I do not know how her son addressed her, but he took great pleasure in suddenly saying to me, "*Ami-o Bangla bolte pari*" ("I, too, can speak Bengali,") and doing so, though not very well, and with a strong Anglo-Indian accent. He is in Sydney these days, I hear; I wonder if he still speaks Bengali. My Jadavpur University classmate (1976-1977), Patrick Walsh SJ, of Ripon Street, in his adulthood and during his novitiate, had learnt to speak Bengali fluently, albeit also with an Anglo-Indian accent, and to write it well. He used to correspond with a Bengali nun in Bengali.

In 1989 in Ballarat, Australia, a fair Anglo-Indian academic, who looked like Shakespeare, said spontaneously to me, "*Amra Bangla-bhasha bolbo*" ("We will speak Bengali-language,")—not actually an idiomatic sentence, but it was gratifying that he tried. At the Melbourne Reunion, on the train-ride, a lady born in Chakradharpur said equably that, yes, they learnt Bengali in school. And the pièce-de-résistance came from my 70-ish friend, Mr. Harold Gomez, a darkish Anglo-Indian of Tamil origin who was a Calcutta taxi driver, and whose wife is from the famous Anglo-Indian milieu of Bow Barracks. He said that he had seen my name and wanted to speak to me. And then he began to speak perfect Bengali, with an accent better than my own! He knows various Anglican hymns and prayers in Bengali, though he cannot read it. And he cultivates such quintessentially Bengali things as *lal sag* (red spinach, or Chinese spinach, amaranth) in his Melbourne garden. (And he speaks Serbian, too!...all the better to communicate with that community in Melbourne seniors' homes.)

In the 2000s, on hearing I was from Calcutta, a recent migrant smiled, "*Ki dada!*" ("What ho, brother!"), in a display of camaraderie, and I heard the same phrase and more, in not very good but very enthusiastic Bengali, just behind me at the meet-and-greet of the Melbourne Reunion. And a recent migrant to Australia in his thirties said to me (Canberra, 2006), "I am Indian and I speak Hindi."

Like David McMahon using language as a testing-ground of Anglo-Indianness, on meeting me some years ago, Keith Butler of the East Indiaman cultural group in Melbourne, started out by asking me how I said the Indian word for lentils (*dāl* versus "dawl"); what I called yoghurt—"tyre" (from the Tamil *tair*, which is what lots of Anglo-Indians call yoghurt/curds); and how I pronounced the fierce curry, *vinDĀHloo*, which so many white people render as the awful "VIN-derloo". The group then passed me as "in effect, an A-I, or 'culturally A-I'", which is fine by me.

On loan-words, more than once I have heard community members sarcastically comment on upward social mobility in the Diaspora, "They were nutth-thing in India; nutth-thing! But outside they go in for a great deal of *phutāni*!"—does the word derive from the Hindi, "to boil or bubble", thus to be inflated?

Anglo-Indians tend nowadays to be more forthright about their racial/ethnic "Indianness" than previously, and in linguistically interesting terms. At the Melbourne Reunion boat cruise, one jovial Anglo-Indian gentleman, who described himself to me as *thoṛā-sā pāgal* (a little mad) said outright, "We're all bloody *kāllu-s* (blacks), men!" At the picnic at Warnambool, the fairish-skinned gentleman who sang *Meri Jaan* (stereotypically one of the three old Hindi film songs Anglo-Indians know, the others being *Goré goré* and, perhaps, *Mera Bulbul*) ended by hailing "you black-and-white darkies".

I did have Anglo-Indian friends in India, but have experienced a perhaps greater spontaneous camaraderie in the Diaspora, as with my railway-station friends. At the Melbourne Reunion, a very courteous gentleman with that familiar, ruddy "English-in-India" skin-colouring, who reminisced about having grown up just over the wall from (perfect Hindi-speaker) Frank Anthony's orchard, actually called me *bhai* (brother) quite unaffectedly.

Joe Bailey of the Canberra Anglo-Indian society wittily referred to me in 2005 as a "baptized Anglo-Indian", on the analogy of a "baptized Christian" as against a born one), and laughingly said to the membership of the Anglo-Indian Society, "Sanjay knows more Anglo-Indians than most Anglo-Indians do." Came the equable response from Mr. Owen Oliver, "Well, we'll have to change his name…" I think that kind of cultural acceptance gracious.

And I think the language-related point in what Messrs. Bailey and Oliver said interesting, as is all Anglo-Indian linguistic practice. I am told there are just a few scholarly studies of it; I hope there will be more.

Endnotes

1. Attempts were made to correct my facial deformity. I had 11 operations in Vellore, India, between 1945 and 1947 (the surgeon was Dr. MacPherson), and 11 more operations in Northwestern Memorial Hospital, Chicago, Illinois (surgeons: Dr. Stuteville, 1955, and Dr. Sidle, 2005). I now look almost normal.
2. Breen, M. and Marshall, R.T., An automated fluorometric method for the direct determination of magnesium in serum and urine using o,o¢dihydroxyazobenzene: studies on normal and uremic subjects. *Journal of Laboratory and Clinical Medicine* vol. 68, pp 701-712, 1966
3. The rupee had 16 *annas*, before it went decimal.
4. It took Australia until 1968 to start winding down its whites-only policy; a major factor was the reality that it had to trade with its Pacific Asian partners.
5. It's difficult for later generations of Anglo-Indians to appreciate the impact of the book and film at the time. I watched the movie with a colleague from *The Statesman*. He left the cinema numb with despair and hurt.
6. A Conservative Party Right-winger, who frequently attacked Britain's immigration policies. His most infamous speech included the line: "Like the Roman, I seem to see the River Tiber foaming with much blood."
7. A title he gave himself because he runs Daphne's household when I'm not around.
8. A traditional Maori ceremonial dance, involving chanting.
9. Uttar Pradesh. Famous for its pottery and ancient fort. Also a major railway junction.
10. Now Guwahati, Assam.
11. Amotz Asa-El, *The Diaspora and the Lost Tribes of Israel*, 2004. Hugh Lauter Levin Associates, Inc.
12. A townhouse.
13. The Indian Constitution guaranteed Anglo-Indians a number of reserved jobs in services such as the Railways, Customs, Post and Telegraph, and Police. These guarantees came to an end by 1960.
14. MRA (1938) is a nondenominational revivalist movement that grew out of the Oxford Group founded by an American evangelist, Frank N.D. Buchman, in the 1920s. It sought to deepen the spiritual life of individuals, and is still active in India. In 2001, MRA changed its name to Initiatives of Change.
15. This hostel was set up 12 years ago by Rodney Almeida through Melbourne's Anglo-Indian Association. Over the past 18 months I've visited a number of times—interviewing residents, and others, about being in the home, their life in India, and their decision to leave.
16. Pseudonyms have been used throughout this piece.
17. Chipu heads the team of helpers who provide 24-hour care for Daphne, who is crippled with arthritis. Chipu chose his own title because he's been with the family since he was 10 and does not see himself as a servant. He takes my place when I return to America every spring.
18. In India it's quite common for people to combine Hindi and English words in the same sentence – hence Hinglish.
19. Iranians who settled in India within the past few centuries; distinct from Parsis, who arrived from Iran more than 1000 years ago.
20. A member of a Scheduled Tribe living mainly in Western and Central India.
21. Indian measure. One *tola* equals nearly 12 grams
22. *TWWA* is using the city's traditional name in this article because CAISS and many other organizations, and even the city's newspapers, cling to the old one.
23. Not her real name.
24. I have discussed these ideas with Anglo-Indians in Calcutta and abroad. It seems that while the idea of a non-gender-biased definition may solve some problems, it would raise others. There is still, however, a real problem which, in my view, needs to be addressed for the sake of gender rights and personal identity.

25 Adi-Dravida or AD are people belonging to the low castes or outcasts; sometimes referred to as Dalits.
26 In India, homeless people often take shelter on railway station platforms—hence the saying.
27 A Christian organization which offers training in handicrafts and other skills for (mainly) young women from poor Anglo-Indian families. It also provides accommodation for the very poorest.
28 Oil-rich states of the Middle East which attract a lot of workers from South Asia and elsewhere.
29 Since I cannot claim to belong to the community, my justification for appearing in this volume rests on the fact that, during the 1990s, I lived in Chennai and conducted a social anthropological study among Anglo-Indians there. At the time, they numbered between 10,000 and 15,000, which made them the largest such community in India.
30 There are numerous publications dealing with this topic. For example, B. Anderson *Imagined Communities* (1983); M. Banks *Ethnicity: Anthropological Constructions* (1996); A.P. Cohen *The Symbolic Construction of Community* (1985); J. Friedman *Cultural Identity and Global Process* (1994); U. Hannerz *Cultural Complexity* (1992); and N. Thomas *Colonialism's Culture* (1994).
31 The Eurasian and Anglo-Indian Association in Calcutta (later to become the All-India Anglo-Indian Association, based in Delhi) was established in 1876, followed soon after (1879) by The Eurasian Association (later The Anglo-Indian Association of Southern India) based in Chennai. Indeed, as early as 1829, there were reports in the *Asiatic Journal* that arrangements were in hand to establish an East Indian Association in that city.
32 *The Eurasian* was a periodical published in Calcutta c. 1907-08. The *Eurasian and Anglo-Indian* (Madras, 1879, 1881).
33 The South Asian Women's Community Centre (SAWCC), Montréal, founded in 1981 and currently marking its 27th anniversary.
34 The phrase "reasonable accommodation" comes from the *Canadian Charter of Rights and Freedoms*, which guarantees accommodation to ethnic minorities. In Quebec there have been several cases where accommodation of religious sensibilities was contested in the public or legal domain. This unleashed fears, anxieties, and insecurities around questions of identity, particularly as they related to minority religions, mostly with respect to dress codes and gender. A Quebec commission released a report early in 2008 which sought to calm the situation.
35 Pejorative term for Gujaratis once popular in Britain.
36 I use this term, of course, in its current usage. In Kipling's day, "Anglo-Indian" referred to domiciled Britishers in India, "Eurasian" to Indians with European blood.
37 "His Chance in Life," in *Plain Tales from the Hills* (Oxford: OUP, 1987), 59. Page references to this story and to this edition, hereafter appear in parentheses in the body of my text.
38 "Shooting an Elephant," essay in anthology, *New Writing*, 1936.
39 Salman Rushdie, "At the Auction of the Ruby Slippers," in *East, West: Stories* (New York: Pantheon, 1994), 94.
40 Renamed Kolkata in 2001. Since the writer deals mainly with past events—and even local organizations and newspapers still call it Calcutta—TWWA has chosen to use the former name.
41 Automobile Association of Eastern India

Meet the Authors

Quentine (née D'Souza**) Acharya** (*Maxwell Piers—One Who Stayed On*) grew up in Nagpur, India, where she completed a BA in English Literature. She earned a Master's degree at Northwestern University's Medill School of Journalism in Evanston, Illinois. Later, she moved with her husband, Abhijit, to the Washington, D.C., area, where she raised her three children; taught in elementary schools; ran a catering business; and taught Indian cooking at L'Academie de Cuisine in Bethesda. Quentine now lives in Saratoga, California, and is an Adjunct Professor in English Composition at San Jose's Evergreen College. Her articles have been published in *The Washington Post* and the *San Jose Mercury News*.
E-mail: vizycal@comcast.net

Robyn Andrews (*A day at St. Joseph's Hostel, Melbourne; A Calcutta Christmas*) is a lecturer in Social Anthropology at Massey University, New Zealand. She has recently completed her doctoral thesis titled *"Being Anglo-Indian: Practices and Stories from Calcutta"* (2005). This work was based on research over a three-and-a-half-year period, and included collecting life stories of Anglo-Indians. She was particularly interested in portraying what it means to be Anglo-Indian living in Calcutta in the 21st century. She is involved in further research with Anglo-Indians—both in Calcutta and in the Diasporic community.
E-mail: R.Andrews@massey.ac.nz

Moira Breen (*Never Give In*) was educated at the Lawrence Memorial Royal School, Lovedale, and Queen Mary's College. Her career spanned the next 45 years and eight universities, of which the first was the U. of Madras and the other seven were in America, where she obtained a Master's degree in Physiology from Vassar College, New York, and a PhD in Biochemistry from Northwestern University Medical School in Chicago. Her primary position as a medical scientist was with the Federal Government of the USA, working in the Research Service of a large hospital near Chicago. She is now retired and is living happily in the Midwest of America. E-mail: moirabreen@sbcglobal.net

Patricia Brown (*February*) grew up in various cities because her father, an army officer, was transferred every two years. She attended La Martinière Girls' High School, Lucknow, and graduated from the Convent of Jesus and Mary, Pune. She has had several short stories, poems, features, and culinary articles published in Canada, India, and Malaysia. In 1998, Penguin published her *Anglo-Indian Food & Customs*, which was a huge success. A Tenth Anniversary Edition containing more recipes, further anecdotes, and sketches by the noted graphics artist, Jim Peters, will be available in the summer of 2008. E-mail: pat.brown@rogers.com

Lionel Caplan (*Close Families in Chennai; The Boundaries of Anglo-Indian Culture*) attended McGill University in Montreal and later studied Anthropology at the University of London, where he was awarded a PhD. He taught for many years at the School of Oriental and African Studies in London, and is now Professor Emeritus of South Asian Anthropology and Professorial Research Associate at the School. He has conducted research in Nepal and India, and his most recent book is entitled *Children of Colonialism: Anglo-Indians in the Postcolonial World* (2001), which arose from his research in Chennai during the 1990s. He is married to the anthropologist Pat Caplan; they live in London. E-mail: lionel.caplan@yahoo.co.uk

Kathy (née Browne) **Cassity** (*Distances*), born in Seattle, Washington, is descended from an Anglo-Indian family. (Her father, the son of a Madras police inspector, emigrated from India to England and then to Canada, before finally settling in Seattle and working as an aeronautical engineer.) Kathleen, who holds a PhD from the University of Hawaii at Manoa, now lives in Honolulu, Hawaii, with her family and works as Assistant Professor of English and Chair of the Writing Program at Hawaii Pacific University. E-mail: kcassity@hpu.edu

Geraldine Charles (*Inheriting The Patchwork*) MSc, FLS, FRGS, was born in Bangalore, India, but grew up in the UK. She originally trained as a biologist but latterly has pursued a museum career, predominantly as an archivist. She feels it is of great importance that the history of the Anglo-Indian Community be preserved for the generations to come. Her specific interest is in Family History. She is a Trustee of the Families in British India Society and has lectured on Anglo-Indian genealogy in the UK and Australia. E-mail: Geraldine.charles@hotmail.co.uk

Joy Chase (*Five Flags*) was born in Coimbatore, Tamilnadu. She studied at Breeks Memorial School in Ootacamund, where she obtained her Senior Cambridge certificate. She received a BA from Queen Mary's College in Madras and an MA from the University of Wisconsin—Madison. She is a librarian in Silicon Valley, California. She loves to travel and visit her family under all the various flags where they live.
E-mail: joyjoy@gmail.com

Dolores Chew (*Coming Full Circle*) was born and raised in Kolkata, India, and has lived in Montréal, Canada, since 1975. Dolores is an historian. Among her areas of research and publication interest are the gendered aspects of the lives of Anglo-Indians and Eurasians. She teaches at

Meet the Authors · 269

Marianopolis College and is active in the Diasporic community. Among other involvements, she is a founding member of the South Asian Women's Community Centre, which began in Montréal in 1981.
E-mail: D.CHEW@marianopolis.edu

Margaret Deefholts (*A Passage to Canada*) grew up in India and immigrated with her family to Surrey, British Columbia, in 1977. She is the author of *Haunting India*, and her award-winning short fiction has been published across North America. As a professional travel writer, many of her stories focus on India, but she also writes about her adventures all over the world. E-mail: deefholt@shaw.ca

Susan Deefholts (*Inheriting Remembrance*) is a critic, writer, and editor. Apart from writing, Susan's interests include dance, music, working out, and reading. Achievements: publication at Oprah.com and various freelance articles and short stories in periodicals. She lives in Waterloo, Ontario, with her husband Tom and two cats.
E-mail: susan.deefholts@gmail.com

Mark Faassen (*Beyond the Raj*) Born to a father from Rotterdam, Holland, and an Anglo-Indian mother from Chennai, India, Mark grew up in Toronto, Canada. He is a freelance visual researcher for documentary film and television, and the director of a forthcoming documentary about Anglo-Indians from a contemporary perspective—*Beyond the Raj*. He has an MA in Political Science and is going to law school this fall, much to the delight of his mother. Website: www.markfaassen.com.
E-mail: mark@markfaassen.com

Sheldon Fernandez (*Unravelling the Mosaic*) was born in Toronto, Canada, to parents Carol (Chittagong, Bangladesh) and Eugene (Kolkata, India). He has a degree in Computer Engineering from the University of Waterloo; he co-founded Infusion Development Canada, which provides software and consulting services to the investment banking industry in North America. Besides his role as a Chief Technical Officer, Sheldon continues to be closely involved with the University of Waterloo in an academic capacity as an Adjunct Lecturer at the Waterloo School of Optometry. Sheldon graduated Alpha Sigma Nu with a Master's of Theological Studies degree from the University of Toronto, and has also studied writing at the U of T and Oxford.
E-mail: sfernandez@infusion.com

Chris Francis (*Just off the Boat*) was born in Secunderabad, India, in an Anglo-Indian family of five brothers and two sisters. He graduated in Commerce from Osmania University and has spent the last 12 years as a

Finance Operations Executive. It was because his father, George Francis, used to collect the scraps of paper he wrote on that first inspired Chris to write. "Just off the Boat" is his first published story, about his recent move to the USA with wife Anne—they recently became the proud parents of a baby girl, Cathryn. He spends his free time blogging and volunteering time with CTR. E-mail: chrizfrancis@gmail.com

Ed Haliburn (*What If?*) studied at Campion High, Trichinopoly, then read Maths at St. Joseph's College, University of Madras. He spent five years in the Indian Customs at Madras and Vizagapatnam. He and his wife Hazel (née Laporte) immigrated to the UK in 1961. They have two daughters, both graduates of London University. Ed spent most of his UK working life with "number-crunching" computers in the petrochemical oil and gas industry. He was a member of many associated professional bodies and has travelled extensively. He is now retired and lives between England and Spain. He is a keen gardener, a DIY enthusiast, golfer, and tennis player. E-mail: e.haliburn@sky.com

Alan Johnson (*Globalization and Anglo-India*) teaches post-colonial studies in the English Department at Idaho State University. He concentrates on India, where he was born and raised, and recently completed a book on literary depictions of colonial Indian spaces. His current projects involve Anglo-Indian literature, globalization, and Bollywood. E-mail: johnala2@isu.edu

Nancy Lilly (*An Epistolean's Legacy*) Eldest daughter of Claude and Rosa Rixon, Nancy was born and raised in Dhaka, Bangladesh. As an aspiring teen writer, her short stories were published by *The Morning News* in Dhaka, but her writing was largely deferred when she became a wife and mother, which duties took her to England, the USA, Sudan, and Vietnam. Nancy and her husband, Peter, live in Rowlett, Texas. Her 23-year-old son, Robbie Sidell III, is also involved in sustaining the Anglo-Indian identity. Her hobbies include reading, genealogy, and travelling. E-mail: cyann14@hotmail.com

Lionel Lumb (*Denial and Pride*) was born in Lahore, Pakistan, and began a lifelong career in journalism at *The Statesman* in Calcutta. After immigrating to Britain in 1963, he worked for Reuters and *The Scotsman*, before joining BBC Television News. In 1973, he moved with his wife, Shirley, and three children to Canada. After nearly 20 years as a documentary-maker and executive producer in television, mostly for the Canadian Broadcasting Corporation, he became an Associate Professor at Carleton University's School of Journalism and Communication. He retired in 2003, returning joyfully to his first love, writing fiction. In

Meet the Authors · 271

2007, he was in charge of communications and publicity for the 7th World Anglo-Indian Reunion in Toronto. E-mail: lionel.lumb@rogers.com

Esther Lyons (*My Bow Barracks*) is a high-school teacher (with a graduate diploma in Special Education and MEd.) and a journalist. She grew up at the Anglo-Indian Trust Property, Allahabad, India. She now lives in Canterbury, NSW, Australia. Her interests include painting, drawing, travelling, and reading. She has three published books to her credit: Non-Fiction—*Unwanted* and *Bitter Sweet Truth*; Fiction—*Peacock in the Gum Tree*. She is a regular writer of short stories for children in *India Post*, a Sydney-based newspaper. E-mail: lyonsfab@optusnet.com.au

David McMahon (*Identity Cadre*) was born and educated in India, where he began his career in journalism, travelling the world as a sportswriter. He has lived in Melbourne since 1988, where he is the business editor of *mX* newspaper, a News Ltd. publication. In 2002 he was shortlisted for a Walkley Award, the Australian equivalent of the Pulitzer. An internationally published photographer, his first novel, *Vegemite Vindaloo*, is published by Penguin India. E-mail: bestmacs@bigpond.com

Dorothy (née Doyle) **McMenamin** (*Collisions of Life and Love*) was raised in Rawalpindi, Pakistan, a fifth generation in colonial India. With her family, she moved to England in 1963, thence to Australia in 1970, and finally settled in New Zealand in 1978; she is married with four children. She lectures in Indian History at the University of Canterbury, and is an oral historian involved in various projects about Anglo-Indians in New Zealand. She has published several articles and presented papers on Anglo-Indians, and is currently compiling an anthology drawn from the interviews. E-mail: dorothym@inet.net.nz

Joyce Mitchell (*Journeying through Life*; *Ginger Wine*) was born in Ratlam, India, and loves to travel—she has lived in nine different countries, thanks to her career as a flight attendant for Air India and her marriage to Joe Mitchell, a Boeing representative. She resides in Seattle, Washington, and spends her winters in India, the home of her heart.
E-mail: memsahib100@yahoo.com

Pamela S.C. Moore (*The Year of '72*) was educated at Wesleyan School, Calcutta, and Dow Hill, Kurseong, before the family immigrated to the UK in 1947, where she married and had two children. She has been a teacher (B.Ed, Southampton), a quality controller in the cosmetic industry, and an art-gallery owner. She immigrated to Australia in 1987 and is now married to Ralph N. Moore. Until her retirement, she was employed as curator of the Western Australian Museum in Kalgoorlie. Pam's interests include painting and bridge. E-mail: pammoore12@iprimus.com.au

Ralph N. Moore (*I Say, Men; Upended Down Under*) was born to a railway family in Kharagpur. After school, he joined the Calcutta Police, but left to spend two years working in Canada and Australia. On his return to India, he worked for the next 29 years at Ludlow Jute Mills, near Calcutta. He has three daughters—Ilka, Lynn, and Jane—from his marriage to Phyllis Ritchie. He now lives in Kalgoorlie, Western Australia, with his second wife, Pam. E-mail: pammoore12@iprimus.com.au

Peter Moss (*Raking Through the Ashes of That Bonfire of the Vanities*) Born in Allahabad into an Anglo-Indian railway family, Peter Moss embarked on a journalistic career at the age of 15, and pursued it on an overland bus journey from London to Delhi. His three volumes of autobiography—*Bye-Bye Blackbird*, *Distant Archipelagos*, and *No Babylon*—recount, respectively, his experience of the end of Empire in India (1947), Malaya (1957), and Hong Kong (1997). His first novel, *The Singing Tree* (Bloomsbury), was described by the *New York Times* as "a little gem".
E-mail: petermoss@yahoo.com

Peter Gordon Nailer (*"My India" No More*) Born in Kharagpur, West Bengal, he left India in 1950 with his parents and settled in Perth, Western Australia. He is married to Jenny, who is a nurse, and they have four adult children. Peter describes himself as semi-retired. He is interested in genealogy and its associated history and cooking (Indian cuisine).
E-mail: Nailer@bigpond.com

Gerald Platel (*A Long Journey in Search of an Identity*) Born in Karachi, he attended the Karachi Grammar School, graduating in 1949. An amateur musician, he played trumpet in Karachi's first teenage dance band. His nickname was "Buju". Peter went to England in 1961 and then on to Canada in 1974. Now retired in Toronto, he stays busy by keeping in touch with old friends and writing his family history.
E-mail: geraldplatel@sympatico.ca

Lesley-Anne Raymer (*When Two Worlds Collide*) was born into an Anglo-Indian family in Mumbai, India, and attended St. Peter's High School, Mazagon. After obtaining her Bachelor of Commerce Degree from the University of Bombay, she became a flight attendant with a Middle Eastern airline. She now lives in Ontario, Canada, with her husband and daughter, and works in the legal field. E-mail: diles@istar.ca

Daniel Riggle (*A Woman from Ajmer*) worked in factories and as a labourer before joining the US Army in 1975. Trained in the cavalry, he served in

Kentucky, Korea, and Texas, returned home, and went to college through the GI Bill, receiving both Bachelor and Master's degrees in English from Northern Illinois University. He has taught writing and literature at colleges and universities part-time for 18 years. Still teaching occasionally, he works full-time for a non-profit, higher education association in Washington, DC. His essays, fiction, and poetry have appeared in the *Chicago Sun-Times* and *Towers* magazine. E-mail: RiggleD@aascu.org

Cheryl-Ann Shivan *(The Way We Are at Pondicherry)* is from Pondicherry, South India, from a family that has resided in the Union Territory for many generations. She is a Lecturer in a College of Education, teaching English Literature and Education. She has a PhD thesis on Anglo-Indian Literature, with special reference to Anglo-Indian women, due to be submitted to Pondicherry University at the end of 2008. She is married to Mullankandy Pamban Shivan, and they have two daughters, Rhea and Zoe. E-mail: cherylshivan@eth.net

Sanjay Sircar *(Matters of Language)* MA, PhD, is based in Canberra, Australia. He is an independent scholar in the junior and marginalized areas of literature and society (children's literature, women's literature, folklore). He has assisted two Anglo-Indian gentlemen with their accounts of "being Anglo-Indian"—Warren O'Rourke (see www.vsdh.org/vsdh/warren/loc.html) and "R.B." ("Blue-Eyed and Brown-Skinned: Uncovering a Hidden Past", *Kunapipi*, Vol. 25, No. 2, 2003, 128-136), and is interested in Anglo-Indian history and culture.
E-mail: Sanjay.Sircar@environment.gov.au

Sylvia Staub *(As the Bough is Bent)* Born in an Indian railway town, Sylvia was educated at schools in Naini Tal and Darjeeling. After Independence in 1947, she worked for the Indian Government in London, Geneva, and Paris before immigrating to the USA. Her career has been as a copy editor with *Time-Life* and as Copy Chief on *Emerge* magazine, a spin-off from *Time*. She lives in Tucson, Arizona, where she writes creatively, edits, ghost-writes, and makes contemporary totems (acrylic on wood).
E-mail: swstaub@yahoo.com

Marina Stubbs *(What's in a Name?)* was born in Croydon, South London, to Anglo-Indian parents and now lives in Brighton with her husband, two children, and pet snake. Marina has always loved words, and has spent the last 20 years working with them in her role as a speech and language therapist. She is about to complete the Creative Writing Certificate at Sussex University. Her current work covers the themes of identity, belonging, and the Anglo-Indian experience. This is Marina's first published story. E-mail: marina.stubbs@gmail.com

Deborah (née Lumb) **Van Veldhuizen** *(Becoming Myself)* is an Anglo-Indian who lives in Ottawa, Canada. She has a BA in English Literature and Philosophy from Carleton University and an MA in English Literature from McMaster University. She teaches Communications courses at Algonquin College in Ottawa. In 1994, she was the Grand Prize Winner of the "Margaret Atwood Quiz", held by Bantam Books Canada. In her spare time, she enjoys reading and volunteering. Deborah is married to Ben and lives in Ottawa with him and their daughter, Angela. E-mail: deb_vanveld@sympatico.ca

John Walke *(My Irish Grandfather)* was born in Karachi, Pakistan, when his family migrated there from New Delhi at Partition in 1947. He attended grammar school in England, followed by university in the USA, where he has lived since 1963. He has published stories in literary magazines beginning back in the late 1970s, essays in newspapers, and broadcast readings of his works on *Valley Writers Read* on Valley Public Radio in Fresno, California. He appeared in both *Voices on the Verandah* and *The Way We Were*, and recently in the magazine, *Anglos In The Wind*, published in Chennai. E-mail: walke@cvip.net

Blair Williams *(An Examined Life)* is a Chartered Engineer from London, who worked as an officer on the Indian Railways for 15 years, before emigrating to the USA in 1976, where he was a manufacturing executive for 20 years and a professor for the last five. His passions are CTR, a charity helping Anglo-Indians in India, and publishing books preserving Anglo-Indian culture. *The Way We Are* is the fifth book he has published on the Anglo-Indian ethos. He loves golf and his wife, Ellen. E-mail: blairrw@att.net

Noreen Wood *(The Edge of the Page)* was born in the Nilgiri Hills of Southern India and educated at the University of Madras; she immigrated to Canada in 1982. She lives with her family in Montréal, and has worked as a Chartered Accountant in Montréal and Toronto for more than 20 years. World travel, home décor, and entertaining are some of the things she enjoys, when she is not working. E-mail: woodnoreen@videotron.ca

Glossary of Indian Words and Phrases

A

Adivasi(s)
Indigenous tribal peoples of India.

Aloo chops
Mashed-potato rissoles stuffed with mince, chopped onions, chillies, etc.

Anna
Old coin valued at one-sixteenth of a rupee.

Ayah
A native nanny, usually unlettered, but a storyteller, comforter, and companion to children in her charge.

B

Baba
Young child.

Baby-ji
Little girl.

Baki
Literally, Hindi for remainder; or goods bought on credit; an Anglo-Indian term would be "on tick".

Baksheesh
Tips, gratuities.

Bearer(s)
Manservant who waits at table and who also acts as a valet in some instances; and would also serve.

Bed Tea
Beloved Anglo-Indian custom of waking up to an early morning cup of tea in bed; often served with a banana or some other fruit.

Bhaji
Cooked curried vegetables; also uncooked leafy vegetables, such as spinach.

Bhangra
A type of popular music combining Punjabi folk traditions with Western pop music.

Bhindi
Okra, usually called lady's-fingers by Anglo-Indians. Often sliced small and fried with spices, to make a dry-ish dish.

Biriyani
A spicy traditional Muslim rice dish cooked with succulent pieces of chicken, mutton, or fish, and sautéed onions, etc.

Brinjal
Aubergine; eggplant.

Bustee
A slum or shantytown.

C

Carrom
A popular indoor game played on a large, square wooden board, with a heavy circular "striker" and lighter disks called carrom-men.

Cha; Chai
Tea.

Charpai; Charpoi
A bed with woven canvas-strips, or sometimes a network of sturdy jute rope strands fastened onto a light wooden frame.

Chota peg; Burra peg
"Chota" indicates a single peg; "burra" indicates a double measure.

Chowkidar, Chowkidhar
Watchman.

Churidhar
Pantaloons, snug around calves and ankles.

Curry patta
Curry leaves, essential is dishes like mulligatawny.

D

Dahi
Yoghurt.

Dak
Post or mail.

Dak-bungalow
A travellers' rest-house located in rural areas. Originally a stopping station for runners carrying mail.

Dal; Daal
Split pea lentils cooked in a variety of ways in India. Anglo-Indians would often pronounce the word as "dawl" or "doll".

Dekchi
Cooking pot.

Derzi; Durzi; Darzi; Durzee
A tailor.

Dhoti
Loin-cloth worn by men.

Dhobi(s)
Washermen.

Divali; Diwali;
A major Hindu festival of lights, celebrating the victory of good over evil.

Dol-dol(s)
A special Anglo-Indian Christmas sweet, usually made with black *puttu* rice flour and coconut milk

Dukan
Shop, store.

Dupatta
Also known as *chunni*: a kind of stole worn with *salwar-kameez*.

H

Haldi
Turmeric.

Housie
Anglo-Indian name for Bingo.

I

Idli-sambar; Idli-dosa
South Indian dishes.

J

Jaldi
Fast in Hindi, as in *jaldi karo*: "hurry up".

Jamun; Jamoon
Purple-skinned, fleshy, round, acrid-sweet fruit.

Jeera
Cumin.

Jhat Bhai
Literally translates as "country brother"; more generally interpreted as "kinsman".

Ji
Respectful suffix to a name or title.

Jungli
Hindi for wild (animal), from the word jungle. Also used to describe an uncouth, unsophisticated person.

K

Kameez
The tunic or "shirt" North Indian women wear over *salwar* (pantaloons).

Kati-Kebab
Skewered pieces of meat, marinated in yoghurt and spices, and grilled over charcoal.

Khana
Food.

Khansama
Cook; chef.

Kheema
Curry with ground meat: beef, lamb, chicken.

Khud
Precipitous hillside; also, deep valley.

Kofta
Spicy meatballs.

Korma
A dish with lamb, beef, or chicken marinated in yoghurt and spices and sometimes garnished with almonds.

Kraal
Afrikaans word: enclosure for livestock, or stockade around a village.

Krait
A highly venomous snake, more deadly than the cobra.

Kul-kul(s)
A traditional Christmas sweet involving a rather complicated preparation process. Regardless of the time and effort involved, many expatriate A-Is all over the world still take pride in turning these out to celebrate the Yuletide season in time-honoured A-I fashion.

Kurta
Tunic.

L

Langra
A type of mango grown mainly in West Bengal, Uttar Pradesh and Bangladesh. Small seed, juicy and sweet.

Lungi
A tubular cotton garment, simply knotted at the waist.

M

Makhan-roti-chini
Literally, butter-bread-sugar,

this is the traditional lullaby for babies in India.

Mango-fool
A milkshake using green mango pulp.

Masala
A variety of curry spices—whole, powdered or in paste form.

Masala dosa
A South Indian crêpe made from rice flour and ground lentils, with a spicy potato filling.

Mofussil
Outlying districts, away from the big cities; similar to "upcountry" in Anglo-Indian usage.

Morah
An Indian stool fashioned from cane, sometimes with a padded seat.

N

Nawab
From Urdu, usually a Muslim ruler.

Nimbu Pani
Freshly squeezed lemon juice, sugar, and water.

Non-Veg
Indian term for meat dishes.

P

Paanwallah; Paan
A vendor of *paan*—a betel leaf wrapped in a triangle around a variety of condiments, including crushed betel nut. Some *paans* are sweet (with honey, powdered coconut, and cardamoms); others are acrid, with tobacco and lime paste.

Paisa
Monetary unit, 1/100th of a rupee. Known as pice until India went metric.

Pakora(s)
Indian snack—deep fried, chick-pea-flour coated, spicy vegetarian or non-vegetarian titbits.

Parathas
Wheat flour fried flat-bread.

'Phallies
Slang for peanuts; Hindi: *moongphalli*.

Pice
Old Indian coin: four pice equalled an anna; sixteen annas made up a rupee.

Pound party
The custom of bringing a contribution to a "social" or pound party, similar to a modern "pot luck" party: some kind of light foodstuff to be shared with other guests. These were often tea time treats (a pound cake or cheese straws, for example) or snack items and finger foods rather than a main course contribution.

Pukka
Ripe. Often used to describe a proper or correct person, e.g., "pukka sahib", or denoting a firm commitment, e.g., "pukka arrangements."

Puttu-rice
A sweet-tasting black rice made into desserts, mostly in South India.

Pulao; Pullau; Pilaw, Pilaf
Fried rice enlivened with cloves, cardamom pods, and cinnamon sticks. Usually garnished with sautéed onions, peas, and slivered almonds.

Punkahs
Ceiling fans; also refers to hand-held fans.

R

Raja
Ruler of a princely state.

Rasna
A colouring agent but also an important Ayurvedic medicinal herb used for rheumatism and allied disorders.

S

Salwar; Shalwar
Pantaloons worn under a tunic (kameez) by women in North India.

Sari
Traditional ankle-length women's garment consisting of a single length of material, usually between six and nine metres long.

T

Tahari
A tasty snack, usually rice and vegetables.

Taka
Originally, the Bengali word for rupee; the official currency of Bangladesh.

Tola
Indian unit of mass, nearly 12 grams.

V

Vindaloo
It was first brought to Goa by the Portuguese. Historically, this was a pork dish cooked with plenty of wine, vinegar, and garlic, known as "Vinha d'Alho." However, it soon received the Goan treatment, which added plentiful amounts of spice and chilli. Popular in Indian restaurants in Britain, though rarely cooked with the authentic flavour, it is sometimes referred to as "vindy", and dreadfully mispronounced there as vin-der-loo.

Z

Zenana
That part of a house (usually Muslim) reserved for women.